Beethoven: The Late Great

33 Personal Variations

The Royal Philharmonic Society bust of Beethoven
and Dean Corey frown together (Photo by Kaly Corey)

Beethoven: The Late Great

33 Personal Variations

DEAN COREY

Philharmonic Society of Orange County

Published by the Philharmonic Society of Orange County
2082 Business Center Drive, Suite 100
Irvine, CA 92612

Library of Congress Control Number: 2013958034

Hardcover: ISBN 978-1-939758-54-5
Paperback: ISBN 978-1-939758-55-2

Cover design by Deborah Shaw and Marie Songco-Torres
Interior design by Dotti Albertine

In harvesting the fruits of wonder,
we came into our own as a species.
—Jesse Prinz

Contents

L'histoire

Illustrations

The Music with Big Shoulders

Two Poems

The Last Five Quartets

Coda

Editor's Note

Dean Corey doesn't look like what he actually is: one of the most erudite, eminent musicologists on the planet. Instead, he looks like the guy who's already in his seat next to yours before kickoff at a college football game, the guy who buys you a beer just because he's about to buy himself one, the guy who knows the game inside out and backwards and has forgotten more about football than the head coaches on either team ever knew.

Now forget the football metaphor and apply it instead to music.

Dean offers an extraordinarily rare combination of down-to-earth likeability and deep knowledge of pretty much everything there is to know about serious music. He knows the composers, the artists, the musicology, the money, the instruments, the gossip and rumors, the donors, the concert halls, and the history. He knows what's going on in New York and Vienna and Palm Springs and Paris and, of all places, Orange County.

When it comes to classical music, Dean Corey pretty much single-handedly put Orange County on the map. As President and Artistic Director for more than twenty years of the Philharmonic Society of Orange County, Dean is responsible for creating programming as well thought-out and desirable as anything one could find in a traditional hotbed of culture (albeit with much better weather). He has built the Philharmonic Society's massive cadre of donors, volunteers, and concertgoers through the strength and friendliness of his own personality and his voluminous contacts in the concert world, all across the planet.

Now Dean turns his attention to a composer who is known to the general public for just a few notes, really—the opening bars of the Fifth Symphony and the "Ode to Joy" melody in the last movement of the Ninth. But there is so much more to Beethoven than even dedicated music lovers could imagine. Nine symphonies, 32 piano sonatas, five piano concertos, several dozen string quartets, an opera, many overtures, the *Missa Solemnis* (which Dean marvels over the fact that it premiered the same night as the Ninth Symphony) and on, and on, and on.

But who was Beethoven? Yes, he was a musical genius, but he was also a human being. You could say as much about Dean. Which makes Dean Corey the perfect person to introduce you to the real Ludwig van Beethoven, not the mythic composer and not just the figure with whom Lucy constantly had to compete to gain Schroeder's attention.

So crack a beer, or pour yourself some fine champagne, or read what follows without adult beverages. Either way, one great man and musician is going to introduce you to a buddy of his, another great man and musician. You're in for an awesome ride.

Michael Levin
Irvine, California
December 2013

Foreword

One of the first things my new editor said to me when I got the job as music critic at the *Orange County Register* was, "You have to meet Dean." My editor, Scott Duncan, had been the music critic at the newspaper before me, so he knew. I don't believe he mentioned anyone else on the beat that required a special meet-and-greet session. At any rate, Scott arranged for the parlay at an Irvine eatery, and the three of us duly repaired there after work one evening to get to know each other over beers.

Dean Corey—the president and artistic director of the Philharmonic Society of Orange County—wasn't like any executive head of an arts organization that I had met before. He was friendly, for one thing. Also, unguarded, just one of the boys. But more than anything he was loquacious; he had the gift of speaking freely. I was a little taken aback. Arts administrators just didn't talk to journalists—music critics, no less— in this manner, not in my experience. Dean assumed we were friends immediately, on the same side. I don't recall the details of the conversation that night, but if it was anything like the many conversations I've had with him since then, it wasn't about business and it wasn't about getting to know me (and my credentials) or me getting to know him (and his credentials); it was about music. Dean likes to talk about music more than anyone I know, and that's all right with me.

The book you hold in your hand is Dean all over. Reading it you get a good idea of what it's like talking to him. Despite the potentially academic subject matter or, at least, the hard-to-talk-about subject matter—the late music of Beethoven—the book is personal, friendly and easygoing. His enthusiasm for music is also much in evidence. Just the idea of writing such a book, 33 personal essays on Beethoven's last works—what other arts administrator ever did that?—is special. To Dean, music is just too important a thing not to talk about, in plain language if possible. The book is chatty in the best sense.

Characteristically, Dean comes at his subject from many angles. "Only connect," E.M. Forster once wrote and that's what Dean does, bringing many strands of the story together. Safe to say, there is no other book on Beethoven that includes an interview (and a fascinating one at that) with the widow of Charles Schulz, the *Peanuts* cartoonist. There are other interviews here too (one with a cook), some recipes and poems, disquisitions on Schubert, Berlioz, Sainte Foy and Napoleon, pre-concert talks and straight essays on the music. I particularly enjoyed the snippets of autobiography that he has included as well, interesting in themselves, but also because they fill out the picture of my friend with stories I had never heard before. He must have been a terrific French horn player. He had amazing parents.

As a journalist I've also had the pleasure of interviewing Dean on many occasions, on record, about his organization. Again, uniquely in my experience, he has always been straightforward and honest, never trying to hide anything from a prying member of the press. (Or maybe he just does it better than others.) His account of the debacle that was Zingaro—an artsy horse show in a tent, with music by Boulez and Stravinsky—was typical. After telling me about all the money the Society lost in presenting it, after recalling the dangerous spike in his blood pressure that it caused him, after taking the blame for the whole thing, he said: "Although I would do it again." In all the years I have been reviewing his concerts, he has never once complained about anything I wrote, not even when I had negative things to say about his biggest projects. Rather, he has been one of my biggest supporters and cheerleaders here.

He's generous, perhaps to a fault. When Dean read in *The New York*

Times about a lowly Russian orchestra, on tour of the U.S., whose members were being paid $40 a concert with no per diem for food, he had a Mexican dinner waiting for them when they came to play for the Philharmonic Society. In the event, the orchestra wasn't the greatest, but at least it was well fed.

Orange County has been lucky to have Dean Corey all these years. In a place still developing its artistic tastes, he could have settled for less, and saved a lot of money in the process. Instead, he continually gave us the best and brightest of the classical music world and, with the Eclectic Orange Festival, the most progressive. A young writer moving down here from L.A. into what he had thought a cultural backwater found himself in the middle of things, a kingdom of classical music. His old friends in L.A. envied him. The Orchestre Révolutionnaire et Romantique didn't go to L.A. to perform the nine symphonies of Beethoven. The Berlin Philharmonic and Claudio Abbado didn't go to L.A. right after 9/11. The Vienna Philharmonic with Bernard Haitink played three nights here, none there. O.C. became the better place to hear the world's greatest orchestras and recitalists, thanks largely to the author of this book. He made my beat an exciting place.

A few years ago, the folks at the Philharmonic Society decided to make Dean "the face" of the organization. They gave him a blog. He began to give pre-concert lectures. He now makes short introductory remarks at concert time. Some of you may know him only from the last, but they are a good capsule portrait. He shuffles out onto stage, a little distracted perhaps, microphone in hand, orchestra in place, extols the sponsors, apologetic and amused at having to point out the emergency exits and tell us all to turn off our cell phones. (If anyone's does go off during the concert, he warns, he or she will have to perform an oboe concerto with the visiting orchestra.) He always makes it quick and painless. The music's the thing, and he'd rather be listening to it, and knows you would too. This book is about listening to it more intelligently and emotionally. "Please…enjoy," he says, as he goes off stage. He means it.

Timothy Mangan
December 2013

LIST OF ILLUSTRATIONS

(Following Page 150)

Figure 1. *Ludwig van Beethoven* (Beethoven © Georgios Kollidas - Fotolia.com)

Figure 2. *Dean Corey and Marino Formenti* (Photo by Amy Carson Dwyer)

Figure 3. *Detail of the tympanum of the Last Judgement, Conques, France* (© Fulcanelli - Fotolia.com)

Figure 4. *Dr. William Meredith, Director, Ira F. Brilliant Center for Beethoven Studies, San Jose State University* (Photo by Everett Taasevigen)

Figure 5. *Lock of Beethoven's hair* (Photo by Dr. William Meredith, Director, Beethoven Center, San Jose State University)

Figure 6. *Charles Rosen, John Gingrich (not Brahms) and Dean Corey at the Bar Boulud, New York City* (Photo by Kaly Corey)

Figure 7. *Sound artist, musician, composer, and inventor Trimpin in front of his Sheng High installation* (Photo by Matthew G. Monroe)

Figure 8. *Charles and Jean Schulz in the late 1980s* (Photo by Giovanni Trimboli courtesy of the Charles M. Schulz Museum and Research Center)

Figure 9. *Schroeder prepares for the Hammerklavier Sonata* (Detail from Peanuts, January 15, 1958; PEANUTS © 1953 Peanuts Worldwide, LLC. Used by permission of Universal Uclick. All rights reserved.)

Figure 10. *Dean Corey and his mother Becky* (Photo by Kaly Corey)

Figure 11. *Sir John Eliot Gardiner and Dean Corey at the Mandarin Oriental Hotel London* (Photo by Kaly Corey)

Figure 12. *Napoleon's Elephant of the Bastille* (Elephant of the Bastille in Greenwich © KarenDMartin - Fotolia.com)

Figure 13. *Beethoven and Goethe and the Teplitz incident* (Depicted by Carl Rohling, Beethoven and Goethe meeting the imperial family, July 1812; The copyright in this work has expired. This work was published before January 1, 1923 and is in the public domain in the United States and other countries.)

Figure 14. *Johann Nepomuk Hummel* (© Georgios Kollidas - Fotolia. com)

Figure 15. *A portion of Beethoven's manuscript draft of the 2nd movement of String Quartet No. 13, Op. 130* (Gertrude Clarke Whittall Foundation Collection, Music Division, Library of Congress, Washington D.C.)

Figure 16. *Beethoven's letter to Karl Holz which accompanied the 2nd movement of String Quartet No. 13, Op. 130* (Gertrude Clarke Whittall Foundation Collection, Music Division, Library of Congress, Washington D.C.)

Figure 17. *Kaly avec ses tournesols à « Les Rêves à La Coste » Guizerix, France* (Photo by Fiorenza de la Fuente)

OTHER PHOTOS

Front cover. *Sunflowers* (Photo by Karen Evarts)

Page ii. *The Royal Philharmonic Society bust of Beethoven and Dean Corey frown together* (Photo by Kaly Corey)

About the Author. *Dean Corey* (Photo by Kaly Corey)

Back cover. *Sunflowers* (Photo by Kaly Corey)

INTRATA

Variation 1

PRELUDE

IF COMPOSERS BACH, Haydn, and Mozart were suddenly brought into the present, they would be astounded to learn that we are still playing their music. They usually wrote their works for specific occasions—symphonies, cantatas, or operas performed a few times and then shelved for future performances, if any. However, if Beethoven also reappeared today in Orange County and observed what the Philharmonic Society is doing in celebrating his late works, he wouldn't be surprised in the least. He would expect it.

Beethoven believed he had a moral responsibility for his actions. He was the greatest composer in the world at the time and he knew it. Because of this, he felt he was responsible for doing the best work he was capable of and giving it back to the society in which he lived, as well as to the future world where the rest of us would make an appearance. This is the message the Philharmonic Society means to convey in our *Beethoven: The Late Great* project—find your talent (or the best you can do, whatever it is), develop it, and give it back.

This compilation of thirty-three variations you are about to read are indeed personal. They come in many forms and from many uses—lectures, program book letters, articles, interviews, recipes, and a variety of musings on the subject. They take the form of essays, memoirs, travelogues, book reviews, hagiographies, and poems. Beethoven's pursuit of joy for all mankind was oft times borne of traumatic circumstances where collective strength is found when we band together as brothers and sisters. We are strongest when we act in concert, in harmony. This is the other message.

I deal with the music mostly in the form of pre-concert talks. The first one was delivered prior to Marino Formenti's performance of the *Diabelli Variations*, which was splendid.

The concert was a bit controversial. Marino had commissioned Evan Gardner to compose a new variation, which had its North American premiere that evening. Rather than try to write a 34th *Diabelli Variation*, Gardner chose to write a variation on the most famous composition of the late John Cage, whose 100th anniversary was in 2012. Of course, I am referring to the piece 4'33". True to the original work, the pianist's hands do not touch the keyboard. Instead, Marino wore a special pair of gloves that activated microphones placed in front of speakers, producing feedback from the ambient sounds in the hall while he depressed the sustain pedal. This "silence" lasted about ten minutes as opposed to Cage's original four minutes. Some interesting sounds were realized. The audience response was reasonable. There were a couple of boos, of which I was so proud. They were the first in my more than 19 years (at that point) with the Society. I had finally earned my stripes.

I discuss the last Beethoven five string quartets, the Bagatelles, Op. 126, the *Missa Solemnis*, the Ninth Symphony, and Berlioz's *Symphonie Fantastique* from a historical perspective and also in a play-by-play fashion. I would encourage you to get recordings of all of the works and listen to them as you read that portion of the essay dealing with the music itself. I wrote these parts of the essays as I was actually listening to the music.

While all of these variations are written from a personal perspective, none are more personal than "Mom, Dad, and Beethoven;" the poems "A Christmas Eve" and "Les Tournesols;" the variations "I'll Have What He Is Having," "Taft Music Bungalow," and "A Tale of A Thousand and One Nights (and Weekends);" and, of course, the final variation, "Bows."

I have included essays about Beethoven's effect on other composers such as Schubert, Berlioz, and Elgar. I have also interviewed some individuals connected to *Beethoven: The Late Great*, including Bill Meredith, Director of the Ira F. Brilliant Center for Beethoven Studies at San Jose State University; Jean Schulz, widow of cartoonist Charles "Sparky" Schulz; and Seattle-based sound artist Trimpin. Also in my plans was an interview with Charles Rosen, who passed away before I could talk with him. I have still included something about him.

A number of writers have influenced me as I've developed my writing style. Leading the pack are M.F.K. Fisher, Rebecca Solnit, Michel de Montaigne, and Charles Rosen. I am grateful for their examples. Because many of these variations are from my letters and public talks, I repeat a lot of information. Always the marketer, I often think in the style of promotional copy. This is why some of my writing about *Beethoven: The Late Great* may sound like a stump speech. I beg your indulgence. My writing style for these variations is purposely casual and conversational. I have a hard-wired passion for music, and it has always been my goal to spread my enthusiasm to others.

I want to give special thanks to Chantel Chen Uchida for being my right hand in this entire project. I am indebted to Jean Hsu for her brilliance and invaluable talent. I want to thank my wife Kaly for her total support and David Lieberman for taking me to Moisés Kaufman's play *33 Variations* in New York, which started me on this project in the first place. I will recognize other important people in the last variation, "Bows."

I am especially grateful for what I have learned while on this great adventure, the realms to which my imagination was inspired to take me, and the opportunities that have arisen from it. I look forward to continuing this process with music and many other subjects well into the future.

Please…enjoy!

Variation 2

The Unattainable

A President's letter for the January 2012 Segerstrom Center for the Arts program book for the Beethoven's Diabelli Variations performance by Marino Formenti.

Dear Audience,

"Let us strive with all our might toward the unattainable." So said Ludwig van Beethoven. Ludwig did indeed walk the walk, especially in his late works—the final quartets, *Missa Solemnis,* Ninth Symphony, and the *Diabelli Variations.* He seems to have distilled this concept of striving upwards into a tight focus that guided him through the distorted sonic horror of his deteriorating sound world. He continues on, organizing this surrounding cacophony with selected notes on paper and transferring it subsequently through instruments and voices into a voyage beyond the mortal world—into the heavens, into the essence of joy.

The Philharmonic Society of Orange County is excited to join in this journey toward the unattainable. We are presenting all of Beethoven's major late works over a number of months—the last quartets, the big choral works with orchestra, and, tonight, the *Diabelli Variations* for piano. Inspiration is like a football that is handed off or passed from player to player towards, at times, a seemingly unattainable goal. While winning may be important, it's the game and the techniques that really matter. I received this inspired football idea from playwright Moisés Kaufman after seeing his play *33 Variations*, first on Broadway and then in Los Angeles. The play gained notoriety largely due to its star, Jane Fonda. She did a fine job portraying a terminally ill musicologist who is trying to discover, in the time that she has left to live, why Beethoven would go to the trouble of writing thirty-three variations on a rather insipid tune by his publisher, Anton Diabelli. Ultimately, the play provokes a lot of thought. While it does explain the reason why Beethoven did what he did (one reason at least), the play inspired me to look further into the composer's late creative period. As a presenter of music, there is no better way to conduct such an exploration than by organizing live performances of the late major works and then talking and writing about them.

Kaufman, the playwright, was in a record store seeking a CD of classical piano music. The store's resident expert suggested the *Diabelli Variations*, saying it was a mysterious creation—Beethoven's great obsession. "The question I had was, *why?*" says Kaufman. "Why, when he was working on his eighth and then his ninth symphonies, would the genius choose to focus on the mediocre? It's not like he had all the time in the world. Beethoven was the one who said, 'Life is short, art is long.' So, by the time I got home from the record store, I knew I had to write this play." (This also begs another question for me: where are all of those wonderfully knowledgeable salesmen who worked in the classical music section of the now defunct Tower Records? Every one of those stores had them, across the nation. So sad for the state of music in this country, but I digress.)

I had an opportunity to chat with Kaufman during a break at the play's rehearsals at the Ahmanson Theatre in Los Angeles. He was driven to write and direct his play the same way Beethoven was motivated to write those variations—on a smaller scale, of course, but with no less intensity. I was determined to pursue the presentations of these late works. And, above all, I wanted to make them attainable for the enjoyment of our public. A group of Philharmonic Society supporters and staff members piled into a bus to join me at a matinee of *33 Variations* at the Ahmanson. I was determined to spread the fever. Everybody loved it, and I can only hope all were inspired to discover more, continuing the chain of completed passes.

To present these great late works, we bring to you the very best. The pillars of the whole project are the performances of the *Missa Solemnis* and the Ninth Symphony. The choice was obvious—the dream musical combination of Sir John Eliot Gardiner conducting the Orchestre Révolutionnaire et Romantique and the Monteverdi Choir, the same fabulous assemblage of English musicians who performed the complete nine Beethoven symphonies for us back in 1999. The only question was how to make the dream come true.

Conversations with Sir John Eliot over tapas in London and then Greek mezes in New York did the trick and the deal was done: he agreed to appearances at both Carnegie Hall and Segerstrom Center for the Arts in 2012. Scheduling the quartets was easy. Every string quartet worth its salt has the late Beethoven quartets in its repertoire.

Now another big issue: who should play the *Diabelli Variations*? Alfred Brendel is retired from concertizing and Maurizio Pollini hates flying to California. Above all, the performer needs to be special, talented, and unique as this is the piece of music that started me on this unattainable journey, but the right choice became clear. Marino Formenti is, I feel, the most renowned pianist for new and avant-garde music. His insight into music is uncanny. In the past, we had enjoyed his presentations at our Eclectic Orange Festival. Formenti has appeared numerous times in Los Angeles. On one of those occasions, he played a little *D minor Sarabande* of Bach with such tenderness and understanding that I was moved to tears. I asked him a short time later, "Do you know the *Diabelli Variations*?" He replied, "No," to which I responded, "Please learn it." He did and in addition, much in his personal style, he commissioned the young American composer Evan Gardner to write a new "variation" for our concert. It will have its North American premiere here tonight, and is inspired by the late American composer John Cage, whose 100th birthday we celebrate in 2012.

We will have quite an evening ahead, celebrating a chain of iconoclasts from the 19th, 20th and 21st centuries—Beethoven, Cage and Gardner. May you be inspired to continue with us on this quest for the unattainable!

Dean Corey
President and Artistic Director
Philharmonic Society of Orange County

Variation 3

HORN A PLENTY

WHILE WRITING THESE variations, I have been pestered by a few folks to write about the French horn. No one in Orange County has ever heard me play it, and in the current condition of my chops, they wouldn't want to. I might take it up again just for fun; maybe I can join a French village band.

I hung up my horn, professionally, in 1983. Being that it is now 2013, I have *not* been playing the horn much longer than I *did* play the horn.

During my childhood in Texas, Mom and Dad were very close friends of Bill and Lucy Jacobsen. Bill was the band director at Carter Junior High School, and Dad was band director at Arlington High School. They would often get together at the Jacobsens' to drink beer, listen to music and complain about the school budget. Meanwhile, my sister and I were relegated to the den to watch TV. Bill was a horn player. On one of these occasions, I saw his horn in the den and I asked him if I could play it. He demonstrated a few basic pointers—how to make a sound and how to use the valves to play a C major scale. I was smitten and spent the whole time trying to figure out how to play the scale, which I mastered by the end of the evening. I was inspired to think about playing the French horn in band when I was finally old enough.

My first band director was Bob Rober, whose wonderful wife Marcia would accompany me on the piano whenever there was a solo contest. We were a winning team, taking first division medals one after another.

By the end of high school, I had decided to major in music in college. The best university in our part of the state was the University of North Texas, and I was already taking horn lessons from its horn professor, Clyde Miller. He was a terrific, if strict, teacher. Of course, I thought I was already a hotshot. From him, I learned a sense of humility with my instrument, discovering how much more I really had to learn. I also took a few lessons from John Barrows one summer at the University of Wisconsin—he was my idol at the time.

During my senior year at North Texas, I received a scholarship offer to study for my master's degree at the Yale School of Music. To this day, it remains the single most exciting piece of mail I have ever received. Having participated in Yale's music festival in Norfolk, Connecticut, the previous summer, I must have made a decent impression.

The timing, however, was problematic. In my naiveté, I thought that I would be able to avoid the military draft because I was going to graduate school. Wrong! After graduation, I got married, went on a weekend honeymoon to Dallas, and started a summer job delivering mail. I came home to find a nicely written piece of mail, a letter from President Richard Nixon requesting my presence at a rice paddy party in Vietnam. I was already working for the government, delivering mail in the blistering Texas sun, so this news came as a double whammy, unfortunate as well as unexpected. Some of my talented classmates saw this coming and wisely auditioned for some of the military bands in Washington—better to make music than get shot at. I made some frantic calls and learned there was a single opening in the horn section of the United States Navy Band in the capital. I high-tailed it to Washington, D. C., played the audition, and got in. I had to enlist for four years, but at least it meant I could continue playing my horn.

As fate would have it, they wouldn't accept me in the military. I had been experiencing back problems for a number of years, and this was a barrier for service. I thought, "I guess I'll just go to Yale after all." What a summer!

I had a tremendous time there, studying with Paul Ingraham. Not only was he a great teacher, but he was also one of the busiest horn players in New York City. I was able to substitute for him often, which gave me a lot of playing time with the orchestra of the New York City Ballet.

I remember my first morning rehearsal with the orchestra. I was more excited than nervous. To think, "Wow, New York City…Lincoln Center"—it was my dream come true! While walking down the hallway behind the orchestra pit, I asked one of the other horn players what music we were going to play, and he responded, "Who cares?" It seemed cynical, but I had been told by people at home that this is how New Yorkers were. I was playing principal horn because I was taking Paul's place. When I sat down in my chair, I opened the folder on the music stand and saw a piece of music called "Who Cares?," a medley of Gershwin songs that Balanchine had choreographed for the New York City Ballet arranged by Hershy Kay. The so-called cynical horn player was Ed Birdwell, a fellow Texan. He and I became great friends and this was a very happy time. I was being well paid for spitting through a coil of brass tubing. I would have done it for free, but I didn't tell that to Ed.

It is said the French horn is the most difficult of all musical instruments. It may be true. My band director Bob Rober used to say that any instrument is difficult to play well. But the French horn is the one instrument that can entertain audiences with the many musical disasters that can befall its practitioners. "Did you hear those horns? Dreadful!" has been uttered at many an intermission of orchestra concerts or operas throughout music history.

What is the problem, then? To answer that question, we must explore how a brass instrument works in the first place. Sound is produced by a vibration that is carried on waves of air at a frequency we can hear. Vibrations can be caused by striking a surface, plucking or bowing a string, blowing on a reed, or, as in the case of brass instruments, buzzing the lips on the end of a hollow tube. A steady vibration, which can be described as having a certain pitch, volume, duration and timbre, is a musical tone.

A musical tone can be produced on a brass instrument by steadily buzzing the lips on a conical or cup-shaped mouthpiece. Its funnel shape directs the vibration into the hollow brass tube to which it is attached, causing the column of air within to vibrate, producing a musical tone. Increasing or relaxing the lip tension can produce higher and lower tones. Different pitches correspond to a series of overtones. Without going into acoustical science as to how this happens, these overtones have a set pattern for all brass instruments. You may be familiar with bugle calls where the player can play a number of notes without the use of any valves. He is playing exclusively on the overtones of the instrument. The lowest pitch on the instrument is called the fundamental tone. Each successive overtone, as one increases the lip tension, grows closer to the next. First they are eight notes apart, then five, four, three, and then two notes apart as you go higher. These are all of the notes that a bugle or valve-less instrument can play, unless you make adjustments. On the horn (short for French horn), notes that are not in the overtone pattern can be played by inserting the hand in the bell (flared end of the tubing) and partially closing the opening until the desired note is found. The sound quality is greatly affected. In all music produced for horn by Baroque and Classical composers, the player must use this hand-stopping technique.

To further complicate matters, if the composer wanted a different key altogether, the player would have to change horns or add or subtract crooks of tubing to get the right key. Therefore, the written music was always in the key of C and the composer would indicate which horn the player has to use—horn in D, horn in E-flat, etc.

On the modern French horn, valves are used to reroute the tubing to change the key of the instrument. Now the player has the full range of the chromatic scale (every note in order). The same goes for the trumpet. The trombone never had this problem because the slide can move the instrument between all of the overtones.

We are getting closer to the innate problem of playing the horn. For reasons unknown to me (probably financial), the modern versions of printed Baroque and Classical horn music are as they originally appeared—the part written in C with the key of horn stipulated. It has not been transposed, which means that we cannot simply play what is written with our valve—chromatic horns. We have to transpose the part in our heads as we play. For instance, if the part is for horn in D and because the modern horn is in F (three notes higher), the player has to play three notes lower than written to compensate. This is a real pain for someone just starting to play the horn, but you get used to it and, eventually, quite good at it.

The real trouble for the horn, on top of everything else, is that those stepwise overtones are in the highest octave of the range. Valves, of course, help, but in that range there several notes that can be played with the same fingering. Not only does it require a great set of chops, but it also mandates an excellent ear; you have to be able to hear the note. The fingers won't do the trick like they do on other instruments. This makes horn playing very complicated. It is slippery territory, fraught with danger.

Mankind can't leave well enough alone. Today, it is almost *de rigueur* to perform Baroque and Classical music on "period instruments," that is, the original (or a replica of) instruments used at the time the music was written—such as gut strings, wooden flutes, and horns without valves. Christopher Hogwood and his Academy of Ancient Music were among the earliest modern practitioners of this style. When this practice started a number of years ago, I thought it was all rather granola. I now love it. Opera director Jonathan Miller refers to Hogwood's orchestra as "The Academy of Ancient Muesli." The sound is more honest, and the period instrument horn players are truly amazing. As a former horn player, I am sorry to have missed out on this change. My joke is that I played horn so long ago that my career predated the ancient instruments.

Beethoven was a horn player and wrote a sonata for horn and piano in his early days. The story goes that its first performance was listed on a publicity poster before he had even written it. At that first presentation, the horn player read from a manuscript part while Beethoven improvised the piano accompaniment.

The nine Beethoven symphonies are fun to play. There are the occasional land mines to be aware of. The *Eroica* is especially effectively written for horn. In the Ninth Symphony, there is a very exposed solo in the third movement for the fourth horn, a player not generally used to the spotlight. It would be difficult enough for a player with a valve horn, yet on the open horn, where you only have the overtones and your trusty right hand—it is murder. That passage of music is strewn with the graves of many of the best horn players.

The next time you hear the horns struggling, think of what you now know about how the instrument works. The modern valve horn, with its valves and extra security triggers, can be likened to the temperament of a golden retriever—it is comfortable and familiar, with only the occasional mishap. The valve-less period horn is more like a domesticated wolf, capable of viciously turning on you at any moment. Difficulties and all, there is nothing quite as satisfying than the sounds emanating from the horn section of an orchestra—a horn section that is having a really, really great day. At intermission, you want to overhear your wealthiest patroness tell her friends, "What marvelous horns!" This is the reason we horn players go to all the trouble—horn players both new and old.

Variation 4

BEETHOVEN'S TOOLBOX

A NOTE FROM the author:

Before you read too deeply into these personal variations, I thought we might take a peek into Beethoven's musical toolbox—his bag of tricks— and explore the materials, techniques, and forms that he used, especially in his late period. Some of the terms I will explain directly within the text of the variations. There are others—possibly very familiar to some, partially familiar to more, and brand new to others. I am not trying to force a musical degree upon you. I merely wish to clarify a few things to make it all more comprehensible. I will give you a good deal of the basics of music without having to ask much—everything you've ever wanted to know, for as little effort as possible.

Audience members encounter these terms over and over, often without knowing what they mean. Due to the fact that many of these folks have long experiences with concert going, they are embarrassed to ask. Once, after giving a long lecture about a fugue in one of the Beethoven works, a gentleman later approached me and quietly asked, "What is a fugue, anyway?" I realized that I had not reached him with my presentation, and I am certain he was not the only one.

For those of you who consider yourself a musical expert, please read William Kinderman's wonderfully dense introduction, entitled "Overture," to his book on Beethoven—and guide me through it. For those of you who are musically knowledgeable, you can skim over the next dozen or so paragraphs. As for the beginners and the curious—I hope this helps.

So, here it goes—the following covers some of the basics of the music: pitch, notation, speed, rhythm, and expression.

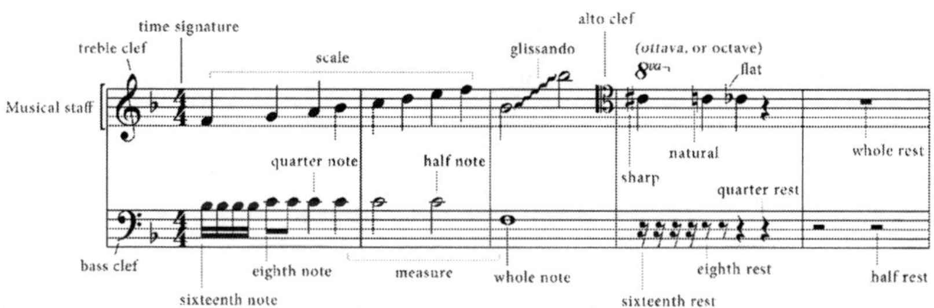

A **musical tone** is a sound that can be described as having **pitch**, a steady vibration of sound—often referred to as a **note**. This note can have duration or length, be it very short and crisp or quite long and drawn out. These notes can sound higher or lower, depending on the frequency of the vibration. A musical tone also has a sound quality, or **timbre**. This timbre helps us differentiate one instrument from another; timbre can also be thought of as subjective—the squawk of an oboe versus a particularly gorgeous sounding oboe, sometimes obvious and at other times a more subtle matter of taste. Notes can also be varying degrees of volume, referred to as **dynamics.**

The composer writes these musical notes on a kind of graph called a **musical staff**. It has five horizontal lines, with four spaces in between. The notes on the staff are represented two ways:

Fundamentally, each note is placed on a line or space of the staff, ascending in pitch as the notes on the staff go higher (and descending as they go lower). Each differently pitched note is designated by a letter, A through G. After G, the next note is A again, which matches the lower A but sounds higher. This space between the two A's or any other similar arrangement is called an **octave** because they are eight notes apart. A **scale** is a pattern of notating all of the notes on the lines and spaces in ascending or descending order, one after the other. By scraping your thumbnail up or down the white keys on a piano, you are, in effect, playing a scale. This sometimes cheesy technique, made famous by Liberace, is called a **glissando**. Beethoven uses *glissandi* on rare occasions to great effect, such as in the first concerto or the *Waldstein* Sonata.

There are **clefs** (such as **treble, alto, tenor**, or **bass**), which are placed at the beginning of each staff of music encompassing a particular line, the name of a particular pitch that sets the pattern for the other lines and spaces. The treble clef encompasses the note G. This clef is used for higher pitches, commonly played with the right hand on the piano. The bass clef encompasses the note F that handles the lower pitches, commonly played by the left hand. For notes that extend higher or lower than the lines and spaces in the clef, the composer draws a little line and places that note on, under or over it. The note follows that pattern dictated by the particular clef. For extremely high notes, a symbol *8va* is written above along with a horizontal line above the notes that the composer wants played an octave higher. This symbol is an abbreviation for the Italian word *ottava*, or octave. The alto clef (used by the violas) and the tenor clef (used sometimes by cellos, bassoons and trombones) both indicate the pitch C, and are placed in such a way on the staff as to avoid many of the little lines above or below that staff, making the music easier for the musician to read.

Secondly, there is the duration of the note, indicated by changing the shape of the note itself.

Then there is the question of making notes that need to sound together. A steady beat pattern is generally required. The time signature is placed next to the right of the clef containing two numbers, one above the other. The top number indicates the number of beats in a measure, which is designated by a vertical line on the staff. The bottom number indicates which shape note gets the beat. One of the most common time signatures is 4/4, or common time. It means that there are four beats in each **measure** (also called a **bar**) and that the quarter note gets the beat. This **quarter note** (♩) can be then divided into **eighth notes** (♫, two per beat) and **sixteenth notes** (♬, four per beat). Two quarter notes tied together equal a **half note** (two per measure). Two half notes tied together equal a **whole note** (one per measure.) In music, it is important to regularly have some spaces between the notes. This is accomplished by placing rests (silences) of various durations between the notes. The musician treats these rests rhythmically just like the note. Rests have the same length relationship as the notes—whole, half, quarter, eighth, and sixteenth notes correspond to **whole, half, quarter, eighth** and **sixteenth rests**.

Rhythm is the movement of a regular pulse or beat. In common time C, the four quarter notes occur on each of the four beats—they coincide with the pulse. The beats can be at different tempos (plural, *tempi*)—very slow to very fast, depending on the desires of the composer and the performer. Jazz uses a concept that gives it "a good beat" by using rhythms that may not coincide with the pulse, thereby giving more importance to it. This is called **syncopation**. The resulting sound is either a bit too soon or slightly after the expected note sound, and is often used in improvisation. Otherwise, it encourages emotion and is used to create excitement and intrigue within the music. Beethoven was no stranger to this device. My English friend and music devotee, Tim Mahon, defines syncopation as an unsteady movement from bar to bar—I am positive he was referring to music rather than the early days of our friendship.

Of extreme importance, especially when two or more instruments are playing together, is agreement on a standard set of vibrations for each note. In the United States, the standard is the A on the second space of the treble clef, 440 vibrations per second. It is a standard set by our government. Countries in Europe generally use a slightly higher A. The Vienna Philharmonic uses A at 443 variations per second. We run into problems when the music they are going to perform needs a celesta, a bell-sounding keyboard you have heard used in the *Dance of the Sugar Plum Fairy*. Because these are not easily tuned, we ask the orchestra to bring its own instrument. Playing 440 A with a 443 A produces what is often referred to as a sour note.

The distance between two notes, whether or not they are sounded together or one after the other, is called an **interval**. They are referred to as a number—a second, a third, fourth, etc. A second defines two successive notes that are right next to each other on the scale or staff. In western music—especially that of Beethoven—the pitches rise or descend using a chromatic scale, equivalent to the white and black keys on a keyboard. This is the same palette of notes that Beethoven used, calling each interval between notes a half step. For example, the interval between C and D is called a major second. Raising the C to a note between C and D is called a half step. That particular note is called a C-sharp. The sharp (#) placed in front of a note raises it a half step, and a flat (♭) placed in front of a note lowers it a half step.

Keys in Beethoven are generally major or minor. A C major scale is composed of the white notes on the piano. The intervals between E and F, as well B and C, are half steps. To change keys to, say, B-flat major or G major, the notes must be in the same intervallic relationship as they are in C major. Major scales generally sound happy and positive. Minor scales are markedly sad, moody, or even angry. To change a C major scale to a C minor, the E, A and the B notes needed to be lowered a half step to E-flat (E♭), A-flat (A♭) and B-flat (B♭). You can create a minor scale on any note as long as you keep the same intervallic relationship. The flats or sharps used for a particular key are placed in the key signature after the clef, meaning that all of the notes indicated as sharps or flats are always sharped or flatted, unless a natural sign (♮) is put in front of the note to indicate that, for that one note or measure only, that note is not to be sharped or flatted. To establish the key of a piece, one must center harmony on the notes of the scale in question. For example, a piece in the key of C major uses the notes of the C major scale. The tonic note is C. The tonic triad, C-E-G, is also known as a C major chord.

Harmony is created when several notes sound together at the same time. Pleasing harmonies are referred to as being **consonant.** Harsh harmonies can be called **dissonant.** Harmony can be quite complicated. After causing your eyes to glaze over with all of the above, I would simply state that what I think makes music beautiful is the battle between consonance and dissonance. Composers use consonance for a thought or feeling or idea we can relate to; dissonance is a way to express that which is not entirely understood by the listener—or sometimes even the composer. The dissonance makes the consonance more beautiful; its edgy harmony makes the consonance sparkle. It is transitional, contemplative, and very meaningful—a truly great composer understands the way to use it wisely. To me, that is the essence of what makes music beautiful.

You don't have to analyze it. The average listener without any musical knowledge will feel it, understand it, and appreciate it. It's innately human, like the difference between sweet and sour, hot and cold—it enhances, the contrasts balance each other. Altogether, it is an audible way of asking *why*, releasing a sentiment and meeting the listener halfway. Of course, it is all the same with drama or visual art—you can overdo either and ruin it. The artist creates a balance and makes it beautiful.

One very musical aspect is **melody**. This is something that you can remember, especially if it is a so-called "catchy" tune. Melody is like a sentence, with notes instead of words. People get nervous when they can't perceive a melody. They suspect that the music is not very good. This, of course, is completely not true. I recommend that they just breathe and give it another go.

The original purpose of melodies in early times was to dictate what dance steps would be used—you change to a different melody; you change your dance step, like in a square dance. In the days of the historical epic poem (be it the *Odyssey, Beowulf, Song of Roland,* etc.), the reciter would actually sing the poem to help him remember it. There wasn't notation and many of the reciters and listeners were illiterate; while we are not able to hear the original versions, we have editions that have been handed down through the course of time. While we lack the original melodies, we have the words, which were handed down by those who were fortunately literate. We are grateful to the melody for standing the test of time—yet another example of the timeless qualities of music.

A **melody** is simply an arrangement of notes, pitches, and rhythms in regular phrases. Melody, in vocal songs, serves the same purpose that it did for the ancients—keeping the words straight between the verse and the refrain, like a mnemonic. It acts as the cohesive point between the writer of the music, the player, and the listener.

Melodies can also be called themes when they refer to someone or something, or, especially in the case of Beethoven, when they serve a structural device for holding a piece of music together. The most notable example of this is the first movement of the Fifth Symphony. The memorable opening "dit-dit-dit-DAH!" is used throughout the piece. Beethoven uses this pattern to shape other melodies; he can change keys and break up the theme into little pieces. It holds together brilliantly, because he never lets go of that initial four-note idea. It keeps us engaged as listeners: those few simple notes are distinctive in Western culture—one of his greatest signatures.

Writing a melody that is uncomplicated as well as effective is one of the most difficult things to do. Beethoven's "Ode to Joy" theme in the last movement of the Ninth Symphony is a perfect example of a profound tune that anyone can sing. This movement is a grand set of variations on the "Ode to Joy" melody. By the late period, Beethoven was the master of the variation form. Theme and variations is a form he used throughout his life. His 33 *Diabelli Variations* is the inspiration behind these "variations" that I am writing for you here; the trick is to create a theme—building your own or borrowing from someone else—that has many possibilities for variation, where you can strut your stuff. The simplest variations are technical displays, an opportunity for the performer to show off his skill. A good example is the variations for cornet on the *Carnival of Venice*; certainly not profound music, but very fun. At the other extreme are variations like the *Diabelli* of Beethoven or the *Goldberg Variations* of Bach that transform the theme, making a metamorphosis. Beethoven reached the zenith of variation writing in his late period.

On the subject of **forms**, Beethoven greatly restricted their use in his late period. By the time he had written the *Diabelli Variations*, he had already written all of his concerti, all thirty-two of his piano sonatas, and eight of his nine symphonies. Also done during this time was his last mass, the *Missa Solemnis*, his last symphony the Ninth "Choral" Symphony, and a lovely set of bagatelles, as well as the last five string quartets. Franz Josef Haydn fully developed the classical forms of the sonata, the string quartet, the symphony, and the mass. These were primarily the forms in which Beethoven worked during his last years.

The sonata, the string quartet and the symphony are very similar kinds of music. The **sonata** is generally written for a single instrument like the piano or an instrument with piano accompaniment, as in the violin sonatas. The **string quartet** is written for the obvious four instruments (two violins, viola and cello), while the **symphony** is meant for an orchestra. Typically, all three of these forms are in multiple movements, generally four.

The first movement in general is the most formally constructed in what is known as the *sonata-allegro* form. In this form, the movement is in three sections. The first, the **exposition,** begins in the tonic key, and exposes a main theme, a second theme, and then a concluding theme, which ends in the dominant key, based on a triad pitched five notes above the tonic key. There is method in this madness; the dominant chord has a tendency to lead into the tonic chord. It just sounds right, like the shift between tension and relaxation. It is another example of the kind of contrast that makes music beautiful.

The second section of the first movement is called the **development**. In this section, the composer is free to develop the themes from the first section in any way he chooses, similar to what he might do in the variation form. It is important to build a sense of instability so as to contrast this section from the more organized exposition. To create this effect, it is helpful to change keys, straying away from the tonic and dominant keys, and then gradually working your way back to them so as to begin the final section, called the **recapitulation.**

The recapitulation does what it sounds like it is supposed to—it recaps the exposition in the tonic key, only this time it does not modulate into the dominant key. It stays in the tonic key and moves to a close. This procedure gives the whole movement balance. Sometimes a composer will add what is known as a **coda**. The Italian word *coda* comes from the Latin word meaning "tail." When the recapitulation is not quite sufficient in strength to close the entire first movement, a coda can be used to bring the entire thing into balance. Beethoven often used codas because many of his development sections were long and harmonically complicated. He used codas in the way one would use long tails on very lively kites, to keep them from crashing.

The first movements of most sonatas, quartets and symphonies follow this sonata-allegro pattern. The term *allegro* (fast) is important because most first movements are written to be performed fast, even if there is a slow introduction.

The second movements are generally slower, more song-like. They are comparable to an aria, though usually much longer. Whereas first movements are a bit serious, an opportunity for the composer to show off his mental prowess, second movements are more music for the heart instead of the brain. They are like songs, arias, or ariettas, short songs. This offers a wonderful contrast that we now understand as being important in making music beautiful. The second movement is generally divided into verse and chorus, just like a standard song. Melody is extremely important. Sometimes, it is set in the theme and variations format, like the *arietta* movement of Beethoven's last sonata, Op. 111. This movement is sometimes referred to as the "slow" movement, because the composer will often indicate at the beginning the tempo to be used such as *andante* (walking), *adagio* (slow) or *lento* (very slow).

Whereas the second movement is music for the heart, the third movement is music for the feet. The third movements of Haydn and Mozart were quite often minuets. **Minuets** are derived from a type of French social dance, with three beats per measure. They are generally moderate in tempo, making an elegant dance of small steps. The form can be rather strict—two sixteen-bar phrases with each repeated. Between the tonic, there is harmonic movement, changing to dominant and back to the tonic again. The key of the minuet is generally the same key of the first movement. After this, there is a trio with a contrasting melody and mood in the dominant key. The tempo stays the same; the trio also consists of two repeated sixteen-bar phrases. Then there is a return to the minuet section, this time with no repeats. Beethoven exploited this form and used it to transition into the **scherzo**. The same format is used, except the tempo is much faster—*presto* (very fast). A supreme example of this can be found in the second movement of Beethoven's Ninth Symphony. The word *scherzo* means "joke."

The fourth and final movement, in most cases, is also music for the feet. In concertos, this movement is the third and final movement, leaving out the minuet-trio. The tempo is often very fast (*prestissimo*) or lively (*vivace*). The form can be the *sonata-allegro* and sometimes a *rondo* form; the *rondo* is another French dance form, similar to the minuet-trio. Where the minuet-trio form might be described as ABA, the **rondo** continues the pattern with some added material in a format of ABACA. Because of the complexity of ideas, a coda is often added to keep the movement in balance. The fourth movement generally ends in the same key as the first movement, giving cohesion to the work as a whole. This is where the composer is going for a standing ovation.

Beethoven wrote sixteen string quartets; the last five are known as the late quartets. With these in particular, he dramatically altered the form. Three of the five have more than four movements. In Op. 131, the first movement is a fugue, and a great one. This particular quartet was Beethoven's favorite.

Now I'd like to take this opportunity to clarify what a **fugue** is all about, in response to the puzzled attendee I mentioned earlier. It is first important to know about counterpoint. **Counterpoint** is the concurrence of two melodic lines at the same time. Imitative counterpoint is the effect of the same melody played against itself. First, the melody starts and then a few beats or bars later, the melody starts in again by another voice. The song "Row Your Boat" is an ideal example. This type of counterpoint is called a **canon** or a **round.** No matter how many voices you have join in singing "Row Your Boat," it always sounds right, because the melody is centered around a major triad—therefore, no clashes.

The fugue is a complicated form of imitative counterpoint. More a style than a form, it can be written for more than two voices, though usually no more than five. Like the canon, there is an initial single melody, or fugue subject, followed in the next voice by an imitation of that melody beginning on a different note, followed by more similarly staggered entrances by the remaining voices. When the first voices run out of the theme, they take up new material that can be called a **countersubject**. After all of the voices have joined and completed the fugue subject, then there can begin a further episodic section, like the development section in a sonata's first movement. Here the composer can play around with bits and pieces of what has happened so far, moving through different keys. When he is ready to bring everything to a close, the fugue subject returns in the same key that it started. The other voices follow suit. This is usually followed by a coda, its length in relationship to the overall length of the entire fugue. Again, it is that same kite-and-tail idea.

Fugues, especially those with many voices, can be quite difficult to write. Bach, of course, was the great master, influencing all fugues that were composed after him. Above all, fugues show off a composer's creative ability. Because of their complexity, they can be very dramatic and are very effective when used in especially poignant moments within a larger movement. The word fugue comes from the Latin *fugare*, meaning "to chase." The term *fughetta* is simply a smaller fugue. Due to their exciting nature, fugues can draw a musical conclusion in much the same way that a fantastic car chase brings the end of an action film. The effect can be very powerful.

Beethoven composed two masses, the wonderful Mass in C major, Op. 86, of 1807, and the *Missa Solemnis*, Op. 123, finished in 1822. The name for the latter means "solemn mass," a mass being the sacrament of the Eucharist of the Roman Catholic Church. Although baptized in the Catholic faith, Beethoven was not a devout church attendee. He looked upon the mass primarily for its formal music aspects. The mass is divided into five primary sections: *Kyrie,* a prayer asking for mercy; *Gloria,* an expression of praise; *Credo,* a setting of the belief-affirming Nicene Creed; *Sanctus* with the *Benedictus,* another hymn of praise; and the *Agnus Dei,* asking for mercy and peace from the Lamb of God. In the *Missa Solemnis,* Beethoven was thinking big. Masses after this could be immense—think of the requiems (masses for the dead) of Berlioz and Verdi, or the over-the-top mass of Leonard Bernstein.

Another device that Beethoven employs in his later works is the trill. The **trill** is a rapid alternation between two adjacent notes, an ornamental figure. In Baroque and Classical music, it is used often on the penultimate note of a melody, giving more focus to the ending. Musicians often add them at points of the melody they would like to emphasize, an improvisation. In his late works, Beethoven used them frequently, mostly for the ethereal, dreamy effect they produce. There are many examples in the late piano sonatas, the *Diabelli Variations*, and the late quartets. You will have fun discovering them.

Beethoven used descriptive terms at the beginning of his pieces to give the performer an idea of his intentions. They are primarily Italian terms, the language of the day because so many of the classical forms originated in Italy.

A few of the most common: ***cantabile*** meaning "songlike;" ***appassionato*** says "passionately;" ***grazioso*** means "gracefully," and ***crescendo***, telling the musician to increase the volume. These are words that are good to know and can be easily found with full explanations on the internet. Beethoven also used his native German for more personal, specific instructions. One might wonder how Beethoven's work would have changed had he had access to the Google search engine.

There you have it, a basic introduction to important classical terms. The above is by no means a definitive education—the beauty of it is that we always have something more to discover. I hope that you will enjoy reading my variations and that you will be inspired to continue your exploration of Beethoven, the math behind the sounds, and musical creation.

Piano Pieces and Other Strange Ideas

Variation 5

LITTLE MIRACLES

*A pre-concert lecture that took place on January 7, 2012, prior
to a performance of Beethoven's Diabelli Variations by Marino
Formenti at the Renée and Henry Segerstrom Concert Hall,
Segerstrom Center for the Arts.*

GOOD EVENING, LADIES and gentlemen, and welcome to the Philharmonic
Society's *Beethoven: The Late Great* project. After tonight, we will present
the other great works of his late period—the *Missa Solemnis,* the Ninth
Symphony, and the remaining four string quartets—over this and the
next two seasons. I was inspired to curate this series after seeing Moisés
Kaufman's play *33 Variations* in both New York in 2009 and later in Los
Angeles. Moisés told me he ran across a CD of the *Diabelli Variations*
and, after listening to the sales associate in the classical section expound
on the significance of the variations to Beethoven and the world of music,
he was inspired to write a play about it.

The Philharmonic Society presented a performance of the *Diabelli
Variations* in April 2002, when Alfred Brendel performed it in the second half of a recital. The day started with an early morning, when we
took Brendel to the Irvine Barclay Theatre to meet piano technician Ron
Elliot. Before our arrival, Ron had already tuned the piano—a select one

from Pro Piano in Los Angeles. Brendel had given us the serial number of the piano he wanted a few months before, as he knows where all the great ones are stashed around the world. He is a very serious and thorough artist. Mr. Brendel and Mr. Elliot sat next to each other in front of the keyboard, where the technician proceeded to voice each and every note under Brendel's careful direction. Voicing a piano consists of loosening and hardening the felt on every hammer, an incredibly tedious and time consuming process. The result is to create a perfectly even sound over the whole keyboard. After this was complete, Brendel began his warm up, and I took a seat in the back of the empty hall to listen to the master for a few minutes. He worked his way through various exercises, and, in his noodling, started in with the actual Diabelli waltz. I was struck by what must be a most enormous task, remembering all of the variations, while demonstrating technical prowess and energy. Physically, mentally, and emotionally, this was an exhausting piece. To perform this in public would be a monumental achievement. He proceeded to the first variation, then the second, the third, and on and on until I realized he was going to play all thirty-three of them. I glanced at my watch, trying to mentally reschedule the rest of my day. Slipping out quietly was not an option. The last thing I wanted to do was to disturb his concentration. I then realized what an enormous opportunity it was, to have a private performance of the *Diabelli Variations* by one of the greatest pianists in the world. That experience, and my new interest in the *Diabelli Variations* itself, attracted me to Moisés Kaufman's play.

Appreciation aside, I had a bigger question: "Why did Beethoven create this enormous work?" It began as a challenge by his music publisher Anton Diabelli, a rather mediocre composer, who wanted him to write a variation on his own banal waltz. Diabelli thought his tune was rather catchy and had the idea of commissioning fifty of Vienna's most prominent and up-and-coming composers to write a variation on the theme. Being a better marketer than a composer, his plan was to publish the waltz and the fifty variations in a single volume and make money while creating a public relations coup. At this point in Beethoven's creative life, circa 1819, he had already completed his 32 piano sonatas, the piano concerti, violin concerto, eight of his nine symphonies, and eleven of his sixteen string quartets. So why would he take up such a challenge? Was it for the money? What did he hear in this unremarkable tune, and what would inspire him to invent thirty-three variations on it? It took him three years to complete it, during which time he was writing the monumental *Missa Solemnis* and sketching out his Ninth Symphony.

Genius aside, Beethoven was not above composing for the sake of making a buck. Testament to this was his instrumental bombast *Wellington's Victory*, which was composed to commemorate the defeat of Napoleon's brother Joseph at Vitoria, Spain. It is both fun and, at the same time, a sort of dreadful piece for mass consumption that provided a surge of celebrity to Beethoven's already huge public reputation. He enjoyed the income, but still had more to say. But due to failing health and his almost complete deafness, he felt that time was working against him. He knew it would only be a matter of time until he was no longer able to write like he wanted to do. It wasn't so much a fear of death (which would occur in 1827), as it was the distress that his time as an artist was running short. Beethoven felt a powerful need to maximize the gifts he knew he possessed and sensed a moral obligation to give of his gift to the people of his time and generations to come. He was the world's greatest composer and he knew it.

Diabelli's project ran into trouble when Beethoven took more time than was expected to deliver a single variation. The publisher ultimately managed to get 50 variations composed without Beethoven, including ones from Czerny, Schubert, and the boy Liszt. Later, when Beethoven completed his 33 variations, Diabelli added them all to the edition of now 83 variations by now fifty-one composers, compiled under the strange name of *Vaterländischer Künstlerverein*, or the "Patriotic Artists' Association." Diabelli realized that he couldn't call it a collection of contemporary Viennese composers unless it included something by the greatest composer himself, Ludwig van Beethoven.

So why 33 variations? Johann Sebastian Bach's 32 *Goldberg Variations* (if you count the aria and its reprise) were, up to that point, the most significant set of variations yet written. Was Beethoven trying to compete with Bach? The beginning of the answer, I believe, is found in the dramatic difference between the themes of each set of variations. Bach's *Goldberg Variations* are spun off an elegant aria of his own devising. Beethoven's variations are shaped from a tune from another composer, Diabelli, that is nowhere near as originally elegant. Did he hear in it some possibilities that were musically worth exploring? I think so, and also believe there was a deeper significance.

Ludwig van Beethoven was born in Bonn, Germany, on December 16, 1770, the second child to Johann Beethoven and his wife, the widowed Maria Magdalena Leym. We traditionally celebrate his birthday on the 17th as that was actually the day he was christened. An earlier son, Ludwig Maria, died after only six days. Of the next five siblings, only his brothers Carl and Johann survived. He was the namesake of his grandfather, who was the *Kapellmeister* of the elector court, a post that his father Johann, a court tenor, was unable to achieve after his father's death. Johann was an angry man, a fierce drunk and an abusive father. The young Ludwig's grandmother was also an alcoholic who was institutionalized by the *Kapellmeister*, her own husband. Beethoven's grandfather never approved of his son's marriage to the widow Maria, and this kind of family dynamic did not make for what one would call a happy home life. Maybe Diabelli's little tune was a reminder to Beethoven of where he had come from. Taking this into consideration, I think Diabelli's tune sounded to him more like the music of a beer hall "oom-pah-pah" band rather than a conventional waltz.

As far-fetched as this seems, perhaps this information is the key to the comprehensive set—33 characteristic miniatures containing a fair amount of parody—some playing on Diabelli and other composers, including his own self-satire. He first dismissed the whole idea, calling Diabelli's little theme a *Schusterfleck* or "cobbler's patch." Of course, we are not as accustomed in modern times to having the soles of our shoes redone—we just throw them out. But this was not the case in the nineteenth century, when shoes and boots were expensive and everyone walked a great deal. When the soles of shoes wore out, one would hire a cobbler to add a patch on the scuffing. As time passed, more and more patches were added. And you can hear these "re-patch" jobs in the theme with an upward harmonic progression device in each half of the piece (first the left shoe, then the right, I suppose).

I believe Beethoven had fun writing these variations. The composer's secretary and early biographer Anton Schindler says the work "amused Beethoven to a rare degree, bubbling with unusual humor." Not something we might expect of Beethoven at this late stage in his life. It seems to me that Schindler was perfectly accurate in this description. Referring to the following set of variations, Alfred Brendel says, "The theme has ceased to reign over its unruly offspring. Rather, the variations decide what the theme may have to offer them. Instead of being confirmed, adorned and glorified, it is improved, parodied, ridiculed, disclaimed, transfigured, mourned, stamped out and finally uplifted." I think this is an excellent summary of the work as a whole. Each one is a part of a whole, but can stand on its own, a forthcoming Romantic ideal. In his late period, Beethoven was not so much out to change the Classical forms but to transcend them, finding fresher methods of expression.

A week ago, my wife Kaly and I came home from spending the holidays in France. We went to the medieval village of Conques in the Aveyron, where I wanted to visit the famous abbey. For the last couple of years, I have been very intrigued with the story of Sainte Foy. Her relics are at the abbey and I see a parallel between her story and that of Beethoven. Of particular interest is the famous lock of hair snipped from Beethoven's head by the 15-year-old Ferdinand Hiller, shortly after Beethoven's death. The lock has had quite an adventure in the twentieth century. Sainte Foy was a 12-year-old girl in Agen who was tortured and executed by the Romans in 302 A.D., after repeatedly refusing to recant her deep Christian faith. Her name, Foy, means "faith." Many miracles are attributed to her, some of which were recorded in a very interesting collection called "Liber miraculorum sancte Fidis" written in the eleventh century by the monk Bernard of Angers. My wife and I were fortunate to see the original manuscript which was on display at the abbey. It is comprised of four books, most of which I have now been able to read. The most important is the first book, which contains the stories of 34 miracles, one more than Beethoven's *33 Variations*—which is one more than Bach's 32 variations. The dawning significance to me is that we might be able to refer to the *Diabelli Variations* as "little miracles."

And little miracles they are, indeed. And by little, I refer to their length. Some are less than 30 seconds. The big fugue, No. 32, is five minutes, while 15 other variations are only one minute or less. In listening to them, I feel each has its own character, and it's important to just let them spin out. The first variation is a march, not unlike the marches that the teenage Beethoven wrote in Bonn. It is rather pompous, ridiculing Diabelli's theme. Others are like finger exercises, again poking fun at Diabelli, who was chiefly a composer of pedagogical pieces. Aside from the more playful pieces, there are some others that are quite beautiful, presaging Chopin, Mendelssohn and Schumann. Rather than "variations," Beethoven called these pieces *Veränderungen* (alterations or ramblings). There are many ways that he elaborated on the theme. I recommend the in-depth study by William Kinderman, who provides an excellent play-by-play account. The variations primarily stay in the home key of C major, moving briefly into C minor with only the fugue, but variation 32 is in a contrasting E-flat major. They all roll along, revealing Beethoven's extraordinary imagination and resourcefulness. The advent of Beethoven himself, I feel, was a miracle.

He wrote the first 19 variations only to be interrupted with working on other pieces, family crises, and illness. All of this, of course, was driving Anton Diabelli to distraction. A deadline is a deadline—unless, of course, if you are dealing with Ludwig van Beethoven.

Variation 20 is probably the most puzzling, and the yet the most moving variation through the midpoint of the variations. Pianist Jürgen Uhe describes it as "frozen motifs contained in a crystal."

There are great influences of Bach and Mozart. Beethoven's early studies in Bonn were with the composer and court organist Christian Gottlob Neefe, who had studied in Leipzig with Johann Hiller, Bach's successor as *Kantor* of the Thomaskirche. The young 11-year-old Ludwig's primary early study pieces were from the *Well-Tempered Clavier*, though it was not commonly available in print during the 1780s. In the *Diabelli*, the three great Bachian moments are the extremely tasteful *fughetta* variation 24, worthy of the *Art of the Fugue*; the 31st variation, *Largo, molto espressivo*, reminiscent of the *Goldberg Variation* No. 25, *Larghetto*, and the penultimate variation 32, which is a quintessential Beethoven triple fugue. This connects directly through a mysterious series of triads to the last variation, the 33rd, a minuet that sounds like the one in Mozart's *Don Giovanni*. Variation 22 is a direct quote of "Notte e giorno faticar," Leporello's aria from *Giovanni*. In this song, he complains about the Don in the same manner Beethoven might grumble about Anton Diabelli: "Day and night slaving away, for someone who is never satisfied." Actually, Beethoven was probably referring to himself as the Don and writing Anton Schindler, his amanuensis, as Leporello. Beethoven finally reaches his most uplifting moment in the final half of the minuet, as I remember Alfred Brendel's performance. Here, the composer parodies himself as he returns his audience to the sound world. The *arietta* movement of this last piano sonata, the great Op. 111, is music in its most perfect form. After a truly moving listening experience, Beethoven has the final word in probably the best set of variations ever written.

Variation 6

BAGATELLES, OP. 126

A talk given to the Alta Bahia Philharmonic Committee in November 2011.

THE LATE PERIOD of Beethoven's creative life was a sea change. He left the sonatas and concertos behind. From around 1819 to his death, with his sound world deteriorating and the daily drudgery of painful health challenges, he managed to change his forms of expression. As if newly inspired, he reached deep inside for the artistry that he instinctively knew he was destined to give the world. It was a message of transformation from his innermost being, expressing a need for joy, peace and engagement, miraculously articulated for the billions of people who have enjoyed his music in generations to follow. He explored the innovations that were developing at the time, the style trending into the Romantic movement. His Op. 98, *An die ferne Geliebte,* written in 1816, was the first song cycle ever written, presaging his new creative direction. This would later be seen in examples such as the Bagatelles, Op. 126. He would still utilize theme and variations, as well as fugues, although much more intricate and grand in other late works. We might liken this to new wine in some older bottles. The substance is both substantial and curious.

William Shakespeare coined the term "sea-change" in *The Tempest* and I think it describes Beethoven's transformation to a tee. Here is the passage where the spirit Ariel sings a song of solace to comfort Ferdinand over the death of his father:

> Full fathom five thy father lies,
> Of his bones are coral made,
> Those are pearls that were his eyes,
> Nothing of him that doth fade,
> But doth suffer a sea-change,
> Into something rich and strange,
> Sea-nymphs hourly ring his knell,
> Ding-dong.
> Hark! Now I hear them, ding-dong, bell.

The Bagatelles, Op. 126, were composed at the end of 1823. Beethoven referred to them as *Kelinigkeiten* (cycle of trifles). The scholar Maynard Solomon calls them "romantic aphorisms," or a cycle of bagatelles. The composer gave the pieces to his brother Johann, saying "many of them [are] being considerably developed, and [they are] probably the best of their kind which I have written."

From earlier sketches, it appears that Beethoven finished these pieces after the Ninth Symphony was in his mind. They are unified by the key of each one being separated by a major third—except for the first two. These Bagatelles were pledged to his brother in 1824, and published by Schott in 1825.

No. 1 *Andante con moto, Cantabile e compiacevole* (agreeable): This is a gentle declamation, a sort of preamble. It plays song-like, with a *coloratura melisma* midway through. Beethoven was writing a number of songs at this point. His *An die ferne Geliebte* was probably the first song cycle, a form that would be important to notable composers like Franz Schubert, Robert Schumann, Johannes Brahms, Hugo Wolf, and others. These artists championed the Romantic ideal to which Beethoven tipped his own composer's hat. It is not certain that Beethoven and Schubert ever spent any significant amount of time together, even though they were active in Vienna at the same time. Beethoven was quite the celebrity, while Schubert was practically unknown. They were talented contemporaries, Schubert passing away only a year after Beethoven. This first bagatelle is also reminiscent of *"Of Foreign Lands and Peoples,"* the first piece of Robert Schumann's cycle *Scenes from Childhood*. It has the same sentiment and introductory nature. Having a strong melodic line, it could have been made into something bigger.

No. 2 is marked *allegro*. It is a piece of romantic form in the sense that it is programmatic and descriptive even as it is still absolute music, meaning that it is not really about anything in particular. It sounds as though it could be. To me, it represents an exchange between two individuals—one, a very agitated person, as represented by rapid sixteenth notes sounding *Ra ta ta Ra ta ta ta,* and the other is a more soothing individual, demonstrated by legato eighth notes to counter the tension of the former. It is written in two repeated sections, the second marked *cantabile*, where the soother begins and predominates until the *Ra ta ta tas* interrupt and seems to take over until there seems to be a conciliatory close. Here again, this could have been written by Schumann.

No. 3, marked *Andante cantabile e grazioso,* could have been a famous, beloved slow movement of Beethoven's piano sonatas, if he were still writing them. But his sonata phase had ended with the completion of the 32nd. The No. 3 is really a truncated theme and variations, a form that was very important to his later works. It brings to mind the third movement of the Ninth Symphony or the *Diabelli Variations* in much the same way. Especially notable is the use of a mini-cadenza. It is a noble piece with no repeated sections, quite wonderful.

No. 4 is marked *presto* and is the longest of all the bagatelles in this set. It resembles a sonata finale, with initial energy contrasted by a more dreamy section. This segment harkens nature, a distant shepherd's flute along with the drone of a faraway hurdy gurdy, quite appealing, yet a bit curious. There is a brief attempt at counterpoint in what starts off like a fugue, another form that Beethoven relied upon in his late pieces. We see here again, like the Ninth's fourth movement, a *fugato* finale on the themes of the first and third movements, and, of course, the *Diabelli Variations* 24 and 32. Beethoven is not really writing fugues in this set, but is more interested in the cyclic nature of the six pieces, much like the

String Quartet, Op. 131. That is what makes these pieces smack of the Romantic Age. The fourth movement is written in B minor, very rare. The only other major movement in B minor was his *Agnus Dei* from the *Missa Solemnis.*

No. 5, marked *quasi allegro,* is one of the loveliest moments in all of Beethoven's music. In two repeated sections with a little coda, he gives us a lyrical melody contrasted by a gentle lullaby, or serenade, drifting over the accompaniment of a quiet harp. This momentum slowly builds, in Beethoven's usual fashion, until he seems to become self-conscious of the beautiful mood he has just created. The piece ends with the original theme working its way into the clouds as it softly plays itself out.

It is believed that Beethoven had pretty much worked out the majority of the Ninth Symphony in his head before he wrote these bagatelles. This is borne out in No. 6, marked *presto,* followed by *andante amabile e con moto.* The opening six bars give the impression of a clattering carriage as it pulls away at breakneck speed—with a similar sound that so shockingly begins the choral movement. What follows is a noble section, much like the grace of the Ninth's third movement, and reminiscent of the elegant 33rd *Diabelli Variation.* It moves toward some rather inspired closing chords with Beethoven at his immortal best, only to be blasted away with the return of the opening breakneck passage. There, the Bagatelles, Op. 126, abruptly end.

Like most composers, Beethoven was not above writing music for the sake of making money. Certainly, his bagatelles are very approachable for the average pianist—unlike the *Hammerklavier* Sonata, which few pianists could play. Those who couldn't, usually bought that score as an impressive decoration to been seen by parlor guests as it sat on a music rack on the piano. But, as noted, the Op. 126 bagatelles are different. Beethoven's level of creative expression is quite high, as it is believed that he wrote with the sense that these would be the last pieces he would compose for the rank and file pianist, which turned out to be true. He would have very few published works after this set, namely the last five string quartets.

Variation 7

BEET STRETCH

A President's letter for the November 2007 Segerstrom Center for the Arts program book for the Colburn Orchestra, St. Petersburg Philharmonic, and Yo-Yo Ma & Kathryn Stott performances.

Dear Audience,

Welcome to our first Beethoven concerts of the season, the first of several concerts where we have programmed the odd-numbered symphonies. We are indeed fortunate to have pianist Vladimir Feltsman return to perform Beethoven's Third Piano Concerto and the Orange County debut of the Colburn Orchestra performing the *Eroica*. I like to think of the Colburn School as the Juilliard of the West. Its founder and great benefactor, Richard Colburn, was the greatest philanthropist of classical music that I had the pleasure to meet. He was a great friend to music in Los Angeles, to the Salzburg Festival, to the Philharmonic Society, and to me personally. Without his interaction, we would have never brought the Vienna Philharmonic here. He is greatly missed, but his legacy lives on through his foundation and the many fortunate recipients of his largesse. This afternoon's performance, which you are about to enjoy, is a brilliant example of his inspiration. I welcome all of those with the Colburn School who are joining us today.

With the big celebration of Mozart's 250th birthday recently concluded, I have felt Ludwig's spirit impatiently lurking in the wings expecting a reprise of sorts of the Beethoven Festival we presented in 1999. It is now the twenty-first century, and Beethoven's music is as important to us as ever. I feel, however, that things have changed. There are still nine Beethoven symphonies but now there are only eight planets. With this revelation, our pop science understanding has taken quite a hit and I feel it is high time for another voyage through Beethoven's sonic inventory to reassure us that it is intact.

A visit to the odd-numbered pieces would do it—his only violin concerto, his 3rd piano concerto, and Symphonies Nos. 1, 3, 5, 7, and 9. We will encounter some new views. Symphony No. 1 will be a micro-listen, condensed into one of my *What Makes Music Beautiful?* talks. Symphony No. 9 will be a macro-listen, lasting 24 hours. The rest will be in real time, a not-so-narrow view of a music that transforms reality, performed by some of the leading musicians of our time.

I am very excited about the guest artists and orchestras scheduled for this project. Beethoven's only violin concerto and the Seventh Symphony will be performed by the Royal Philharmonic Orchestra and Pinchas Zukerman. The Philharmonia Orchestra of London, conducted by Christoph von Dohnányi, will conclude our "Odd Beethoven Festival" with a performance of Beethoven's Fifth Symphony, possibly the most famous piece of classical music ever written.

To complete our tour of the odd-numbered Beethoven symphonies, I have tapped into the far side of my imagination. The Ninth Symphony, normally 65 minutes in length, will be stretched over a 24 hour period. *9BeetStretch* is a piece of idea art, a soundscape, conceived and implemented by Norwegian artist Leif Inge. It was realized at the NOTAM sound production center in Oslo. Those familiar with the real-time version of the work will recognize it, even though it is dramatically slower.

The delightful Mr. Inge will be with us, overseeing the sound installation at the Orange County Museum of Art. *9BeetStretch* will begin at 11am on Saturday, April 26, 2008, and finish at the same time the following day, Sunday. We will make available for purchase by attendees brunch, lunch, dinner, and midnight snacks.

Referring to this Beethoven Festival as "Odd" bespeaks both the emphasis on the odd-numbered works, the peculiarity of the contemporary renditions of the First and Ninth Symphonies, as well as the oddity that a genius such as Beethoven ever walked the earth. Colin Wilson wrote, "He reminds me of a man driving the car with the handbrake on, but stubbornly refusing to stop, even though there is a strong smell of burning rubber."

Music, art with sound, is certainly a temporal art. It has beginnings and endings separated by durations. This is true of any music—whether it be by Bach, John Cage, or Spike Jones. As interminable as Wagner's *Ring* or our *9BeetStretch* may seem, the above is still and always true. This means that we can—and must—continually revisit, reexamine, and replay our collective art-as-music. It may not seem the same to us each time, but that is a part of its mystery and beauty. Music will exist as long as there are human beings alive to hear it. We may now *not* consider Pluto to be a planet, but it is still out there.

Please…Enjoy!

Dean Corey
President and Artistic Director
Philharmonic Society of Orange County

Variation 8

I'll Have What He Is Having

*Music is the wine that inspires one to new generative processes,
and I am Bacchus who presses out this glorious wine for mankind,
and makes them spiritually drunken.*
    —Ludwig van Beethoven

Of my many personal passions, you should know that I love the music of
Beethoven, and I love to eat and to drink. Beethoven loved the very same
things: *his* music, eating, and drinking. We know this because Beethoven
was a packrat and kept not only his manuscripts but also scraps of paper
about everything, including shopping lists, recipes, receipts, and, of
course, old letters—a musicologist's dream. A good number of his conversation books have survived, giving a record of one-way conversations
where visitors would write questions, to which the deaf Beethoven would
verbally respond (or not). From this documentation, we can get an idea
of how the discussion was going, often times what must have been awkward circumstances. Anton Schindler, Beethoven's amanuensis and early
biographer, preserved many of these conversation books for posterity,
reportedly destroying some where the conversation was not going in
Schindler's favor. Since Beethoven's bicentennial in 1970, there has been

a great deal of study concerning any piece of paper related to Beethoven. And now we have many of the letters that he sent to others—many of them asking for wine, ordering firewood, and giving critiques of his cooks and housekeepers.

Beethoven primarily ate to feed the engine. He did, of course, have the opportunity to enjoy a good repast when present at the dining tables of his noble benefactors. This is most assuredly where he refined his palette, especially for wine, the same way I've refined mine (though not with "nobles" per se, but with the generous supporters of the Philharmonic Society and previous musical organizations with which I have had the honor to associate through the years). Like Beethoven, I share a fondness for simple but well-prepared food and wine—especially the "jammy" reds.

Beethoven was particularly interested in Gemischter Satz, a blended white wine commonly associated with Vienna and the surrounding area. It is made from a variety of grapes that are grown and harvested side-by-side, and fermented together. The flavor and quality varies depending on which grapes are having a good season. As far as cities go, Vienna is still one the largest producers of wine. In 2006, our dear friends Willy and Veronica Khristov invited my wife Kaly and me to stay for a few days at their home in Vienna before we all went to the Salzburg Festival together. It was the Mozart year (his 250th birthday), and Veronica had arranged for a tour of all of the city's top music spots—especially those involving Mozart, Schubert and, of course, Beethoven. I felt like an eager ten-year-old boy, enjoying Disneyland, space camp, and skydiving all in one day. We ended up in the village of Heiligenstadt, at one time a small municipality when Beethoven stayed there in the summer of 1802, now completely surrounded by Vienna. We dined in a local *heuriger*, a wine tavern where we could enjoy the locally produced new white wine. This is an annual tradition in Germany and Austria. There was plenty to drink, tons to eat and *Gemütlichkeit* to be shared by all. I am sure Beethoven would have enjoyed his time more if he had not been so preoccupied with his depression over the onset of his deafness.

Beethoven loved soups, vegetables, fish and, especially, macaroni and cheese. I love macaroni and cheese, though I can't have it much—only once in a great while when I can get away with it. Most of us have fond memories of macaroni and cheese, the kind that came in a store-bought blue box. Having prepared this same dish for our grandson, I was brought into the painful, Twinkie-less present. Many times, things aren't nearly as good as they used to be, or at least as we thought they were. In recent years, chefs (fancy or not) have tried to recapture this dream with way too much cheese and cheap tricks, such as adding lobster or truffles.

So, Beethoven being Beethoven, what was the version of macaroni and cheese he was so passionate about? There are some recipes and I would now like to refer to a recipe for Beethoven's macaroni and cheese assembled by the eminent Beethoven scholar William Meredith, director of the Ira F. Brilliant Center for Beethoven Studies in San Jose, and a wonderful friend and great cook. Here it is:

BEETHOVEN'S MACARONI & CHEESE
(or Traditional Austrian Spaetzle with
Cheese and Sweet Caramelized Onions)

1. Either buy or make the pasta or dumplings. If you want to purchase them, buy either 10 ounces of macaroni or dried spaetzle (available at import stores). If you buy them pre-made, cook according to the package's directions till done. If you want to make your own spaetzle, it's really easy and fun! Here's the recipe. Mix together in a bowl 3 cups of flour, 4 beaten eggs (free range if possible—it makes a big difference to use high-quality eggs), 1 teaspoon of salt, and 1 cup of milk (whole milk best). Dough will be sticky.

2. Using either a spaetzle maker (they sell them at kitchen stores for only $15) or a colander with large holes (minimum 1/4 inch holes), press the noodles into a big pot of boiling water (about 1/2 cup at a time). Once all the dough is pressed into the pot, cook for additional 2 minutes. Drain noodles in a colander and then transfer

them gently to a large bowl of ice water. Stir till the ice melts and drain the spaetzle.

3. Whether you purchase store-bought noodles or make your own, once they are cooked (and cooled if you made them yourself), put them in a large bowl and stir together with 1 tablespoon of olive (or peanut) oil. Add freshly ground pepper and salt to taste.

4. Oil a 9x13 casserole pan, add the noodles/spaetzle, and dot the noodles/spaetzle with 1-2 tablespoons of butter cut into small pieces.

5. Spread anywhere from 5 to 8 ounces of grated cheese over the top of the noodles and bake at 400 degrees for 20 minutes. Beethoven is supposed to have liked Parmesan cheese on his macaroni and cheese, but the classic Austrian recipe uses Gruyere, Emmentaler, or Appenzeller cheese. (American Parmesan is too mild and boring for this dish.)

6. While the noodles are baking, put either 1 or 2 diced onions and 1-2 tablespoons oil in a skillet and cook on high heat until softened for 1 minute. (I always use 2 onions, preferably ones like Vidalias or Hawaiian sweet onions.) Reduce heat to low and cook until caramelized, which takes the rest of the time until the noodles are cooked. When the noodles are done, scatter the caramelized (now sweet) onions on top of the noodles and serve.

Thank you, Bill! This dish is delicious, but leaves quite a dilemma—what to do? Make it myself, or more wisely, get Kaly to make it? Eat alone, or share it with friends and music lovers? I decided to use it as a promotion, as I am always trying to hustle extra tickets—and that is exactly what we did.

On Sunday, April 21, 2013, the St. Lawrence Quartet gave a concert, performing Beethoven's String Quartet No. 12, Op. 127, at the Irvine Barclay Theatre as a part of our *Beethoven: The Late Great* project. We paired the program with a dinner to follow at Britta's Café; owner Britta Kvinge Pulliam offered a typical Austro-German meal featuring the Beethoven/Meredith macaroni and cheese. We made this performance and meal arrangement after being inspired by the Glyndebourne Opera, where you can buy a ticket and order the evening's dinner in a single online transaction. We had done this once before, when pianist Louis Lortie performed the complete Liszt's *Années de pèlerinage*. The experience began in a matinee and continued in an evening performance, after a luxurious sort of intermission dinner at a choice of restaurants. Patrons pre-selected their restaurants and menus, and enjoyed shuttle transportation to expedite the schedule.

With the Beethoven/Britta's event there was no performance after dinner, so a tight schedule wasn't critical. Our promotional copy:

Music and fine dining go hand-in-hand! Make the most of your concert experience and include a four-course dinner specially created by our partner restaurant, Britta's Café, along with your ticket purchase.

Attend the St. Lawrence String Quartet performance at 3pm, and after the concert, head to Britta's Café to enjoy your gourmet dinner. Dinner reservations will be set for 5pm. The dinner package includes dinner, a beverage of your choice, tax and gratuity. Dine out without ever taking out your wallet!

Please select one entrée and one dessert:

1ˢᵗ Course
BEETHOVEN'S KÄSESPÄTZLE
Beethoven's Macaroni and Cheese

2nd Course
GEMISCHTE SALAT
House Salad

~

3rd Course – Entrée
Choice of

(3A) JÄGERSCHNITZEL
Pork cutlet with Wild Mushrooms

(3B) RINDSROULADEN
Roulades of Beef

(3C) GEBRATENES HUHN
Roasted Chicken

(3D) EINE PLATTE DES GEMÜSES
A plate of Seasonal Vegetables

(3E) BRATWURST UND SAUERKRAUT
Sausage and pickled cabbage

~

4th Course – Dessert

Choice of

(4A) ROTE GRÜTZE
Red Berry Pudding

(4B) APFELKUCHEN
Apple Cake

It was brilliant. We attracted a new audience to the concerts and had forty for the post-concert supper. Britta's team did a wonderful job. A few days later, I spoke to her about the experience in the café.

DEAN: I did—I ordered the apple cake and Kaly had the red berry pudding, so I ate off of her plate. All scrumptious. Your grandmother lived close to the water, so did you have a lot of seafood?

BRITTA: Oh, yes, but also German land food. We would have *Käsespaetzle* with knockwurst, kind of traditional. When she came to California, she wanted to eat the same food. She came here in the 1930's when she was twenty-one.

DEAN: You changed the cheeses from what Beethoven would have had.

BRITTA: Emmentaler is kind of the traditional cheese. But I love Cowgirl Creamery Wagon Wheel. It really works well and I like to eat locally.

DEAN: I have been to their stores in Ferry Street Market in San Francisco and next to the Pike Street Market in Seattle. They are paradise to cheese enthusiasts. California cheeses are quite something. Your *spaetzle* wasn't this globby thing that one might end up with. How did you make it with such perfect consistency, using the cheese?

BRITTA: Emmenthaler doesn't break down when cooked. My grandmother added a little heavy cream in there with the onions—not like American mac and cheese, which might be swimming in it, but just enough to coat the onions.

DEAN: Caramelizing the onions makes a huge difference.

BRITTA: I lightly caramelize them. If I wanted them very dark, I would add a little sugar.

DEAN: That worked out very well with your bratwurst.

BRITTA: Bratwurst on top of potatoes and sauerkraut—you can't go wrong with that.

DEAN: How do you communicate your ideas to the kitchen staff?

BRITTA: I essentially gave them the recipe that I gave to Cathy Thomas [for her *Orange County Register* article on this project] and enlarged it. I made the spaetzle myself. I'll send you the recipe. You have to have a spaetzle maker.

DEAN: I'll be honest; this whole idea of promoting a Beethoven dinner is as much a marketing ploy as much as it is an educational interest. We had 40 for the dinner and a great crowd at the concert, with a lot of new people. You could tell they were new because they clapped between every single movement. The first piece was the Haydn Quartet, Op. 71, No. 2. The first violinist for the St. Lawrence Quartet, Geoff Nuttall, spoke to the audience. I thought he was going to chastise them, but no—he brilliantly described what the reality of clapping between movements was in Haydn's time. In those days, they not only clapped between movements, but also when the music got louder or suddenly changed. Everyone today assumes that his Surprise Symphony was written to wake people up, but it was really written to elicit applause and cheers. Now in our time and culture it has become the tradition with classical concerts that people have to restrain themselves from expressing their feelings—unlike with pop or rock concerts. He did say that there are times when it may not be appropriate to clap when a little space or silence may be necessary to connect two contrasting movements or to reflect on what was just played. The audience totally got that, and later, during the Beethoven Quartet they knew not to applaud after the very emotional slow movement.

What is your emotional experience with cooking or in running a restaurant?

BRITTA: There are many aspects for me, being an owner/operator. It is a fitting question, because just last night I was visited by the man who had been my very first paying customer. He is 85, and his wife passed away a few months ago. They came every day when I had the restaurant in Balboa, and three times a week when I moved to this location. They became a part of the family, so it went far deeper than the appeal of the food. Special events, like the one we just did with you, are also incredibly inspiring. There are some regular customers, like my early customer, Mr. Burch, and other music lovers who also come here all the time.

DEAN: It's really about the people; we all have to eat.

BRITTA: It's beyond the creative part of it.

DEAN: The connection is all about participating in life. What did you take away from the Beethoven project?

BRITTA: I love doing themes. It forces me to be creative, which is always great and fun.

DEAN: What got you into this business?

BRITTA: Spaghetti Bender—I started there when I was 14 years old. It's still there. They are like my family; I say that I am half-Italian, by association.

DEAN: I'm glad you are here, German, Italian or however you see yourself. Thanks for a splendid time on Sunday and for our visit today.

~

Beethoven loved wine and had it on his mind even during his final hours. Having asked for some of his favorite north German wine to be delivered for many weeks, it finally arrived, although too late. It was close to the hour of his death, and he responded that it "was a pity." The lesson here is to live your life fully, enjoy what you do, take care of the people you care about, and to do all this for as long as you possibly can.

SOME COOL PEOPLE

Variation 9
Bill Meredith

Variation 10
Charles Rosen

Variation 11
Dinner with Trimpin

Variation 12
Taft Music Bungalow

Variation 13
Sparky

Variation 14
Schubert

Variation 15
Mom, Dad, and Beethoven

Variation 9

BILL MEREDITH

ONE OF THE great joys in life's journey is the people you meet along the way—people who can show you how life can be better, people who know a lot more than you do. As the old saying goes, "Every being on the planet knows something that you don't." Dr. William (Bill) Meredith knows a ton about Beethoven and a great deal more. He shares his knowledge and passion with anybody—a very Beethovenian thing to do—and he has made a brilliant career for himself.

I was introduced to Bill by Ira Brilliant, the wonderful benefactor of the Ira F. Brilliant Center for Beethoven Studies at San Jose State University. Bill is the Center's director and is on the University faculty. (I write more about Ira Brilliant and Bill in the variation called "Little Faith.")

In 1999, we presented another big Beethoven project with live performances of all nine of Beethoven's symphonies, as well as an exhibit at the Bowers Museum. Bill was a huge part of that project, as he is now for our current *Beethoven: The Late Great*. A few months ago, he was in town for planning meetings with Philharmonic Society staff and the Bowers Museum. He spoke to our Board of Directors, describing the Ira F. Brilliant Center's involvement with our project. I took advantage of his being in town to interview him for this book.

DEAN: What started you on this whole Beethoven thing?

BILL: I've loved Beethoven's music since I was a child, but I didn't start piano until I was a teenager. It was kind of a funny story. My family was saving for college for four kids. We each got to do something. I always had an interest in art, so I got private drawing lessons. My sister got piano lessons, and I was fascinated with them as well as my art lessons. So, I would sit in while she was practicing. And actually, I was doing better than she was. We moved to Birmingham when I was in high school and then I began to take lessons.

DEAN: Where were you born?

BILL: I was born in Anderson, South Carolina—not the most beautiful place in the world. So I started playing the piano in high school, which is past the age when you have the muscle skills. I would never be as good as those who started younger. So then I went to college, and majored in music education. That was at Birmingham Southern College, a private college which, at that time, was incredibly liberal in the middle of Birmingham, Alabama. I got an undergraduate degree in music education and had a very fine music history teacher who did his dissertation on Haydn, but I got excited about Beethoven sometime around then. When I went to the University of North Carolina at Chapel Hill I was very lucky to study with William Newman, the famous Beethoven scholar and also a scholar on the history of the piano sonata. It was his last year of teaching, and I took two classes with him. The University of North Carolina did this fantastic thing that whenever someone took a sabbatical they would hire experts from around the world to take their place. Doug Johnson, a scholar who was at the University of Virginia at that time, came and taught a class on Beethoven sketches. He was there a whole year and Bathia

Churgin also visited from the Bar-Ilan University of Israel. She is an expert on the composer Sammartini and also on the history of the symphony. A lot of people subscribe to the birth of the symphony happening in Mannheim, Germany. It is not that this is *not* important, but she maintains that the symphony developed in Italy and gets transferred to the north. She taught a class on Beethoven, which was rather hilarious. So here we were, Master's students and graduate students. On the first day of class, she asked, "Which Beethoven pieces do you know really well? We won't cover those." Someone said, "What do you mean by 'really well?'"

DEAN: Alfred Brendel well, or…?

BILL: Things like, "What can you tell me about the development section of this symphony?" and other questions like this, to which we responded that, no, we could not answer any of these questions. Normally an undergraduate, unless he is very lucky, doesn't necessarily focus on one particular piece of music. So she said, "Alright, I see where we are." She would give us a list of Beethoven pieces each week along with a list of questions that we should think about. Between Doug Johnson and Bathia Churgin, we got really excited about Beethoven. Dr. Newman then retired, and it was time for me to pick a dissertation. I asked Doug Johnson if he would supervise me so that I could work on Beethoven sketches. This was during the middle of the Beethoven sketch renaissance when lots of people were writing about the sketches, so we went through them.

DEAN: What made it a "renaissance"—the post-war years?

BILL: Doug thinks it was because of the focus on Beethoven's bicentennial.

DEAN: 1970?

BILL: Yeah. There was a lot of activity related to that. There were a lot of discoveries being made about how to do sketch studies in a more scientific, reliable way—things like looking at the watermark. Also, if you had a sketchbook, how many pages were missing and where were they missing? Where did those pages go? Are they in some other collections? Do they even exist? Was the sketch in a big blank book that Beethoven might have bought at a shop or did he put together a bunch of papers? It got a lot more sophisticated.

Doug and I looked at a few of the existing sketches that no one was really writing about at that time. Two of the choices were the late quartet in B-flat, the second movement of which is in the Library of Congress, and the other was the Piano Sonata, Op. 109.

DEAN: That's a couple of great projects to choose from.

BILL: Most of the materials on Op. 109 were either in Berlin or in Bonn, which made it more difficult, so I received a grant for a German academic exchange for five months. It started in the summer with an intense German language course. I was in Bonn and Berlin before the wall came down. I could only officially use the money I received in West Berlin, but there were things I had to see in East Berlin so I didn't report them when I went over to the other side of the wall.

DEAN: So you went to East Berlin?

BILL: Yes. I went to the German State Library on Unter den Linden. It is actually not too far from the Russian Embassy, but it was just inside East Berlin on the other side of the gate.

DEAN: How did you get back and forth?

BILL: There were different ways to do it. You could go to Checkpoint Charlie—I was advised not to do that. At Checkpoint Charlie you walked across. Depending on the political climate of the day, or if spies were being exchanged, it could close and you would be waiting for hours. You could take the subway that goes in a ring around Berlin. In the part that went under East Berlin, the government in the west had made a deal with the government in the east that you could get off at certain stations, but for the privilege of allowing the westerners this access, the West Berlin government had to pay the East Berlin government around 20 million marks a year. You could get off of the train and walk up and outside, and go through the customs people there, which was not as harrowing as going through Checkpoint Charlie. Sometimes there would be lines, the guards would be in a really bad mood for some reason, and it could take forty-five minutes or more. One time I was in line and they pulled this young woman out of line and took her off. She came back in tears. The incident made us all very nervous.

There were funny stories. At the end of the time, I wanted to say thank you to those that were so helpful to me in the library. Whatever they earned—and they were a hard-working people—most money was sent to Cuba or East Africa so there wasn't a lot of it around to pay decent salaries. The flower stalls in East Berlin were pretty pathetic, like branches that had been cut off of trees that were about to bloom and a few little daffodils. I got flowers from West Berlin, where they are crazy about them and the selection was great. The last week, I took the flowers to the east where the border guards were suspicious of them. They asked me, "What are you doing?" I replied that I was working at the library. I had my coat and tie on. They asked why I had roses. I wanted to thank the people at the library who had helped me by bringing them some roses. I didn't find out until later that the American servicemen used to take either stockings or roses to the prostitutes for payment so the guards probably thought, "Yeah right, you're taking these roses to 'librarians.'" The librarians were really moved because they had not seen roses like that in a very long time. Each night someone got to take them home and they would bring them back in the morning so that someone else could take them home the next day.

DEAN: Do you correspond with any of those people to this day?

BILL: Most of them have retired by this point. It was an incredible experience to work in the library because you were working with actual Beethoven manuscripts. You would go down to the cafeteria and eat your greasy sausage and bread. But there were no napkins so you had to bring your own, as well as toilet paper. There was also no soap. So here you were, working with the actual manuscripts.

DEAN: You wore no gloves?

BILL: They would give you gloves, but they didn't insist that you wear them.

DEAN: This was real paper—of real Beethoven—not linen, correct?

BILL: Right.

DEAN: It is astounding that any of this material still survives.

BILL: Anyway, there were some advantages to life in East

Berlin. It wasn't as materialistic. The whole experience of working there and working in West Berlin was dramatic. Most of the German graduate students could never imagine that the wall could come down. The West Berlin library was literally two hundred yards from the wall.

DEAN: The last time we were together, we talked about Kerry Candaele and his film *Following the Ninth*, which is now finished because we got a generous couple to finish paying for it. The first Orange County screening will be at the Newport Beach Film Festival in spring of 2014 as a part of the final months of our *Beethoven: The Late Great* project. Have you seen it?

BILL: I have seen parts of it.

DEAN: In the film, there is a scene regarding East Berlin. There is a young woman who was a student around the time of the wall coming down. It is very moving. She describes wanting to come over to the west and how her boyfriend's brother made a break for it across no-man's-land. He was, of course, shot to death. Two weeks later, the wall came down. They just didn't know that this was going to happen.

BILL: It was very strange. Did you ever see it when it was up?

DEAN: No. I've only been to Berlin once in 2000 when it was down.

BILL: Through the middle of the city it was very heavily guarded. Once you got outside of town, there were barbed wire fences. The people in West Berlin used to spray paint the wall all the time with protests like, "We are watching you over there." It just seemed permanent. It is interesting, when Bernstein conducted the Ninth Symphony in East Berlin after the wall came down; there was still a tradition from the mid-nineteenth century that Beethoven meant to say "freedom" instead of "joy" in the choral movement of the Ninth. Instead of "joy" Bernstein inserted the "freedom" because of the circumstances. He caught a lot of grief for that.

DEAN: Is it true that Beethoven meant to say "freedom"—really?

BILL: There is no real evidence for it. I don't think anyone knows for sure. You would need Beethoven's copy of Schiller's poem.

DEAN: Freiheit versus *Freude.*

BILL: Right.

DEAN: Actually, who cares? Both words work.

BILL: It is the perfect piece to celebrate the falling of the wall. Nothing else would work as well.

DEAN: This film that Kerry made has four different stories that follow the Ninth in modern times in which the Ninth Symphony is the background score. It is about 78 minutes and at the end you realize, "Wow, we just heard the entire work." I asked Kerry how he found the attractive young woman from East Berlin to formally interview. She was perfect. I believe he said Craigslist. He asked for people in the L.A. area of a certain age who were in school in East Berlin at the time the wall fell. He heard from about six people. Her selection was brilliant. When you see it, you will be very moved. We are a crazy people, we humans.

BILL: Also, when you looked across at the wall from the library, you could see the site of the bunker where Hitler killed himself. You have this combination of looking over where the bunker was and this place from which people were trying to escape. It brings up some fundamental issues about what matters in society. The people in East Berlin kept saying that the people in West Berlin were too materialistic, obsessed with appearance and not obsessed with things that matter a lot. If you went to West Berlin then it was decadent—still is, to some degree.

One day I was in East Berlin during lunch and walking around. There was this long, long line to buy oranges from Cuba, maybe 300 people. I thought nobody in West Berlin would stand in a line ten people long for anything. The things we take for granted.

The East German government had some money to send people to work in West Berlin. There was a scholar who did this from Leipzig that I met. He was working, I think, on Mendelssohn. This Canadian friend of mine offered to give him some money to buy something in West Germany. She gave him twenty marks, which wasn't that much money. But to him it was a lot. He decided he would buy some bananas because he had a four-year-old son who had never even seen a banana. He had seen pictures of one but had never had one. Again, I thought, "We take many things for granted in the west."

DEAN: Kaly and I were in Berlin in 2000, our only time to this point. It is ironic; the bombing during the war seemed to do more damage on the west side. You noticed so many more new buildings because they replaced the ones that were destroyed. It was like the modern building was the gravestone of the old one. But today, the hip places to go are located on the east side— clubs, restaurants, etc. The cool Berlin is all over there. When you imagine all the sites of the new architecture once being rubble, you come to realize how horrible it must have been.

BILL: The museums were really terribly bombed. When I was there, a lot of them were still closed or you could only go on certain days, to certain galleries—very unpredictable.

I'll never forget, in East Berlin, all of the signs on the buildings that were advertising things were still there but had faded. This was in 1980 so they were 35 years old by this time. Then you'd go to West Berlin where there were all of these flashy signs telling you to do this, buy that—all of this excess, like being in California. You go to the mall. Advertising is everywhere, trying to get us to buy things that we don't really need and can't really afford. It's about creating a need that wasn't there before.

DEAN: It's called marketing. *Mea culpa.* Okay, let me switch gears on you. How did the whole thing with Ira Brilliant get started? The Beethoven Center was already up and running before you got there, correct?

BILL: Right. [San Jose State University] decided to set up a center around the collection of Beethoven first editions that Ira had donated to them. They formed a search committee for a director. I found out about the search and I applied, but thought they had already selected their short list. They decided that there wasn't anyone on that list that they were looking for in terms of being a combination of what they wanted. What they wanted first was a famous scholar to come, so then Doug Johnson, who was my advisor, was hired to write a plan. He wrote them a letter and told them, "You don't want a senior scholar. First of all, you only have these first editions right now; you want a young scholar who is just starting out."

DEAN: Those first editions, were they all from Ira?

BILL: Yes. There were about seventy of them. So they decided

at the end of their search that they would search again. I
applied again for the next round. They brought three people.
What were they looking for? A few years before, I applied for
the position of director of the music collection at the Library
of Congress. They actually said in the job description from
the federal government that they wanted someone who is an
impresario. Just to make sure, I looked up the word. They
wanted someone to put on programs *and* do research. There
wasn't supposed to be so much fundraising with that job, but
they wanted someone who knew people. I ended up being on
the short list of three people for that job. The Beethoven Center
is the same kind of job. In the first 28 years it has been growing
the collection, raising money and doing all of this while in
a really underfunded state institution that is not a research
school. People were asking Ira, "Why aren't you giving these
editions to Harvard?" And, "If you are going to give them to a
university in California, why not Berkeley or Stanford rather
than San Jose State?"

DEAN: And his answer was?

BILL: Part of his answer was he had talked to Arlene Okerlund
at the college of humanities and arts. She is a Shakespeare
scholar and she had asked him if there were anything like the
Folger Library for Beethoven in the United States. He said,
"No, there is not. The only other place is the Beethovenhaus
in Bonn." She said, "Let's think big and think about starting a
Beethoven Center." Arlene contacted the university president,
who was a woman. A part-time professor in math had talked to
Ira, who said he had offered it to Arizona State University and
they turned him down.

DEAN: Because of the expense? Ira is from Arizona. It would
make a lot of sense.

BILL: It is not quite clear why they turned it down. They did say they thought it would take five or six years to put it together. Ira wanted a class on the Beethoven items so people would look at them, and he wanted Xerox copies of the scores he was contributing. They gave him the run around. When he talked to Arlene, she responded, "We could have a course on Beethoven next semester. They are called trial courses. You can do them right away." The folks at Arizona just didn't want it. Arlene called Gail Fullerton, who was the president of San Jose State. Gail was a sociologist and loved the arts. Her husband was a painter. She had worked really hard to help the football team so that the games wouldn't be embarrassing. This was in 1982 and it happened quickly. There was a fair amount of resistance from the School of Music and Dance at the time.

DEAN: Is it that usual internecine war between faculties?

BILL: I think really this goes back to a lot of the problems always having to do with money and who gets it. The Center decided they wanted to have a fortepiano. Ira gave the money, which I think was $17,000, and told Arlene that he and his wife wanted to name this after their daughter (who had died when she was young). Arlene wanted to talk to the piano faculty about how to find a fortepiano. They went ballistic. They wanted a new Steinway piano. They really did need one, asking, "Why would we need something else?"

DEAN: Ira wants something else and he is paying for it, that's why!

BILL: They weren't interested in how music sounded during Beethoven's lifetime or what sound Beethoven had in mind.

DEAN: They were holding onto an old idea that was just about to crumble. The whole period instrument movement started right after that.

BILL: It was already going. It was a big deal at Chapel Hill when I was there. Also, we had an orchestra and a faculty string quartet. Ira happened to mention at one point that he would like to have a professional string quartet be in residence. That really upset all of them.

DEAN: Oh, yeah. I can see it now.

BILL: Then there was a man who was director of the wind ensemble who felt that he should be the director of the Center. There were problems that way. Arlene went outside of the school to get the first acting director for two years, so they picked this really wonderful person named Tom Wendel who was in the history department. Tom knew everybody on the board of the San Jose Symphony because he had been writing program notes for them for years and years. Arlene gave Tom that money and said, "This is how much you have. Please start working on this." Tom called Malcolm Bilson, who is the most famous fortepianist in the country. He responded, "There is a husband and wife team in the central valley. They are making great instruments. You should hire them to do it."

DEAN: Who knew? Are they still around?

BILL: They are. They got divorced because of different kinds of arguments, including how to build pianos. When I arrived, there was just a bunch of broken fences. There was a lot of hostility. I was explicitly told, "You have to mend all of these fences."

DEAN: When did you first hear of the whole "Hair" thing?

BILL: That was interesting. It was the fall of 1994. We always get advance sheets about what is coming up for auction at Sotheby's and Christie's. We got the sheets and there was a first edition of Opus 1, which we always wanted, and there was also this lock of hair. Patricia and I got really excited about it.

DEAN: Has Patricia been at the Center the whole time?

BILL: She came one year after me.

DEAN: Did she regret the purchase because of the notoriety of the object?

BILL: People will come into the Center and want to see the lock of hair. To her there is so much more than that and it has gotten so much notoriety over the years. I told Ira that I really think that we should get this. He responded that what he was interested in was Opus 1, but then he got Dr. Guevara to put in $5,000 for the hair, and then Tom Wendel put in $500, and a woman who was a friend of his put in $500, and I put in $1,000. We got it for a steal.

DEAN: Did he get the Opus 1?

BILL: No, he didn't. He was outbid. So we ended up with the lock and when it came, Ira and Dr. Guevara started asking each other, "Besides its value as a relic, are there things that you could learn about Beethoven's life?" There was a lot of news about it. At first it was in the newspaper. A book agent in Denver read the notice and cut it out. She called Ira and asked if he would be willing to have a book written about this. Then she found Russell Martin…

DEAN: Russell Martin lives down here, doesn't he?

BILL: He lives in Los Angeles. He and his now ex-wife did a children's version of the book. *Beethoven's Hair* is still in print. It has been translated into a dozen languages. That book has legs. I have never minded the publicity. If it brings people into the Beethoven Center then we can get them excited about Beethoven. We can show them the pianos and the other things that are there.

DEAN: I am amazed by your Betty Hummel collection and finding that little watercolor of Haydn's birthplace. That was a moment.

BILL: I have always wondered, "Where is that picture of Haydn's birthplace that Beethoven owned?" I am not positive that this is it. If it is not, I do not know of any better explanation. It is signed on the back by the artist, plus it was with their stuff that was from Johann Nepomuk Hummel's collection of Beethoven material. He was there during the last days of Beethoven's life. He brought the young Ferdinand Hiller who clipped the famous lock. Beethoven was sweet on Betty Hummel.

DEAN: Maynard Solomon lists her as one of the possible immortal beloveds.

BILL: She is not a really strong candidate because she got married. He definitely liked her. This is one of those things that I often tell people. When I went to graduate school I had no idea of the different things I would get involved in, like how to test hair and find out what is in it.

DEAN: It has all changed. Some of that technology is relatively new.

BILL: Some of it is new, but DNA has been a total failure from the beginning. I don't know whether it is because of *CSI* or what, people will come into the Beethoven Center and ask, "Did you get DNA evidence?" It is very hard with older samples to get DNA. It is not what people think it is and it is destructive. You don't want to keep doing it too many times.

DEAN: You want to get it right the first time or as close as you can. It is the same danger you get when you put an early instrument into playing condition. You get a sound but you destroy the history.

BILL: Right.

DEAN: Talking about notoriety for the Center, what challenges do you face for the future?

BILL: The Beethoven Center is set up as what is known as an organized research unit or ORU. ORUs are meant at some point to become self-sustaining. Being a part of the humanities and arts, funding is a big problem. The American Beethoven Society raises the money that we have to do projects with. My dream at the moment is that I would like to set up a small museum across the street from the University with two or three floors. We don't have enough room to show many of our things right now. On one level, the next thing for the Center to do and for the Beethoven Society to do is to figure out a way to see if we can buy one of these apartment houses and turn it into a Beethoven Museum. That is my dream. When I go to Europe, I love these museums that are in houses where you look at maybe a hundred objects. There is only so much one can look at. In this day and age especially, if you look at fifty things seriously, you have looked at a lot of things.

DEAN: And there is a limit to the number of things to look at in the first place.

BILL: Although we could definitely fill two or three stories of a house. So there is the problem of funding my salary as the director of the Beethoven Center and also how we are going to have more space in the future. One thing I am not at all worried about: Modernism can come and go, Post-modernism can come and go, Post-post-modernism can come and go—but Beethoven is never going to lose his appeal to people around the planet. He is not a dead old white guy. His music always sounds modern and just as the movie shows and all of our experience shows, there is just something about the music that transcends his identity as a white European male from 200 years ago. It becomes a kind of internal message that speaks to people.

DEAN: There is a little book I read on Kindle by Jonathan Biss called *Shadowing Beethoven*. It's about his process of recording the sonatas. He is very articulate. He talks about Beethoven's influence on various composers in the Romantic period and even up to and including Schoenberg. It goes beyond and then it is a matter of people being inspired by this music or trying to go the opposite direction of Beethoven. So basically, no matter what music is going on anywhere, Beethoven is always in the room. That's a great line. Beethoven is walking in here now. His influence is so huge and it gets bigger and bigger.

BILL: One way that he is especially in the room is that the biggest composer in Beethoven's lifetime was Haydn. Mozart had this idea that music is beautiful. It could never step outside of that. He couldn't write ugly music. Haydn writes music that is beautiful also, but he couldn't take it to that next step.

His music doesn't have the same depth of philosophy that Beethoven's music has. You can listen to Beethoven's pieces early, middle and late and you have this sense that there is some powerful message in it.

Last week I was teaching a class at Stanford in continuing education and we were talking about the Fifth Symphony. We were listening to the third movement and I was talking about how the symphony was used during World War II. When you listen to the third movement you just have this feeling of mighty forces at work.

DEAN: Exactly.

BILL: …and mighty forces at work today, not two hundred years ago—Napoleon and his armies.

DEAN: A number of the variations in this book are derived from talks I have done, especially to the Philharmonic Society's volunteer Committees and ticketholders. I have told them on numerous occasions, "If Mozart and Haydn were suddenly brought to the present, they would both be astounded that we are still listening to their works. They wrote their music for occasions and weren't that concerned if they were performed over and over. If Beethoven could be transported to today in Orange County and saw what we were doing for this *Late Great* celebration, he would not be surprised in the least. He would expect it because he wrote that way."

BILL: …and it has to do with this quality. His late period is often referred to as the transcendental period. It's about getting rid of everything that is superficial and focusing on the things that count. To me, I don't know how many composers before Beethoven were willing to sit down and write a piece of music like the *Holy Song of Thanks* (*Heiliger Dankgesang*) he wrote before he almost died. Here is Beethoven. He almost dies and he has this experience, thinking, "How do I express that in music?" He does it and it is something that no one had written like it or will write anything like it. What is it like to come very close to death, to the point where, I think, you are ready for it and then to be drawn back into life because you are getting better? To almost have a sense of regret that you didn't pass?

DEAN: Because you were almost there.

BILL: The transcendence…who thinks of something like that? To take raw experience at its most fundamental level and to transform that into music without words, using music symbols.

DEAN: And the thing of it is, people get it. They don't have to be sophisticated at all. In some respects it might be better if they weren't that sophisticated because they probably have a more open heart and mind than somebody who prejudges everything and makes decisions on something they have never heard before.

BILL: They don't have to know the "title" to get it.

DEAN: No, not at all.

BILL: I have a friend who used to be the president of the university. He told me he liked to turn on music frequently because it shuts out the noise of the world that he really doesn't need to be hearing, so when he is with someone to hear music or if he wants to talk to someone, he will turn it on. So he has the luxury of plugging back into the world. To Beethoven, the noise of the world began to be turned off around 1817. He didn't have a choice, but the longer he survived the more it is happening inside him. The less the external world is keeping him down physically or directly. It is a really interesting statement. This president is thinking, "I get to tune out all of that rattle, racket, and all those things that distract me from the things that are important. When I want to hear something important, I turn it back up and I start to tune back in."

DEAN: January of 2012, we had pianist Marino Formenti perform the *Diabelli Variations*. He is primarily an avant-garde pianist, a real champion of contemporary music with a keen understanding of the past. In the first half of the program, he performed a work by a young composer, Evan Gardner, whom he had commissioned to write a variation, not necessarily a 34th Diabelli variation. He chose John Cage, whose 100th birthday was celebrated that year and did a variation on 4'33", the so-called silent piece. It is an interesting angle of dealing with silence in the Beethoven sense. Cage maintains there is no such thing as silence. In Gardner's piece, Marino did not touch the keyboard, but pressed the sustain pedal and wore special gloves that when moved in the air interacted with speakers and microphones that were placed close together, picking up the ambient sounds of the hall to create feedback. Some very interesting sounds were produced. This was a special handling of "silence."

What's the most fun you have being director of the Center besides being interviewed by me?

BILL: I would say there are probably two things. One is when we find something we thought never existed before, like the Betty Hummel stuff. One of her living descendants calls me up and says, "My mother is the great-grandchild of Johann Nepomuk Hummel and she has this collection of objects." When you find out something that completely surprises you that you didn't know existed, that's the one thing that is very exciting, like the painting of Haydn's birth house. Because those objects pinch together time so that we feel like two hundred years has disappeared and you are dealing with objects that Beethoven dealt with on the last day he was alive. In the collection is his last real quill pen and it is stained with ink. It is like you are there. Betty Hummel is there.

The other thing, we had a group of junior high school choir students come in this week. We showed them around the Beethoven Center and they were so excited to learn about Beethoven. To have those pianos, to show them the life mask that is mounted the same height as Beethoven was, and the lock of Beethoven's hair. People get very excited about it. It is easy to communicate the excitement about this person.

DEAN: It is great to see other people excited about something you really care about. That gets me going.

BILL: …and especially younger people. There is a Russian piano competition in San Jose. Two years ago they had a young man in the competition who lives in the Midwest. I always talk to the students. This young man was 14, maybe 15, and he was playing the Op. 109. I let him play it on our original piano from 1827. This kid was a knockout. He sat down and played. It really meant so much to him to play on a Broadwood grand that was only a couple of serial numbers away from Beethoven's own piano—to hear the music the way Beethoven meant for it to be heard. He wrote me this incredible letter thanking me for it. If you have these things around, somehow they manage to compress time. We can't go back and ever see Beethoven but we can get in touch with the things that excited him.

DEAN: Last question. What broad changes do you think are ahead that might affect the Center or how we feel about Beethoven? The world has changed. What do you make of it?

BILL: I have two responses to that. One is I heard last week on NPR that children nowadays spend more than 50 hours a week on electronic devices and they spend less than 40 minutes a week outside doing something. That made me think about my childhood, how much time we spent outside when the weather was good compared to watching TV, which we didn't do that much. That could be a good and a bad thing. The good thing is that people need to go hear music live. I keep saying, "Listening to recordings of music is like kissing phonographs." If you find that satisfactory, then that's good for you. That's not music the way I think of it. Music has to be heard live. When you go hear a symphony orchestra, if you are not struck by all of this color and sound, everything being created anew, then you need your ears checked. I love visual arts too. We change how we look at a Van Gogh but the painting is always the same. Music always has to be created anew by a performer interpreting the music. I hope that young people don't get more and more hooked on listening to music electronically and give up on going to concerts. That's true music, where it happens.

DEAN: The other great thing about live music is that you share it. When you are at a concert you are sharing it with others. You are often with somebody and you are sharing it together.

BILL: And now with this "50 hours of electronics" that kids deal with in a week, you can use it. As you know, we put the Charles Schulz, Beethoven, and Schroeder exhibit online for people all around the world to be able to see. But at the same time, I don't want people to stop going to concerts.

In the last few years we are all more distracted. I have been trying to teach the skills of conscious listening, about mindful listening, having your mind present when you are listening, music not just as background sound—to really stop and focus on the sounds that you're hearing. That is a skill that you have to work at this day and age.

DEAN: I am listening in the car right now to all of the Beethoven piano sonatas recorded by Rudolf Buchbinder. I am thinking about having him come to perform all of them here. If I am trying to find an address while driving, I have to turn the music off so my mind can focus on where I am supposed to be going.

BILL: You hear someone fantastic one time; you have that experience with you forever. Some people will say, "Why should I go through the hassle of going out to hear great music when I can hear it at home?"

DEAN: Then I would quiz those people, "Would you do it? Would you actually sit down and listen to an overture, concerto, new work and Mahler Symphony in your media room in one sitting (with a 15 minute intermission)?" By not going to live performances, a whole lot of music will pass you by. That would be a real shame. Life is too short as it is.

BILL: I think we need to talk about: what is the point of that communal experience? Small concert hall? Large concert hall? No, it's people gathering together to say, "This is something that we value. This is something that we want to experience together."

DEAN: It makes you listen to the music. You could say, "I want to be a doctor, and I am going to study on my own." You know what? You're not going to do that. You are going to pay some place a lot of money to make you learn it. If you are in a live concert, you have to listen to the music that is there.

BILL: People also think that their CDs accurately capture the sound of an orchestra.

DEAN: No.

BILL: They can't.

DEAN: I have the same issue with digital recording. I have a friend who has this Jadis amplifier. It takes the digital signal and puts in back into analog. There are pieces of music that just don't work well in the digital recording format. One of them is Ravel's *La Valse*. It is an analog piece of music. It is designed for the ambience of a concert hall. The piece is constructed with no instruments playing long phrases. Each player has small bits they weave together giving this dream version of a waltz. On a digital recording you hear every detail, the bits and pieces, the strands of the weave. Ravel didn't want you to hear all of that detail. The brain captures every piece of the puzzle. It becomes irritating.

BILL: All of those little spaces that are missing in the music are gone. When I haven't been to an orchestra concert in a while and I sit down at one of Michael's rehearsals with the San Francisco Symphony, the sound is overwhelming at first because if you listen on CDs it is such an impoverished thing.

DEAN: Absolutely. We had an extraordinary time with John Eliot Gardiner here. For the *Missa Solemnis* we were packed and for the Ninth Symphony as well. People are still talking about it. Most of the audience had not heard the *Missa* before. It was an amazing experience.

BILL: Beethoven thought it was his greatest piece.

DEAN: I completely agree. It is so glorious.

BILL: In the beginning of the *Credo*, all of the parts keep saying, "Credo, Credo, Credo" (I believe, I believe, I believe) almost like Beethoven is making himself believe in an institution.

DEAN: Then when he gets into the areas of doctrine that he was not completely comfortable with, the writing gets so complicated that it becomes all about the music and not about the words anymore.

BILL: The Brahms *Requiem* is unimaginable without the *Missa Solemnis.*

DEAN: Brahms would have had a hard time existing without Beethoven coming before him.

BILL: Yet they are so totally different.

DEAN: Beethoven was so intimidating to him. He didn't compete with the sonatas but utterly failed to write any string quartet better than Beethoven's. Those string quartets of his are just not as good.

BILL: I still love his music.

DEAN: Me, too. I have to let you go on with your life. Thanks so much for this very interesting time.

BILL: Thank you.

Variation 10

CHARLES ROSEN

He has no immediate survivors.

THIS IS THE final sentence of David Ng's obituary for Charles Rosen in the *Los Angeles Times*—a very sad one indeed. In my view, however, Charles' true family is the thousands of people who have been inspired by his masterly writing on classical music and the many that were able to hear the man play the piano. It was our privilege to experience all of this when he came to talk to us about Chopin and then gave a memorable recital of the composer's music at the Irvine Barclay Theatre in the year of Chopin, 2010. Before the lecture, Kaly and I had arranged to pick him up at the Westin Hotel, where we found him sitting rather dourly in the lobby. This was the first time I met him. He was dressed plainly, and his shuffle to the car gave me some concern that he may not have the energy to get through the night. But once in the car, he began to talk. His energy returned and he became the Charles Rosen that I expected him to be.

I was grateful to have dinner with him twice during this visit. On the first evening, I took copious notes on everything he said and was moved to make an Amazon order the very next morning. Among the titles, I thoroughly enjoyed *Renaissance Art in France* by a close friend of Mr. Rosen, Henri Zerner, and *The Art of Cooking with Steam* by another of his friends, Jacques Manière. Sabra Bordas, Kaly and I had lunch with Charles and his manager John Gingrich at the Bar Boulud in New York. This occasion taught me about the magic that can happen when great food, great wine, and great conversation combine. It was an experience of true connection—unhurried and sincere—the kind of event that seems to be so threatened in our modern age. I knew Charles wouldn't live forever and that this would be a significant memory.

This past fall, John Gingrich and I were talking about the possibility of Charles doing a recording and then touring with the Beethoven *Diabelli Variations*. I was extremely excited. Charles was fighting prostate cancer at the time and John was concerned that he was experiencing depression—not a surprising concern, considering the circumstances. I told John that I would love the opportunity to talk with Charles about the *Diabelli Variations*, thinking it would be a great bookend to our *Beethoven: The Late Great* project, even if he was unable to perform it live. Such a meeting would have taken place in January 2013.

Charles' many books on music are a tremendous legacy for us all. There are many obituaries about him now to be found in numerous print and internet publications. He was a unique and talented human being. Like Beethoven, he knew he was among the best and went to great lengths to share his gift with us. I am most grateful.

Variation 11

Dinner with Trimpin

One of the great pleasures of collaboration is the opportunity to work with fascinating people, the kind who adds depth to your life experience. One such person is Trimpin, the renowned installation artist from Seattle. I have invited him to create a sound installation that plays the "Ode to Joy" theme from Beethoven's Ninth Symphony as a part of our *Beethoven: The Late Great* project.

Born in Germany, Trimpin creates artistic contraptions that are fascinating to look at, to hear, and to contemplate. He is a 1997 MacArthur Genius Grant recipient. It was our privilege to work with him during the 2001 Eclectic Orange Festival, when we presented an exhibit called "You Are Hear" at the Orange County Museum of Art. The inspiration behind the exhibit came from my own curiosity about people who are enthusiastic about contemporary visual art, even being avid collectors, but who are unenthusiastic or even hostile to contemporary music. I thought that placing music in a museum exhibit format might prompt interest and answers. Unlike public concerts, where audience members are stuck listening to music (especially new music) that they don't care for, visitors to museums can easily control the dosage of what they take in; the choices are to ignore it, walk quickly through the galleries, leisurely stroll, slide into the gift shop, stare at the work for an hour, return on a regular basis to stare at the work for an hour, etc. An alternative title for the exhibit was "Music Machines at the Museum." The team that worked on this project was incredible, using the imaginations of Justin Urcis (my artistic administrator at the time), the late Naomi Vine (director of the museum), Elizabeth Armstrong (former curator), and myself.

Justin immediately suggested that we include György Ligeti's *Poème symphonique* for 100 metronomes, as well as some Conlon Nancarrow pieces for player piano. Nancarrow had recently died in Mexico City, and a collector in Switzerland had purchased his specially prepared player pianos. What to do? The ever-resourceful Justin suggested that we contact the Seattle-based installation artist Trimpin, who had worked with Nancarrow and had realized some of his pieces on his machines. I paid a visit to Trimpin at his Seattle studio. I was scheduled to spend the morning with him and then meet my sister-in-law for lunch. But because he was so fascinating, the morning turned into a very long and wonderful day, concluding with a late dinner with my very understanding sister-in-law and her family.

The "You Are Hear" show at the Orange County Museum of Art was a roaring success. Trimpin took over the entire museum. His installation included self-tuning and self-playing electric guitars, a room full of toy pianos that played programmed music all at once, and an installation called "Conlon in Purple," which was essentially suspended individual marimba bars, each with its own attached mallet and resonator, playing a Nancarrow piano roll piece that had been programmed into a computer. It was open to the general public, and we arranged for a number of high school groups to see the exhibit and listen to Trimpin explain his art. They, along with our docents, were thrilled.

Besides being a polymath, he is very dedicated to teaching young people. He was in Orange County for a site visit to scope out possible locations for the Beethoven *Ode to Joy* installation. Later that evening, he came over to our house for dinner and stayed the night. It was a great chance for me to chat with him personally about his art. The weather was perfect, so we sat in our gazebo sipping martinis, a tradition that we continue anytime we can get together.

Supper was in its final stages of preparation—Kaly's famous vichyssoise garnished with minced chives and drizzled Pernod, a golden beet carpaccio with toasted sunflower seeds and radish sprouts, followed by seared scallops with a saffron beurre blanc. Life is always good at home. I asked Trimpin about working with kids.

TRIMPIN: Next month there is an opening. Two years ago in Seattle, I was asked to do a workshop for children with disabilities, and I was warned, "They are hyperactive, they have an attention span of about two minutes, they can't do much and most of them are in wheelchairs."

They asked, "Would you still like to do something?" I said, "Yes! Let's do it!"

The plan was to build some kind of contraption. I brought in some wood, pieces of metal, and some other random objects. I wanted to make some sound. I asked the kids, "How do we make it?" They responded, "We could just bang on it." So I said, "Why don't we just do that." But it didn't sound right. I asked, "How do we make this piece of wood sound right?" Slowly through this conversation, I said, "We could tune the wood, add more pieces, and make a xylophone. To tune them we have to find the nodal points. We have to drill some holes in this piece of wood to hang it." You can't just drill all over; you have to drill at certain points. These points are easy to find when we shake salt on it, start to bang and slowly the salt is migrating to points where there is no vibration and we know that's where we have to drill. Everything was visually explained.

Drilling the holes on the wood in the spots where the salt vibrates would kill the sound. You have to drill where the salt settles, where there is *no vibration*. Those are the nodal points. Drilling at the nodal points will make sure the sound isn't affected.

This was in a place called the Children's Play Garden. They have a rabbit, chickens and two ducks. The children pick up and pet the animals. One of the ducks is called Lewis and the other Clark—Lewis and Clark. Unfortunately, I was over there a few weeks ago and the ducks were no more, they had been eaten by coyotes. Each chicken was named after a flower— one was Rose. All of the kids knew them. The chickens were mostly calm, sometimes nervous. Then I told the kids, "OK, let's figure out what happens when I bring in a few duck calls." We had some big balloons and at the end of them we attached a cheap recorder flute and taped over most of the holes, with each balloon sounding a little bit different than the next. They couldn't play a keyboard because their fingers were too stiff and deformed, but they could play the duck calls because they could squeeze objects. I made an interface using baby nose suckers. I bought twelve of them in a pharmacy and I put a sensor on each of these that triggered the duck call. When they were squeezed you got a "quack, quack." There were some twin children who could activate something for the first time.

KALY: With their hands?

TRIMPIN: Right. The kids were smiling. The chickens came. They were curious as to what was going on with these duck sounds. And, of course Lewis and Clark—they were still alive then—they came too. They all came without being asked, they were so curious. The kids are yelling out, "Lewis is here!" It was a great experience for all. We were building a xylophone.

The organization that was doing this is privately funded. We were in a public park that is open to the public. Everyone could come. It is in a neighborhood with many mixed-race families. Many couldn't attend a regular school, but this place is open for the children to come three or four days a week. Parents can leave their kids safely, overseen by the educators there who take care of them.

The next idea was to actually build an outdoor sculpture.

It's a very nice park for kids. They have a mountain that is made out of rubber so that when they fall they won't hurt themselves. There was a little stream running down it where the kids could put sand in it and see how it would flow down. Everything was designed with minimal air, water and nature to make the kids happy—very simple, natural and not toxic.

They had some kind of fence. I thought we could make a musical fence with instruments that could be played by anybody, especially those kids with disabilities. They could pluck it, bang it or kick it. It would have to be approved because it was a public park. It opens on June fourth. They have a tree house and the kids have tremendous support from the teachers. That's my project right now, which has to be done soon. The wooden bars are all in tune. When they bang on the low A, it is 440.

Some people write checks. As of yet, I haven't made a dime but maybe I will by the opening because of fundraising events a few days before. It is part of our environment to deal with children who have no means of playing instruments.

DEAN: How did you get started?

TRIMPIN: My background was in psychology. I have a Master's from the University of Berlin, where I worked with children with disabilities. Actually, it was with kids who were victims of birth defects resulting from thalidomide that their mothers had taken during pregnancy. In response, I designed a light pencil that could be held in their teeth—they couldn't play a keyboard because their hands couldn't reach the keys. So I made a light-sensitive keyboard. They used their feet to feed themselves and they were capable of moving their heads to rapidly change notes smoothly. I worked in this field as a student. After I graduated, my work there was behind an office desk. The German system is all subsidized, but you are basically an administrator, so I never worked professionally in this field. At the same time, I was a set designer. My first job was for the Bertold Brecht Theatre. Rick Cluchey, an inmate in San Quentin Prison, started to perform Beckett pieces in the mid-70s. Beckett heard about this kind of thing. Jerry Brown got Rick out of jail, while he was serving a sentence for shooting someone in the finger during a bank robbery. The next year, Rick was invited to Berlin. He performed in major houses. Peter Stein was running the Shaubühne; Rick was fortunate to be there and he didn't leave for quite some time.

DEAN: Kaly, you know those Dos Equis commercials? Is Trimpin not the most interesting man in the world? …And he is only drinking a martini.

Trimpin, what drives you, ultimately, to do what you do? Aside from all of the fabulous grants you get.

TRIMPIN: The grant money is fine for a while—but it quickly runs out. First of all, I never decided to be an artist. This was never a question in my family. I started to study music quite early, to learn different instruments like my father who gave lessons to different students. He was a cabinetmaker. When he finished his apprenticeship, he made his way to Munich to attend an art and trade school.

On his way, he was drafted into the military—this was in 1939. So his career was over. In 1945, six years later, he came back and saw that everything was gone, everything was bombed. None of my family was ever a part of what Hitler and his supporters did, and they suffered the effects. I am proud that we were different. I have a friend whose father was in the SS, and my friend's life was a complete dilemma. He was obsessed with the fact that his father was part of the Nazis. I don't know what he could do in that situation.

I didn't think I would be an artist. I was excited when

reading about scientists, about thinkers, about artists, about people who contribute something—they were my kind of heroes. Sometimes they had white lab coats, because they were scientists and they were doing something interesting. So, from my young age, I assumed that scientists and artists were the ones that made this world kind of exciting.

My family members were musicians but not into the arts this way, mostly classical music. I remember being introduced as a young child to Jean Tinguely, a Swiss sculptor who did incredible pieces, like the Stravinsky Fountain next to the Pompidou Centre in Paris. These were the people who, as a child, I was very interested in—Tinguely and even Stockhausen, who came a little bit later. It was interesting stuff that I couldn't understand at the time. I grew up nearby in Donaueschingen, a small town in the Black Forest that had a music festival in the fall.

DEAN: Who are people, alive or dead, who are your mentors—who you look to for inspiration?

TRIMPIN: Many different ones—they always changed. I couldn't sometimes tell, even if someone asked me, "What are you listening to?" First of all, I don't even own a CD player. I've never owned a TV. But I have stacks of CDs in my studio that are given to me by composer friends. Most music from the CDs I experienced in the concert situation. I don't open the seals of these CDs because I still have the memory of the music. When I would open the CD, I put it on my computer, which is the only way I can listen to it. It would destroy the memory of live experience.

DEAN: It's not the same.

TRIMPIN: It's different.

DEAN: I had a college professor at North Texas who listened to a piece of music only once. He would never go back and hear it again whether live or recorded. I thought that was rather strange and then I also thought that there is something to that.

TRIMPIN: You know, going back to Beethoven, Brahms, or whoever, they put their concerts on for only a certain part of society. That was how music was performed and appreciated. This was a true kind of experience of what was going on. Today, there are so many ensembles and conductors for someone in your position who has to explore what is going on. So far in my lifetime, I tremendously enjoy a live experience I hear and what I experience. Every time I listen to a CD, it is great for education or for preparing a presentation, but it is not the experience I have at a live concert.

DEAN: Music is so subjective anyway, which is what makes it magic. It's alive.

TRIMPIN: It's only a hundred years that we have had recording; before that you had to remember the music or devise some music machines. These had a very bad reputation because they had no dynamic, expression or soul. It is always the same and it is repeated over and over. So, this was the reputation of mechanical music. It's still going on. Music on the iPhone has much better quality. In an acoustic environment you can turn your head and the experience can be completely different. I don't want to contaminate this kind of experience by just listening to something that I know is not satisfying.

~

Dinner had arrived. Kaly took a seat and I poured a wonderful 2010 Refugio Ranch Tiradora Sauvignon Blanc, a wine that I am very recently excited about. It was a fun evening. Plans were made for Trimpin to return to meet with students and faculty, organizing some workshops after the first of the year when he comes back to install his piece at South Coast Plaza. We plan for passersby to be greeted with the sound of Beethoven's "Ode to Joy" coming from an upended grand piano played upon by various devices that will spread this musical hope and sunshine for months. Beethoven, I feel, would be very pleased. Cheers!

Variation 12

Taft Music Bungalow

A President's letter for the November 2012 Segerstrom Center for the Arts program book for the Philharmonia Orchestra of London and Orchestre Révolutionnaire et Romantique and Monteverdi Choir performances.

Dear Audience,

Welcome to our November concerts. All three of our programs this month are a part of our *Beethoven: The Late Great* project. The first performance, with the Philharmonia Orchestra conducted by Esa-Pekka Salonen features Beethoven's Seventh Symphony (not one of the late works) and also features Berlioz's *Symphonie Fantastique*. The Berlioz is of specific interest, as it helps us contemplate the influence of Beethoven's later compositions and their effect on music that was to come after. The next two concerts include later works—the greatest of them all— the *Missa Solemnis* and the Ninth Symphony. They are given the full treatment by Sir John Eliot Gardiner, the Orchestre Révolutionnaire et Romantique, and the Monteverdi Choir. We are, of course, thrilled to be able to bring these concerts to you. Our special thanks to the Donna L. Kendall Foundation, Shanbrom Family Foundation, The Segerstrom

Foundation and to Nancy Caldwell and Phyllis Jacobs for their special support in making these presentations possible.

These three November concerts have another thing in common. Beethoven had severe health challenges in later life and was profoundly deaf at the time when he composed the pieces you are going to hear. Beethoven is certainly the most widely known composer today, followed and sometimes surpassed by Mozart, whose fame has been greatly expanded by media such as the film *Amadeus* and the plethora of "Baby Mozart" products that are supposed to make us all, especially the wee ones, smarter. Notwithstanding the pop culture surrounding Beethoven—Chuck Berry, Charlie Brown, St. Bernard puppies and the like—this composer is primarily known for three reasons: the Fifth Symphony, the "Ode to Joy," and his deafness. This last factor is what makes him such a wonder—the very idea that a human being, even a talented genius, could come up with such immortal music without being able to hear it. In this way, Beethoven remains an inspiring historical figure. It is his deafness and the circumstances surrounding it that make him endeared by so many people. The great masses of people passionate about Beethoven's music never dig past the well-known works—the first movement of the Fifth or the last movement of the Ninth. And then there are those of us, many of whom are in this room tonight, who want to hear and know every tiny detail. Some of us just can't get enough.

This week (the week I am writing this), I spent some time at Taft Elementary School in Santa Ana. They have nearly 135 hard-of-hearing and deaf pupils from all over Orange County. Steven Longacre is their dedicated principal, and has a hearing loss himself. In the same way that Beethoven's example has been an inspiration, Steve and his staff are champions to the families in our own community, trying to cope with the difficulties of functioning in a hearing world. What amazes me is the fact that the program involves music education, that these kids are being given as many equal opportunities as possible. The music teacher, Eileen Maeda, leads a program that is nothing less than miraculous. As a volunteer with the Philharmonic Society, Eileen knows well the miracles of music and shares our belief that there are no boundaries to the potential of human expression. I have attended her classes at Taft on a couple of occasions and have seen how encouraging and valuable they truly are.

The classroom is divided between the hard-of-hearing and the profoundly deaf. I find it enriching to make a point of sitting with the profoundly deaf kids to have a vantage point that allows me to see their faces and reactions. The music for this class is visually lively, very percussive and extremely interactive, and Mrs. Maeda is a whiz at keeping the interest and energy high. She uses recordings of songs that kids sing and/or sign. It is very loud for obvious reasons, and also the reason that the Taft music bungalow, a temporary structure, is located at the edge of the campus away from the other classrooms. Thankfully, no complaints from neighbors yet. You can see that each child is eager to participate. And there is a great level of personal attention, as there are additional teachers and aides who ensure that all are a part of what goes on. Because so much of the material is repeated in subsequent classes, the students have sufficient time to absorb what is taking place at a pace that they can handle. In this way, their learning is reinforced and personalized. This method helps their confidence grow, as they familiarize and master each new lesson and learn while working with other students. This gives them a measure on how well they are doing. Most importantly, they are interacting with each other, which can be difficult with special needs students. This program allows them a time of creative cooperation that is fundamental to their development. Furthermore, it is fun and each child knows he or she is not alone with their affliction.

While the hard-of-hearing kids can sense the music through powerful hearing aids or the reaction of the sound waves on the body, the most profoundly deaf can only feel sound waves or observe the movements of the other kids. One especially charming little girl, wearing glasses, was slower and could only react after the fact, copying the others after they had clapped or jumped. It never occurred to her that she was behind the beat, which seemed unnatural to me as a musician. But I was moved by her exuberant joy and knew she was incredibly happy. She was a part of the group, playing and laughing, and experiencing life outside of her own isolation.

Isolation. Yes, that is the word that comes to mind. My 93-year-old mother is almost completely deaf and has been getting that way for the last 30 years. My sister and I suffer to some degree of hearing loss, as did our grandmother, a trait of our family genome. I now realize that Mom has been living in a world of isolation. She has learned to deal with the loss by nodding, as if she understands what is being said in a conversation. But I realize that it can be very lonely, to be surrounded by people and left out of every conversation. By now, everyone assumes she can't hear it anyway, and sometimes talk about her in front of her. This is isolation of a terrible kind.

Beethoven knew he was growing deaf by the time he was 28. In 1802, after completing his first symphony, he wrote a letter to his brothers, which was discovered and made famous after his death. It is known as the *Heiligenstadt Testament,* named after the village from which he was writing on the outskirts of Vienna. The letter was meant to serve as a will and was written in reaction to the despair that the young Beethoven felt over his increasing hearing loss. He wrote, "Born with a passionate and excitable temperament…yet obliged early in life to isolate myself, and to pass my existence in solitude. Alas, how could I proclaim the deficiency of a sense which ought to have been more perfect with me than with other men?"

Over the next ten years, Beethoven's hearing worsened, despite his tremendous creative outpouring. The works done during this time would make him the greatest composer in the world of that time, not even counting his late period—seven more symphonies, five piano concerti, the opera *Fidelio, Christ on the Mount of Olives,* the *Moonlight, Pastoral, Tempest, Waldstein,* and *Appassionata* Piano Sonatas—even little *Für Elise,* to name just a few. This is his message: in the letter he advises his brothers, "Recommend *Virtue* to your children; that alone, and not wealth, can ensure happiness. I speak from experience. It was *Virtue* alone which sustained me in my misery."

This is also the message of the *Missa Solemnis* and the Ninth Symphony. Later composers such as Hector Berlioz understood it loud and clear. Thank you for coming.

Please…enjoy!

Dean Corey
President and Artistic Director
Philharmonic Society of Orange County

Variation 13

SPARKY

*Think about the content of **Peanuts**: frustration, loss and fear of loss, insecurity, aspiration of art and heroism, love, lust, sibling rivalry, arrogance, kindness, friendship, disgrace, rebellion, and the existential orneriness of everyday existence. Realize that these grand themes have been expressed with charm and unfailing humor in drawings as simple and evocative as a fine haiku, every day for almost 50 years. Then acknowledge Charles Schulz as one of the century's greatest artists.*
—DENNIS O'NEIL, EDITOR/WRITER OF DC COMICS

I READ THIS quote on an exhibit wall of the Charles M. Schulz Museum in Santa Rosa, California. It is my gut feeling there is a huge connection between the creative processes of Charles Schulz and Ludwig van Beethoven. I think Mr. O'Neil's statement above describes the emotional palette board of both artists. Recently, I decided to check it out.

I am in Santa Rosa, California, in the studio of the late great cartoonist Charles Schulz. His studio is on a beautiful campus that holds the Charles M. Schulz Museum, an ice arena, museum store, and a couple of baseball diamonds for local kids. All of this is surrounded by a grove of redwoods, common in these parts. We are fifty miles north of the Golden

Gate Bridge. It should be noted that redwoods are my very favorite kind of trees. They are awe-inspiring, as is the prospect of talking with Jean Schulz about her late husband, his art, and his characters—especially Schroeder, whose muse was Ludwig van Beethoven. What a thrill it is to be where *Peanuts* was created. The original contents of his studio are displayed across the way in the museum, a memorable place to visit. There are original pictures on the walls, and it is a comfortable space, very easy to move through. I ask Jean about it, sitting across from her.

DEAN: Did Charles Schulz like a sense of constancy in his work environment?

JEAN: Many cartoonists had to draw on the road. They also did roughs that they would ink later once they were home. Sparky [Charles Schulz's nickname] didn't do that. His method of working was that he made scribbles on pieces of paper, only did the barest thoughts about what he wanted to do. Sometimes they were just word doodles, to figure out the right way to say something. It might be like, "What if Snoopy were pushing a baby buggy or Sally were pushing a baby buggy with Snoopy in it?" That might spawn an idea if he didn't have one at hand.

When he did start to work on something, he would sketch just a bare outline, like a circle or two in each panel that he would turn into various characters. He put the dialogue in first. It wasn't until he knew how much space the dialogue would take that he could then draw. He would typically finish the last panel first to make sure the joke worked, because if it didn't, he didn't want to draw three panels for nothing. He didn't like to work on the road, and to answer your question, he did like a set place and routine. His routine was coming here. Leaving the house, having breakfast at the ice arena, talking to a few people, seeing what was going on, coming over here and starting to draw—this was his process. The first thing he did was look at his mail. Cartoonists and probably composers like having a little bit of feedback. It was a way of being in touch with the rest of the world.

DEAN: Beethoven sketched in much the same way. If Sparky got criticized, or if something really upset him, did it affect his work? Did he slow down?

JEAN: I have only one example of something that affected him, and that was a book that came out with the title, *I Heard the Owl Call My Name.* It was an Indian legend. The title means "God or the Great Spirit is calling me." He used that in the strip and he got a letter telling him that it was an inappropriate use of that expression. He didn't know what he was really writing about. He said the person was absolutely right, that he should not have used it that way. The letter writer was a biblical scholar. Maybe you have to write books before you are a biblical scholar. Sparky did a lot of Bible study in his twenties and really loved the Bible. He put the Bible in the comic strip and some people criticized that you shouldn't put biblical passages in something as lowly as a comic strip. He objected to that. He felt that he was using them respectfully and that people would learn more by looking at these biblical verses with humor than hearing somebody say "Thou shall" and "Thou shalt not."

DEAN: On Dennis O'Neil's quote, talking about the full range of human emotions that Charles Schulz used in all of his characters, I see a parallel with Beethoven. This full range of emotions is a source of creativity for both. He talks about the "aspiration of art and heroism." What about that word, *heroism*? I think of Snoopy the Flying Ace battling the Red Baron.

JEAN: If you want to talk about heroism in the comic strip, you might say Charlie Brown is a hero because he continues on in spite all of the things that happen to him, all the things that make him want to weep, the things that send him to bed covering up his head—but he still has hope. I think there is a lot of heroism in that. Snoopy's heroism, of course, is all in his mind.

DEAN: That is a very good point. There are a lot people who think that they are heroes when we don't think of them as heroes.

JEAN: I just think Charlie Brown's resilience and eternal hopefulness is a heroic quality.

DEAN: One of the themes in all of these variations that I am writing that I keep touching on is that Beethoven was writing for generations to come. It is that evergreen message from the Ninth Symphony that we are all brothers. There is strength and hope, there is always that. Beethoven also knew that he was the world's greatest composer, and felt he had a moral obligation to do the best work he could and then give it back. I feel the same way with Charles Schulz.

JEAN: I think that he felt that same obligation to do his best work every day. He realized that when you do a comic strip every day, it's different from writing X number of symphonies or X number of books. There are going to be days that are better than others. He would never have said, "I am the best cartoonist of the twentieth century" because I think he would have felt that wasn't something he could say.

DEAN: Beethoven knew that he had that kind of talent and that kind of responsibility.

JEAN: Sparky knew he had that kind of responsibility. Some people said it is a kind of responsibility to God to do that because God gave you this talent. Sparky wouldn't go that far. It was something he loved and felt his responsibility was actually to his readers to do the best that he could.

I was being interviewed for a documentary on PBS, and the director asks me, "Do you have anything to add, anything else you want to say?" I said, "Sparky worked really hard and he was quite surprised with his success." He asked, "And that is your final summing up?"

DEAN: If we all could be that way!

JEAN: That is why he was so good. He worked hard because he loved it, not because he was making money. If he wanted to make money, he could have let others do some of the drawing.

DEAN: Like other artists do, the cottage industry of cottage painters…

JEAN: So it is the hard work and the obligation to use your talent for the people who are consuming your offerings. There is a parallel there.

You might want to know a little about Sparky's music education. He had a school friend named Shermy—the *Peanuts* character Shermy is named after him. His mother was a piano teacher. In Sparky's childhood days, they didn't play in each other's houses. It was more that the kids gathered up and went off together. Shermy played the viola or violin. Sparky said they used to sit on the front porch and laugh because Shermy had to stay in and practice until he had learned the music he was assigned. Sparky and the rest of the kids had to sit on the porch and wait. He sometimes would hear the mother playing Beethoven and sometimes with students. That was the first time that he heard Beethoven, at Shermy's house in St. Paul.

This was up to age 14. After that, in high school, they didn't get together as much.

Sparky liked other kinds of music. At nineteen he was in the army. We have some letters that he wrote a friend saying he was working really hard and that the *Saturday Evening Post* had bought his second cartoon, "page thirty," so you can see this fellow sharing his excitement at his progress. Then he said, "You won't believe it. I thought classical music was stupid, but I am actually listening to it." This was a fellow instructor at Art Instruction in Minneapolis. They all worked together in their cubicles, correcting lessons that people would send in, on perspective, shading, etc. Most of them were college graduates and were interested in music, literature, and art. Sparky came back from the army not having any of that sophistication. This became his college education. They funneled him into what to read. They all listened to classical music together. I met three of them and one of them told me Sparky didn't know anything about classical music when he came and pretty soon he had the best record collection of any of us. Sparky was that sort of obsessive person, and curious, so he wanted to learn it. He also had a desire to be educated.

DEAN: I have read that Brahms was his favorite composer, but we know that he used Beethoven as Schroeder's muse.

JEAN: That's because he thought that the name Beethoven was funnier in the comic strips. He did recognize him as probably the greatest composer but he loved the emotion in Brahms. We began going to the Santa Rosa Symphony after we were married. I don't how much he went before. He could sit quietly through a forty-five minute piece. Sometimes he would pull a pad out of his pocket and jot something down, then put it back. Later, he could whistle the themes. Because it was a small town, we knew the conductor. We went to his house sometimes with the artists.

DEAN: Was that Jeffrey Kahane?

JEAN: No, it was Corrick Brown. We knew Jeffrey too. When Sparky met the soloists, he could hold his own even though he wasn't trained in music. He could keep those melodies in his head.

We have looked at Schroeder as a little bit like Sparky. Schroeder is hunched over his piano. Sparky is hunched over his drawing board. Everybody is pestering Schroeder all the time, especially Lucy. For Schroeder it is real art. For Sparky it is not real art. He is hunched over a comic strip, not a fine painting.

DEAN: That's interesting. Was he denigrating his own art?

JEAN: No. A fellow artist came up with this. Sparky was modest. He said, "It is not for me to say I'm the world's greatest cartoonist. Only time will tell."

DEAN: The chief cartoon that we will have in our Schroeder exhibit in Orange County is a Sunday strip where he is having a healthy breakfast, is working out, limbering up and dashes downstairs to his toy piano. In the final panel you see him playing and the notes above and no words. It would appear to someone who doesn't know the Beethoven piano sonatas that he must be tackling a very difficult piece. It is in fact the *Hammerklavier* Sonata, one of the most difficult pieces of all time.

JEAN: And it takes muscle.

DEAN: It's a huge piece, almost impossible to play. It is said that Beethoven's publisher questioned him about why he wrote such a hard piece for the piano. Beethoven responded that pianists fifty years from now would have something to work on. It has been almost two hundred years and we are still working on it. To learn the *Hammerklavier* is on my bucket list. The fact that Sparky did that cartoon showed huge insight into the music.

JEAN: Somehow, Sparky understood this without ever playing the piano, probably by reading about it. Every time a biography of Beethoven would come out, he would read it. But the toy piano itself came from a toy piano he bought for Meredith as a little girl.

DEAN: On the TV shows when Schroeder plays his piano, the sounds are from a concert grand. Did Sparky have anything to do with that? Did he make that decision?

JEAN: On those shows, Sparky, the producer, and others had their own spheres. They would discuss things. Animator Bill Meléndez would have said we have to get some great sound from a real master.

DEAN: What we are doing in the exhibit with this particular cartoon is to have an actual Yamaha Disklavier piano there. I am having one of our very talented staff members, Randy Polevoi, play the first couple of pages of the *Hammerklavier* on the Yamaha Disklavier, storing it on its hard drive. When people come by to look at the strip, they can touch a screen on the Disklavier that starts the piece, making the bit really work in an enhanced way.

JEAN: There is another strip that I am sure came before that particular one, where he slides down the banister to get to the piano. It is the same kind of thing. He had to build up enough force to play Beethoven. Again, it shows Sparky's knowledge of the music. *Eine Kleine Nachtmusik* or any other piece wouldn't have worked the same way.

DEAN: Dennis O'Neil writes about friendship. I would think he is referring to the relationship between Snoopy and Woodstock.

JEAN: Yes. That was a relationship he developed after we were married in 1973. Woodstock was named in the comic strip before that. Snoopy called Woodstock "my friend of friends." Sparky said he really liked that relationship. You realize what it did in the history of the comic strip. Each of the other characters in the comic strip was part of a pair, a counter balance. The addition of Woodstock gave Snoopy his own animal friend so that he didn't always have to be friends with humans.

DEAN: I remember when Woodstock was introduced. It was a big deal.

JEAN: The name came from the Woodstock Festival that was a few years before.

DEAN: O'Neil also writes about arrogance. Lucy?

JEAN: When you said arrogance, I immediately thought about Snoopy, since his persona became very arrogant. I think what personifies Lucy best is that she is a fussbudget. You know to be arrogant you have to not know your limitations. Somehow she knows that she is off base. I always felt that Lucy's fussing and belittling comes from a place of insecurity. That's not to say that arrogant people are necessarily insecure.

DEAN: He talks about existentially orneriness. Beethoven was definitely ornery. Did Sparky have ornery moments?

JEAN: Yes, he did. Once, for example, he stood up to the syndicate. He said he had been drawing this strip for 35 years and told them, "I have never caused any trouble, I honor my readers, I have helped you, I do interviews and I think I deserve more of a cut. I am the one who has made it successful. Not you." Of course, in this day and age, a cartoonist would own his own copyright. He did not and he was fine with that arrangement because they gave him a professional place to go home to. It wasn't necessarily that he wanted to break that arrangement, but he wanted more. And he was ornery about that.

DEAN: What character in the strip best personified this behavior?

JEAN: He would say, "I have my crabby Lucy side." Lucy said of herself, "I am just plain ornery." I don't think Sparky was ever as hurtful as Lucy. You would run into people who would say, "Oh yeah, I ran into Mr. Schulz, took my little kids to get him to sign something and he said, 'Can't you see I am seated with five people and eating my lunch?'" And that person would say that he was hurtful. He was basically kind. Things didn't come from a mean place, although when you get pushed against a wall, you do bark back.

DEAN: I have been reading a lot about you guys. He got a Congressional Gold Medal. Was that posthumous?

JEAN: It was awarded before he died. The vote was taken in November before he died in February 2000, but it was presented to us a year later.

DEAN: And Ron Paul was only dissenting vote in the two houses of Congress.

JEAN: I heard that.

DEAN: Congressman Paul, really? When it is all said and done, that's probably what he is going to be remembered for.

JEAN: When he was awarded this, less than two hundred had been awarded in our two hundred-year history. Now they are awarded much more frequently.

DEAN: Things have indeed changed.

People ask me, "Why are you doing this project about Beethoven? Everybody knows about him." Things of such importance you have to keep alive. Generations have done it before us. It's now our turn and we'll pass the ball to the next generation.

JEAN: You keep it alive and you keep finding new things too.

DEAN: We are dealing with Beethoven, the late great, in our project. He developed this late style where he transcended into a new creative realm, where he went beyond what he or any other composers had done. I think he wasn't so much afraid of dying as he was worried about not being able to continue working. Did Sparky go through a similar period of a later style?

JEAN: There was a time when a group of people said that Charles Schulz has done his best work. He should stop drawing, get out of the paper and let others come in. He said that would be well and good but he said his readers still want me in the paper. People still want to read it. He felt that some of his later things were better than he had ever done. He didn't take kindly to those types of comments.

DEAN: Why do people say things like that? Who are they to say to make room for somebody else?

JEAN: It was interesting to be with him when that was being said and to see his reaction. When he did a certain strip that he was particularly proud of, he would say, "Nobody else is doing anything like this." He defended his right to keep working. I suppose people would say that the very early Flying Ace strips were great. There are some 1998-99 Flying Ace strips that are just as clever. It's partly because people always want something new. We have transitioned into things always having to be new.

He did a Sunday page with Flying Ace from something he read about D-Day when he visited Normandy 20 years earlier, in the 1970s. Field Marshall Rommel left what was to be the front of D-Day to attend his wife's birthday in Germany. He wanted to present his wife with a pair of red shoes that he had bought for her. The intelligence that he had received was that there was nothing going on and it was safe to go home for her birthday. Sparky did a version of this in a comic strip. At the end, the Germans had wondered who had informed the Allies that Rommel wouldn't be in command on the front for a brief period. He didn't, of course, use Rommel's name. The last frame of the strip shows Snoopy in a phone booth on the phone whispering, "Woof!" Now, that's brilliant. He couldn't have drawn that in the '60s because he had to grow.

He had to steep himself in the material. In the '60s when he came out with the Flying Ace, it was because his son was making model planes and reading biographies. They talked about it. He was shown the model planes and that stimulated him. He had to live some more of this life, get some information to get to that point late in his career.

In the later years, people would say that he had lost his edge. He didn't have Lucy being so cranky and tearing down Charlie Brown as much. What I liked was when he became a grandfather, you could read grandfatherly things. He was looking back, so that is what I think of as late style. It is a reflection back on things that you can't draw when you are forty years old.

DEAN: At the end, Beethoven was writing fugues. In his early days, he was terrible at it. He thought they were a waste of time, too much mathematics. In his late period, he went back to this very old Baroque form and started incorporating fugues into his pieces that were absolute masterpieces. They didn't sound old, they sounded very new.

Are the *Peanuts* strips you see today written by others?

JEAN: No. They are all reruns; what you see now is a 1966 series. There was a time when different papers were running different strips because of the size format for newspapers. They had to fit them. Now we have resized the strips to fit, which means they may have a little more white space. This is one of the main reasons we did the museum. People have seen all of this material in papers and in books but they haven't seen the beautiful line quality up close when you see it in six-inch squares.

DEAN: He could really draw a line. A simple, tiny curve in the line can completely change the character's emotion. It's extraordinary.

JEAN: It is the haiku of the line. In the beginning of the strip, he did draw backgrounds that came from his house. Later, there might be a telephone, a table, or a bed if he needed it, but he didn't have the decoration that he started out with. One reason is that you have more to do, drawing a background. I also think paring it down to the essentials was an artistic decision. If he had felt that artistically he needed to have some background he would have used it.

DEAN: Charlie Brown never did kick the football.

JEAN: Sparky had emergency surgery and he didn't draw the strip after that. What he had drawn was what he had drawn. While he was in the hospital, he drew a Linus and Snoopy, just to see if he could still do it. He began taking chemo and he knew that he couldn't keep working. It took too much energy, too much stamina to do it. Even if he had said that he was going to end this comic strip, I don't think he would have tied everything up with Charlie Brown kicking the football and Lucy getting to sit beside Schroeder at the piano.

DEAN: Why would you want to end it? That football will always be out there for Charlie Brown to kick if Lucy is brave enough to hold it after having been ecstatic coming from Schroeder's non-existent piano bench. Charlie Brown will always have hope.

Variation 14

SCHUBERT

A talk given to the Alta Bahia Philharmonic Committee in November 2013.

CONTEMPLATING RETIREMENT IN a couple of years, and wondering what I will do with myself (other than chasing my wife around our property in France), I have decided to dedicate myself to making a thorough exploration of the piano music of Franz Peter Schubert. I have created programs of his orchestra pieces, chamber music, and songs for years. My interest began in my formative days as a horn player, when I performed his *Auf dem Strom*. Since that time, I have dabbled in playing Schubert pieces on the piano here and there. But I was more occupied with Bach, Beethoven, Debussy, Prokofiev and other, more adventurous composers. Then I gave up the piano altogether to pursue the French horn, on which I ultimately made my living (in my early days). For me, returning to the piano was a source of pleasure and a distraction, and eased the stress caused by running a non-profit arts organization. Most of that credit goes to the support of my wife, Kaly. From this point on, I envision learning the remaining 32 Beethoven piano sonatas, more than a lifetime of activity, and tapping into the goldmine that are the piano works of Franz Schubert. Here I am today, with Schubert on my mind, in the midst of

Beethoven: The Late Great, bringing a performance of Schubert's first *Impromptu* from D. 899, Op. 90. The D. numbers come from Viennese musicologist Otto Eric Deutsch, who died in 1967, not that long ago. His work is invaluable in keeping organized the overwhelming amount of Schubert's compositions.

Schubert lived his entire life—except for the very last year—within the lifetime of Beethoven. He died in 1828, and was a torchbearer at Beethoven's funeral the year before. The two composers were possibly together only once: when Beethoven was on his deathbed and Schubert, along with others, came to visit. It's most likely that they were never really connected, although they were each so influential in the same period of time. I feel certain that Schubert had noticed the great disheveled composer stomping around the streets of Vienna, but that he was too shy to introduce himself. Here is the striking difference between the two men—Beethoven, the most famous composer in the world, versus the meager Franz Schubert, whose talent was easily just as great, but who was a terrible self-promoter. Beethoven's works were widely published and available throughout Europe. Most of Schubert's works weren't publicly performed or published until after his death.

Of all of the great so-called Viennese composers—Haydn, Mozart, Beethoven, Brahms, Bruckner and Mahler—Franz Peter Schubert was the only one native to Vienna. He was born on New Year's Eve in 1797, and died November 19, 1828. Schubert never even neared the amount of glory in Vienna that Beethoven enjoyed in his lifetime. His father was a schoolmaster who had twelve children (of which only four survived) and taught his students in the home compound. The building is at 54 Nussdorerstrasse in Vienna, and serves as a museum today, having been fully restored to the condition it was in during Schubert's time. It is definitely worth a visit, like traveling back in time.

Beethoven made his second and last move to Vienna in 1792 at the age of twenty-two. He took the town by storm. Through his connections with Count Waldstein in Bonn, he made immediate connections with the area's nobility. Mozart had died the year before, so Beethoven quickly reached the top of the virtuoso pianist list. By 1895, he was making quite a mark as a composer. The *Pathétique* Sonata was from this period. He left his terrible home situation for the glory of Viennese living.

In stark contrast to the Beethoven father/son conflict, Schubert and his father had an affectionate relationship. The young Schubert received violin lessons from his father and picked up the ability to play the piano from his brother, who was also learning music from their father. Franz excelled in both instruments so rapidly that he was placed under the tutelage of Michael Holzer. By 1808, he was admitted to the boy choir of the court chapel and into the Imperial and Royal College. He quickly became the leader of the first violins in the school orchestra and served, occasionally, as the group's conductor, playing Haydn and Mozart symphonies and the more recent First and Second Symphonies of Beethoven. He was an excellent student, and started composing at age thirteen, studying with Antonio Salieri, who was made famous in this country by the movie *Amadeus*. Anselm Hüttenbrenner became a friend of Schubert's while they both studied with Salieri. Later, Hüttenbrenner was at Beethoven's bedside when he died on March 26, 1827.

After his mother's death in 1812, a family quartet was formed, for which he composed his early string quartets. The next year, he began teaching in his father's school, which cut into his time to compose. In 1815, he wrote his Mass No. 1 in F major and discovered Goethe's *Faust*, which inspired his first song masterpiece, *Gretchen am Spinnrade (Gretchen at the spinning wheel)*. This song was the beginning of the great lieder period, songs that would pour forth from Schubert and his disciples during the next 100 years. In 1816, he composed 145 more songs and two more masterpieces, *Heidenröslein* and perhaps his greatest, *Die Erlkönig*.

During this period, he made friends with a law student named Franz von Schober, who encouraged Schubert to leave his teaching and take up composing full-time. The next year, he completed his fourth symphony, the *Tragic*. He was having difficulty getting his songs published because of the strength of the piano accompaniment and his emphasis on the dramatic—these were uncommon qualities in songs up to that time. Many meaningful friendships soon followed. He enjoyed a close network of support, as his friends all enjoyed gathering in each other's homes to listen to and participate in Schubert's works. Such an evening became known as a Schubertiade. It was in this format that most of his works were performed. Ultimately, there were very few public performances of his works. To this very day, there are still Schubertiades in Austria during the summer in the villages of *Schwarzenberg Hohenems*. They feature the very best in classical artists, and are definitely worth a planned visit.

In 1816, Schubert's reputation in Vienna began to grow. He finished his ever-popular Fifth Symphony. While Beethoven was looked upon as the great master of Vienna, the star of the era was Rossini, whose operas took the city by storm. Schubert was influenced by this, most notably in his Sixth Symphony and his overtures in the Italian style, the first of which he converted into his very famous overture *Rosamunde*.

The next year, Schubert became music master to the children of Count Johann Esterházy at their summer residence in Zseliz, Hungary. While there, Schubert composed a requiem mass for his brother, who pawned it off as his own to enhance his chances of getting a position.

1819 brought Schubert back to Vienna; this was known as one of his happiest times, when he composed the delightful Trout Quintet. None of Schubert's many attempts at stage presentations were very successful—his songs were the thing. Hüttenbrenner and other lesser composers were getting their works published, but not so for Schubert. It was "who you know," as opposed to "what you could do." His friends managed to get *Gretchen am Spinnrade* published along with *Die Erlkönig*.

1822 was very productive, seeing the completion of songs with texts by Mayrhofer and Goethe—the *Wanderer Fantasy*, the *Quartettsatz* and the unfinished Symphony No. 8 (which was probably meant to be a two-movement work). After this, Schubert fell ill and was too poor to support himself. This caused him to make a bad business decision, selling a large portion of his work to the publisher Cappi & Diabelli for a meager price. During this period of depression, he wrote two of his greatest works: the cycle *Schöne Müllerin* and the song *Du bist die Ruh*. In 1827, he began work on the cycle *Winterreise*. It is possible that Beethoven may have read some of Schubert's songs on his deathbed, where he is supposedly quoted as saying, "Truly in Schubert there is a divine spark." This was claimed by Beethoven's secretary Anton Schindler, although his is not always the most reliable source. Between 10,000 and 30,000 people attended Beethoven's funeral procession, in which Schubert was a torchbearer.

Schubert's last year, 1828, was an extremely productive one, despite his failing health. He wrote the *Impromptus*, the first of which I will play for you in a moment, the A and B-flat major sonatas, the great C major Ninth Symphony, and, in the very month before his death, *Die Winterreise*. Other than their age disparities, there remains a few major contrasts between Beethoven and Schubert. Whereas the first performance of Beethoven's Ninth Symphony was a grand occasion and a supreme success, Schubert's Ninth Symphony was performed much later, not until 1839—one year after the work was unearthed by Robert Schumann in Vienna, eleven years after Schubert's death. Felix Mendelssohn and the Gewandhaus Orchestra performed the premiere of the work in its entirety. Schubert's own funeral was miniscule in comparison to Beethoven's. A few young students in the Margareten suburb of Vienna at St. Joseph church sang the composer's *Pax vobiscum,* from 1817. He was then buried in the Währing Cemetery, next to Beethoven. In 1888, both composers were exhumed and moved to the Central Cemetery, where, today, they rest next to each other and are surrounded by the graves of other composers. This signifies the historical greatness of Franz Peter Schubert. While Beethoven's reputation has always been elevated, Schubert's is high and continues to grow higher. Knowing the genius of Beethoven, we can better appreciate the talents of his unique and dedicated contemporary.

Variation 15

MOM, DAD, AND BEETHOVEN

MY FIRST EXPERIENCE with Ludwig van Beethoven was with a set of 78 rpm recordings of his Fifth Symphony. I played them over and over on a tiny record player that I had received for Christmas when I was nine years old. Later I was greatly traumatized when I dropped that album set. I remember a loud bang when it hit the floor, as each sleeved record simultaneously cracked in two. I was devastated, not to mention afraid of the consequences. Fortunately, my parents were sympathetic rather than angry. The silver lining was that I discovered a lone survivor—the first disc was still on the turntable unscathed. What remained of the Fifth Symphony was four minutes of the opening of the symphony and, on the flip side, the last four minutes of the last movement finale. This would have to do, for now. Our tiny household was inundated with continuing *dit dit dit dah's* that played much to the dismay, I'm sure, of everyone else.

Around this time, I began piano lessons. Mrs. Patterson, my teacher, bought me an extremely easy arrangement of the Fifth Symphony's first movement. It wasn't long before I encountered the theme to the "Ode to Joy" in one of my John W. Schaum beginner piano books. I forget which color it is, but I believe I still have that book, stored in some box somewhere my garage. I went from playing *dit dit dit dah* on the record player to banging out the "Ode to Joy" on a real piano. I played it loudly, softly, slowly, rapidly, *staccato, legato*—every way possible; it was clear that I wanted more.

My dad bought a pair of tickets to a performance of the Ninth Symphony in nearby Fort Worth—a performance by the Dallas Symphony, conducted by Walter Hendl. This was very special, as it was my very first concert by a live orchestra. The event took place at the Will Rogers Memorial Center in the auditorium next to the Coliseum, the site of the giant Rodeo and Fat Stock Show that my dad and I attended every January. This, of course, was quite a different experience. There were a lot of people in the hall, all of them, I'm sure, strangers to the rodeo. To my dismay, the Ninth Symphony was really long, as I was used to an eight-minute version of the Fifth Symphony. I was elated but weary with the amount of music that came before they got to my beloved theme. When they did, I was ecstatic. Dad was pretty amused, always a step ahead of me. My old John W. arrangement would never feel the same again. It was all I could talk about for weeks—even my elementary school buddies, I could tell, were concerned about my state of mind. They had a profound lack of understanding of what music can really mean to someone, and, unfortunately, I believe many of them still do to this day. From that moment forward, I decided that trying to get people to understand music would be a driving force in my life.

Then the great package arrived.

My mother had responded to a junk mailing from either Columbia Records or the *Reader's Digest* by ordering the complete Beethoven Nine Symphonies with Arturo Toscanini, conducting the NBC Symphony. This was beyond my wildest dreams! Oh my God! I was glad to find that these records were unbreakable, though quite easily scratched. This time, the first disc had the complete first movement of the first symphony, and the last movement (my beloved "Ode to Joy") on the flip side. I enjoyed loading them up on our new hi-fi, and it would play all nine of them automatically—this was new technology, state of the art, ever so very contemporary. Naturally, it started to drive my family crazy. Beethoven became the soundtrack to every minute of household living—laundry, television, mealtimes, everything—Beethoven was always going. For the sanity of the household, sadly, Dad announced a restriction on my time with Ludwig. It was my mother who came up with the brilliant idea—the great save.

Being rather slow to rouse in the morning (it's the same, to this day), I was very hard to wake. Mom would shake, cajole, and call me, and I'd roll over and pull the sheet around my neck. I'm sure Mom would have used a cattle prod if we'd had one. But now, she took a new approach using reverse psychology. She'd play the beginning of a random movement from one of the nine symphonies, not allowing me to come to breakfast until I could identify which one it was. The symphony played away while I was getting dressed and chewed breakfast—it was truly brilliant. I got to where I could identify the movement on the first note. After a while, she started dropping the needle at random in the *middle* of movements, and I soon could identify the movement and symphony again with only one note. Early mornings, my motivation was a hunger for the music, and also for Post Toasties. Needless to say, my mother and my sister became pretty familiar with the symphonies of Beethoven. Over time, I noticed that Mom had the tendency to play the movements she liked, and on consecutive mornings. It didn't matter to me; I was energized, ready to take on the day. My father, of course, already knew them well. He began plying me with more music—Brahms, Dvořák, and my next great passion, Stravinsky. I think I have those Toscanini recordings in the garage, as well. It may be time for an archeological dig amongst the boxes to reclaim cherished musical memories.

A few years later, I took up the French horn in junior high school. I was happy to learn that Beethoven wrote a sonata for horn, and I practiced it over the next few years. I bought a miniature score for all nine symphonies, and used to play my horn along with the Toscanini Beethoven recordings. I began playing the symphonies for real once I entered college and joined professional orchestras. It was a wonderful day when I realized that I had performed all nine of them—many musicians acknowledge this as a kind of a rite of passage. When I began my arts management career with the Chattanooga Symphony and Opera, there was no permanent conductor, and I could program any piece that our budget would allow; and the orchestra could play it as long as it was okay with the guest conductor—a fun position to be in when music is your passion. I programmed the Ninth Symphony with the orchestra and local opera chorus, and was able to engage the very same Walter Hendl from my first concert to conduct the performance. I had met his daughter, a dancer in the New York City Ballet, during my horn playing days. I thought I had come full circle. Little did I know of the path that Ludwig and fate had already laid out for me.

When I became the executive director of the Jacksonville Symphony, I inherited a rather complicated problem. The orchestra had been performing in a 3,000-seat auditorium with a large lobby, but questionable acoustics. There was another hall in town call the Florida Theatre, recently and beautifully restored. It had astounding acoustics. The season before my arrival, the board chairman and the music director made a unilateral decision to move the subscription concerts from the old hall to the 1,800-seat Florida Theatre. The board and the chairman came up with this seemingly brilliant idea that they felt would be the right decision for everyone; all seemed right with the world. There was a huge subscription response and the orchestra sounded terrific. It appeared I had made a great choice to come to Jacksonville.

Then the trouble began. Renewals for the second season in the Florida Theatre were abysmal. What could be wrong? Board members cried, "Numbers were up when we moved to the new hall. What happened?" "You took the subscribers' seats away from them," I thought, "of course the season sales were strong." It was an Oklahoma land rush, subscribers running to claim new territory. I knew we needed to confront this issue. The new board chairman had contacts with a marketing research firm. Being the new kid on the block, it would be unseemly of me to cast aspersions on the previous chairman and our music director. We could, however, masquerade our search for the answer—one that we already knew, which was that the lobby of the Florida Theatre wasn't as conducive to intermission socializing, an important aspect of concert going—with some extensive research about other questions we might have for consumers. I won't go into details with the conclusions, so as to prevent embarrassment for the Board of Directors. The main point is that the chairman and music director had met privately to make a decision about the orchestra's fate without consulting anyone else. This was, of course, their way of avoiding those who held other opinions. In Texas, that process is called SWAG, or "sophisticated wild-ass guessing."

How did we remedy the issue? Beethoven, our superhero, came to the rescue. We moved the main subscription back to the old hall and loaded it with soloists like violinist Itzhak Perlman and narrator John Houseman. In the Florida Theatre, we needed to attract a new audience with great music that would make use of the acoustics. The solution, of course, was to plan for the complete nine symphonies of Beethoven in a series of four concerts. This was a fantastic success, selling out almost immediately. The classified section of the *Florida Times-Union* served as a marketplace for the buying and selling of tickets. Needless to say, some of the diehard subscribers checked it out and realized the value of the Florida Theatre's acoustics.

During the run of my many Ninth Symphony performances, I kept hearing the word *Elysium* in the text. What is *Elysium*? It is a place in our minds, where our heroes rest; it is joy, it is immortality. It is where we come from and hope to go to.

My mother's mother and father are buried in Fort Worth, Texas. Substantial amounts of the rest of her family's early generations are buried in the cemetery in Elysian Fields, Texas. They all grew up around there, in small towns that straddle the Louisiana border; their forbearers came from Alabama and Virginia, and, before that, England. My mother was born in Carthage, Texas.

When I was little, I used to ask my grandmother about Elysian Fields, having been there a few times and not being too much impressed by it. Why would such a plain old town have such a fancy name? She would get a bit misty-eyed while she talked about how special it was. She was a young mother during World War I. She talked about soldiers being buried there, sons and brothers of friends. She said it was peaceful, a place you cannot forget. I didn't quite understand what she was trying to say, would forget about it until the next time someone brought up the town, and I would ask about it all over again, and then forget all over again. This went on, it seemed, for years until finally I had formed my own feeling for the place. I guessed if it was important to her, it was important to me. I know now the Elysian Fields is an ancient concept, a place where heroes go when they are done on earth. It is a place they have earned. It is a place that is important.

My great uncle Louie was a World War I veteran, and he is also buried at the Elysian Fields cemetery. He outlived those awful trenches by sixty years. He grew up with sisters who badgered him to pieces, my grandmother being one of them. While he never married, he had all of the feminine hospitality he could handle. I am grateful to have a collection of letters that he wrote from those trenches in France, plus many more from his nineteenth-century Alabama Van Sandt family. We are tied together in history, sharing a gene pool, certain personality qualities, and a keen sense of humor. Otherwise, he was known as a hearty, tough old cuss. And even though we did not spend much time together, I looked up to him very much. My grandmother and my great aunts adored him—they teased and pestered him with deep affection. And he was a charmer—he could get away with anything.

I didn't know either of my grandfathers. So I figured, even married with children and a grandchild, I am now him, as my son and grandson will be him. Everybody has an Elysian Fields somehow, someway, or another. That is the point. When Friedrich Schiller wrote "Daughter of Elysium" in his "Ode to Joy," he was picking up on this very same concept. We all come from daughters (or offspring, as I like to think of it) of Elysium. Buried in that cemetery is a fellowship of joy, misery, hopes, tribulations, dreams, lies, and truths. We are brothers and sisters in a part of an endless procession of life experiences, united by a singular fellowship. In fact, what he wrote was the phrase *Freude, Tochter aus Elysium* (Joy, Daughter of Elysium). It is this personification of "joy" that is the important bit, the quality we carry around inside us. It is there within us, whether we acknowledge it or not. It connects us, no matter how deeply it is buried under that giant pile of emotional luggage that we spend our lives sorting through. Some of us can access it easily. Others need inspiration of literature, music, or, likely, medication.

Schiller's was the perfect text for Beethoven's inspiration. It is a beautiful contagion and has tremendous ramifications for society. A more important word may be *aspiration*—to be in a better place, ultimately Elysium, the realm of perfect happiness.

For me, it all started with my mom and dad. I believe it begins in similar ways, for most people.

Dad died a few days after 9/11, at the age of eighty-three. He was a highly respected music educator and there was a huge turnout for his funeral at the First Methodist Church in Arlington, Texas. Mom passed away last January (2013) at the age of ninety-three. She was active in the community, much loved and respected; her funeral had a large turnout, too, at the very same church. Besides being a school librarian, she worked with the teachers and students at Corey Elementary School—named after my dad. When making plans for her funeral, we debated on what to serve at the reception. My sister, Carolyn, had a phenomenal proposition. Shortly after Corey Elementary School opened, almost 30 years ago, my mother decided that it would be a cute idea to bake a cookie for each student and teacher; this was something she planned to do every year, thereafter. There were, however, 950 students and at least 50 teachers. This meant that my poor mother was baking cookies day and night, for weeks on end in her tiny oven. Needless to say, that was the last time she baked cookies. Carolyn said turnabout is fair play—she got the Corey Elementary PTA to bake enough cookies for the reception. It was a remarkable amount of home-made cookies.

I thought I might close this sentimental journey with the remarks I made at Mom's funeral at the First Methodist Church in Arlington:

When Kaly and I arrived at John Wayne Airport to fly to Dallas this past Tuesday, we were given the opportunity to take a flight that was leaving earlier than the one for which we had reservations. It was American flight 1952.

With my mind reeling over the events that would most assuredly take place over the next few days and with thoughts and memories of my mother, that number did not immediately refer to a flight to me so much as it did to a year. 1952.

That year, I had a new toddler sister who was walking before she was eleven months old. My dad was working at a high school that we were all a big part of on Friday nights, the only day of the week other than Sunday that I was really aware of.

I remember a wonderful day during that year, or it may have been the beginning of the next, when I was outside in the backyard behind our little house on Peach Street here in Arlington. My new little sister, Carolyn Jean, was exploring the rather scant garden and trying to catch our dog Archie while my mother was hanging sheets on the clothesline to dry. They were billowing in the wind, mimicking the fluffy clouds above and were giving my mother some difficulty, bothering her not in the least. She was singing a song that she often sang, mostly with la-la-la and an occasional lyric. She was very happy, which made me very happy. Carolyn and I were not doing anything in particular, just enjoying the moment, a moment that gathered more magic as the years progressed, before we began to take on the cares of the world and the rest of our lives. It was the type of moment that I fear many kids today don't ever experience.

It was the first really nice day in my memory. It was a time before school days, before Beethoven, before everything. I remember the warm sun, the cool breeze not unlike that of the last few days. When I need to find a happy place today I often think of that moment, its feeling, that fresh breeze, my carefree sister and my mother singing. This is my most treasured memory of her and one of the best in my life—pure happiness. I will have this memory as long as I live. It comes to me every time I breathe fresh air.

We will all miss our Becky very much. She touched so many lives. She lived for her family and her friends yet she was her own woman. Her infectious spirit will always be a part of those who knew her. She was an inspiration to all of us. She was my first love, my first best friend and my longest champion. She was our Mom and our Granny. We will miss her deeply.

L'histoire

Variation 16

La Révolutionnaire

*It's in the deepest dungeons that the most beautiful dreams of
freedom are dreamt.*
—Friedrich Schiller

"Beethoven is the friend and contemporary of the French
Revolution…and he remained faithful to it. Beethoven, that
plebeian genius, who proudly turned his back on emperors,
princes and magnates—that is the Beethoven we love for his
unassailable optimism, his virile sadness, for the inspired
pathos of his struggle, and for his iron will which enabled him
to seize destiny by the throat."

So said Igor Stravinsky, another revolutionary composer whose *La Sacre
du Printemps* is a hundred years old this year. The music of both of these
composers sounds fresh and revolutionary today, even if there is a 200-
year separation between the former's birth and the latter's death. They
are both, coincidentally, my favorite composers.

I have called two of these ramblings "La Révolutionnaire" and "…
et Romantique," after the name of Sir John Eliot Gardiner's period
instrument orchestra, who, along with the Monteverdi Choir, gave such

magnificent performances of the *Missa Solemnis* and the Ninth Symphony for our *Beethoven: The Late Great* project. I have inserted a third essay between these two, concerning Napoleon, a subject so significant in Beethoven's time and to Beethoven himself.

Beethoven's music was revolutionary. But the question is, "Why?" Is it because he was frustrated with music's status quo at the time? Was he influenced by the tumultuous changes going on in Europe? Or was he plainly rebellious by nature, a product of an abusive childhood? I believe it is a combination of all three. It made me very curious to look first into the French Revolution itself for clues.

In anticipation of my move to France, I have been reading a lot about the country's history, trying to fill in the many gaps in my understanding. I have read a number of very interesting and informative books along the way that detail culture, history, and personalities of French importance. My research has been a wildly fascinating process, especially reading about and being in Paris, which is some kind of town. I can't say that I completely understand how the place works—I am not sure anybody really does—but I have gained a better understanding of its impact on the rest of the world at the time of the revolution, and now.

To understand Paris, I think it is best to get a grasp of it as a whole so that individual periods of its history make more sense. Three books are perfect for this.

The first is a great summer read that came out a couple of years ago. It is *The Great Journey—Americans in Paris* by historian David McCullough. There are many surprises in this very accessible book. You get a real view of Parisian sensibility as American artists, writers, physicians and inventors during the mid- to late nineteenth century experienced it. This is the perfect book to read before a trip to Paris.

When you arrive in Paris, you must pay a visit to the English language bookstore, Shakespeare and Company. The selection is overwhelming. We bought a pile of books there, happily satisfied in this most famous literary resource. Here, we found two perfect companions to McCullough's book. They are *Seven Ages of Paris* by Alistair Horne and *Wicked Company—Freethinkers and Friendship in Pre-Revolutionary Paris* by Philipp Blom.

Horne's book chronicles Paris from the middle ages of Philippe Auguste to the unrest at the Sorbonne in 1968. History keeps repeating itself. There is a running theme of alternating brilliance and failure, personified by a series of powerful figures such as Henry IV, Louis XIV, Napoleon and Charles de Gaulle. As the history of Paris unfolds, you realize that one should not be surprised by any chain of events. There is definitely a pattern that can be found in all of human society.

Before the outrageous chain of events in the late eighteenth century, there was the Enlightenment. In Germany, it was called *Aufklärung*. The focus was on knowledge, seeking the truth, nature, and wanting to know rather than wanting to believe. It was a fierce reaction against the nobility and the church. This was an age of science, discovery and invention. While developing more slowly in Germany than in England or France, the court of Karl August, Duke of Weimar, was more progressive and attracted such minds as Goethe and Schiller, two great influences on Beethoven.

The language of the German Enlightenment was French. In visiting the court of Frederick the Great in Prussia, Voltaire said, "I find myself here in France; no one talks anything but French. German is for the soldiers and horses; it is needed only on the road." France was where the great changes in Europe took hold.

Pleasure-seeking was paramount. In Paris, these ideas were discussed over great food and wine. It was the age of some amazing minds and conversationalists, such as Denis Diderot, Baron d'Holbach and Jean-Jacques Rousseau. But it was also a dangerous time to express such ideas. This group called *Les Philosophes* was also known as the *encyclopédistes*. They collected and edited a series of articles for a set of reference books (placing the entries in alphabetical order—a first). Such articles gave them the opportunity to disguise their opinions and beliefs in a subtle manner, avoiding the censors. Diderot spent some time behind bars and Holbach published his own works under the *nom de plume* Jean-Baptiste de Mirabaud. It was at his estate that this group could openly express their Enlightenment opinions with some safety. Many came and went, even Benjamin Franklin, who was the darling of Paris, hailing from the country most famous for its revolution. Blom's *Wicked Company* delightfully captures this entire period.

Not that all of the intellectuals got along, of course. The one contrarian was Rousseau, who fled to Switzerland. He was a very popular writer, of whom later even Robespierre was an admirer. The one thing that the *philosophes* had in common was a strong distaste of Baroque opera. They were fed up with the endlessly alternating recitatives and arias where the singer was more concerned with showing off vocal technique than making the comedic or dramatic roles effective theater. Their hero was Christoph Willibald Gluck, the Bavarian-born composer who brought revolution to French opera. Now music was direct and simply expressive—no more nonsense and excess. It had returned to its Italian roots. Mozart was greatly influenced by Gluck, as were composers Mehul, Cherubini, and later Beethoven.

Ludwig van Beethoven was not yet on the scene, being born in 1770, the year that Marie Antoinette married King Louis XVI. The ideal of free thinking and liberty so championed by the *philosophes* was picked up by the Third Estate, the commoners, and reached an explosive point in the summer of 1789 when they infamously stormed the Bastille in Paris. The First and Second Estates, the clergy and the nobility, were put on notice.

As we come to the French Revolution itself, two books come to mind. The first is Edmund Burke's *Reflections on the Revolution in France* (1790). Written in exquisite English, it rightly predicts the failure of the revolution and urges a return to the *Ancien Régime*. The Terror did follow and subsequently, the rise of Napoleon, all affecting Beethoven's views of humanity.

It was a very dangerous time in Paris. Lucy Moore's *Liberty—The Lives and Times of Six Women in Revolutionary France* is a great book that lays out this amazing period from the uniqueness of a woman's point of view. This book has the feel of being on the streets where the action is happening as opposed to being with old Edmund Burke, safely tucked away in England. These six *citoyennes* each have different fates, and, among other things, were hopeful that the revolution's outcome would grant women rights where the American Revolution had failed to do so. This, of course, did not happen. Some of the ladies survived it—others didn't. The balance between speaking your mind and survival was very difficult. Our own Ben Franklin put it simply: "Any society that would give up a little liberty to gain a little security will deserve neither and lose both." Good advice we still need, unfortunately. We seem to be in the same predicament today, albeit not nearly as violent a time on our home shore. Democracy and liberty will always be a grand experiment, one that should be kept alive and vital. When opposing parties remain on opposite sides of the room like boys and girls at a grade school dance, we are doomed to disintegrate into a society unable to find useful solutions to any cause. In this kind of system, democracy wouldn't matter. The grand experiment would be finished.

On a recent trip to Paris, Kaly and I strolled through the Church of St. Eustace where these revolutionary women held secret meetings with other like-minded females. During the revolution, the church was closed, as were most churches during those years. I felt a sense of the energy that was radiated there by those brave women. The experience left me very inspired. My favorite of the bunch, Germaine de Staël, did survive the turmoil and managed later to get crossways with Napoleon—more about him later.

"I am convinced that Beethoven knew of French Revolutionary tunes and they found their way into his music. He used these tunes to incorporate liberty and revolution in his own music. He wanted musicians to live dangerously; pushing them beyond their limits was part of his aesthetic purpose." So said Sir John Eliot Gardiner, founder and director of the Orchestre Révolutionnaire et Romantique. These songs are not as subtle as you would expect. They are in the middle of the fight—causing it or reacting to it, at least fanning the flames of revolt. In the same sense, Beethoven's compositional style is very direct, expressing his thoughts and feelings in a new manner, going where no other composer had gone before. Sir John Eliot is a most eloquent arbiter of this revolutionary

Beethoven concept. Gardiner associates Cherubini's "Hymne du Panthéon" with the Fifth Symphony. The text of the "Hymne:" *Nous jurons tous...le fer en main* (We swear sword in hand) is echoed in the rhythmic "dit-dit-dit-DAH" motif that opens and glues the entire symphony together. Perhaps those four famous notes are not about fate knocking at the door at all but rather about dying for the republic and for the rights of man, even "la–Li-ber-té." Incidentally, Beethoven was very fond of Cherubini's music whereas Cherubini once referred to Beethoven as an "unlicked bear."

Political music of the time usually consisted of specific masses, funeral marches, parade marches, group patriotic songs, and anthems. Masses such Haydn's *Mass in the Time of War*, Beethoven's *Missa Solemnis* and the dreadful *Wellington's Victory* (which I rather enjoy) all contain the noises of war with pounding drums and blaring trumpets. Beethoven wrote a number of funeral marches and other celebrations of military heroes. There is a striking difference between the French revolutionary music and Beethoven's revolutionary music. One is on the defensive and the latter is a paean to future peace.

Take these words from *La Marseillaise*:

> To arms, to arms, ye brave!
> The avenging sword unsheathe,
> March on, march on!
> All hearts resolv'd
> On victory or death!

...And compare them to Schiller's Hymn to Joy in the Ninth Symphony:

> Joy, beautiful spark of the gods
> Daughter of Elysium,
> We enter, drunk with fire,
> Heavenly one, your sanctuary!

> Your magic reunites
> What custom strictly divided.
> All men become brothers,
> Where your gentle wing rests.

These are two entirely different messages, though both are evocative and moving.

Beethoven's music could be stirring and stormy without being violent. He was appalled by the ultimate end to the French Revolution. The composer was peace loving and initially welcomed the advent of Napoleon, who offered hope of restoring some stability to Europe. But Beethoven, of course, changed his tune, as events changed the course of history.

While his music was revolutionary and is still great as inspiration, Beethoven the man was most unattractive and very unpleasant, an "unlicked bear," as it were. We look up to his great spirit and ideals, but he was impossible to deal with and, because of this, had very few close friends. Writer Bishop Fan S. Noli, in his 1947 book *Beethoven and the French Revolution*, emphasizes three principal characteristics of Ludwig van Beethoven: his extraordinary affection for his nephew Karl, his arrogance, and his revolutionary music. He writes:

> The following suggestion is offered to a painter or sculptor [of Beethoven]: A human gargoyle with bristly hair and fiercely protruding teeth holding a lovely boy with one hand and the Ninth Symphony with the other. The inscription should read as follows: <u>Beethoven the Angel, the Devil and the Rebel</u>.

Variation 17

Napoleon

Glory is fleeting, but obscurity is forever!
—Napoleon Bonaparte, Emperor of the French

After writing the variations "La Révolutionnaire" and "…et Romantique," I realized that I had left out one very significant impact on the life and work of Beethoven—Napoleon Bonaparte. As with any topic in modern European history—especially concerning the great writers and composers of the Romantic period—Napoleon Bonaparte is the elephant in the room, certainly the continent, if not the world, during that period.

It is also interesting to consider both Napoleon and Beethoven in regards to the age-old "Great Man Theory." It describes that "the man makes the history," as opposed to the notion that the historical and cultural circumstances into which each was born make the man. The idea can be applied to thousands of other talented artists and leaders in that pre-modern period. But it is often the exception to the rule that prevails. There is no question that Napoleon and Beethoven collectively changed law, governance, war, peace, brotherhood, and music forever. Certainly, they were different from everyone else. They both made—created—history.

Napoleon was born in Corsica, the year before Beethoven was born, to a family of minor nobility. His older brother was also named Napoleon, but died in infancy. Beethoven had a brother first named Ludwig who died in infancy, as well. For most of Beethoven's life, he regretted not being born of noble blood, and on occasions intimated to his friends that he had been.

As adults, both Napoleon and Beethoven were of the same height. This begs the question of also applying the concept of "short man syndrome" (also known as the Napoleon complex), which insinuates that shorter men tend to be more aggressive and self-promoting than their taller counterparts. And while their respective heights were nearly average for men of their time, they both also shared an unusual amount of antagonistic vigor in their respective activities. The life stories that link these two men's behaviors together have been often repeated.

By 1803, Beethoven had become the greatest composer of instrumental music in Europe, with due respect, of course, to Franz Josef Haydn. Beethoven was preoccupied with writing his Third Symphony. However, he did manage to compose and present his *Christ on the Mount of Olives*. This was a vocal work with orchestra, beginning the voyage of writing his first opera. The first performance of the *Mount of Olives* must have been a wild affair. The C minor Piano Concerto was also on the program, with Beethoven as the soloist. His page turner was aghast that the pages of the piano part contained nothing more than symbols and squiggles; they made sense to Beethoven, but made page turning all but impossible. Beethoven was essentially playing from memory, as he hadn't had time to copy the part—not untypical of him.

In 1804, Beethoven completed his Third Symphony; he had intended to entitle it "Bonaparte Symphony" because of his respect for a hero of a man he believed had brought stability and peace to Europe after the disillusionment of the French Revolution. However, the composer became very angry when he learned that First Consul Napoleon Bonaparte had crowned himself emperor in Paris. He scratched the Bonaparte dedication from the title page and renamed it *Eroica,* or heroic. Instead, he dedicated the third movement as a funeral march to a soldier who died in 1804—not Bonaparte but the soldier he had been, certainly not the emperor he had now become.

By the spring of 1809, Napoleon was occupying the Schönbrunn Palace in Vienna. The noise of the exploding shells caused Beethoven to leave his quarters for a friend's cellar, where he covered his ears with pillows to protect his already deteriorating hearing from getting worse. During this time, a French officer and great admirer of Beethoven visited the composer. Beethoven, meanwhile, was still preoccupied with Napoleon. He asked his young friend, "If I go to Paris, shall I be obligated to salute your emperor?" His visitor responded, "If the emperor knew who you were, he might expect you to, but he doesn't know much about music." In fact, it was reported that Napoleon was an awful singer. He was not a fan of the music of his own country, which he said "was almost as bad as the English, and that the Italians were the only people who could produce an opera."

I want to characterize each man by his own defining moment.

By early 1814, Napoleon found himself at a dead end. He still had formidable forces, but they were scattered and unable to leave their current commitments. These dynamics were a sort of checkmate in the making, the stuff military history strategists and armchair generals live for; at the moment, Napoleon faced four major allied powers that had also suffered heavy losses of their own. He still had France, although the threat of insurrection in Paris was growing daily. The treasury was empty. Negotiations with the allies seemed to be the only remedy, but those opportunities had been cut off. The use of force was the only remaining option.

Louis XVIII was already poised to be the new king of France. Napoleon abdicated the throne and attempted suicide with a combination of drugs that he had carried with him for such an occasion from his campaign in Russia. But it was a desperate failure, and he was exiled to the small island of Elba, located off of the coast of Italian Tuscany.

Now, in effect, Napoleon was emperor of Elba. Here, he was accompanied by more than 600 of his old guard and loyal Polish cavalrymen.

Their duty was to protect their so-called emperor. Napoleon viewed these men as the core of the army he would lead if (or when) he would need to "rescue" the French people from the new regime. He believed it would self-destruct with great chaos—which, of course, it did.

During his brief gig as the island's new leader, he made many changes. He improved the fishing fleet and built forts, roads, schools and gardens. As all of this was happening, conditions began to deteriorate further in France. Refugees sailed to Elba—many of whom were Napoleon's former officers. As a part of his exile agreement, he was to receive two million francs a year from France, although that never happened. Soldiers returned home after their tremendous sacrifices to find no jobs, no funds, and no respect. These continuing reports prompted Napoleon to return to France on the *Inconstant* with 1,000 troops and several cannon. Avoiding the well-defended, crown-supporting port cities, he marched his men across the mountains toward Grenoble, which was defended by his former general Marchand (who had sided with the Bourbons).

Facing Marchand's troops, Napoleon put his own at parade rest and rode out in front, a lone soldier facing the muskets of the enemy. He called across to the opposing troops in an amazing display of bravado, his defining moment: "Soldiers, if there is one among you who wishes to kill his emperor, he can do so. Here I am." Instead of shots, there were shouts of "*Vive l'Empereur!*" The enemy battalion and the entire garrison joined Napoleon. Together they marched north, gathering support on their push towards Paris. Napoleon was reinstated as emperor for a brief time, before he met his ultimate Waterloo, as the saying goes.

Three years after the death of Napoleon Bonaparte on Saint Helena (where some say he was poisoned), Ludwig van Beethoven was presiding over a full house at the Imperial Court Theater, where the premiere of his Ninth Symphony was about to take place. He had put up the money for the concert, paying the cost of the venue, large orchestra and chorus, four soloists, copyists and all of the other expenses in producing such a bold, innovative program. He needed to make a profit. The impact of the music was staggering—*The Consecration of the House* overture; the *Kyrie*, *Credo* and *Agnus Dei* of the *Missa Solemnis*—and, of course, the

Ninth Symphony. At the conclusion, the audience erupted into a roar of appreciation, taking to their feet and tossing hats into the air. Caroline Unger, the mezzo soloist, went over to the deaf Beethoven, who was still facing the orchestra and reading the score, oblivious that the symphony had ended. During an earlier rehearsal, Fräulein Unger had referred to Beethoven as a "tyrant over all the vocal organs." Then she turned him around to face the audience so he could enjoy his defining moment. He bowed graciously. A German review said:

> Beethoven has outdone everything we have previously
> had from him: Beethoven has advanced still further onward!!!
> These new artworks appear as the colossal products of a son
> of the gods, who has just brought the holy, life-giving flame
> directly from heaven.

The legacies these two geniuses left us with is the Napoleonic Code, the tragedy of three and a half million military and civilian casualties, and some of the greatest and most enduring music of all time. As far as I am able to find out, Ludwig van Beethoven never shot anyone.

I will let the composer have the last word. In the year of the performances of the *Missa Solemnis* and the Ninth Symphony (1824), he met Carl Czerny in a coffee house in Baden. There was an article in one of the papers on a table announcing a new book by Walter Scott called *Life of Napoleon*. Beethoven commented to Czerny saying, "Earlier I couldn't have tolerated him. Now I think completely otherwise."

Variation 18

...ET ROMANTIQUE

GOETHE'S *FAUST* DEMANDED the impossible. He demanded much of him-self, as well as his audience, as did many of his contemporaries in the Romantic Period—creative minds such as Beethoven, Lord Byron, Berlioz, Liszt, and Wagner. The artistic intensity of the era was a reaction to the Enlightenment and the Industrial Revolution. Behind the movement was a fierce dynamic—pure artistic temperament—expressing personal feelings of sincerity, freedom, imagination, passion, risk, and moral enthusiasm. The title of this essay, "...et Romantique," is, of course, the second half of the name of the period instrument orchestra founded by Sir John Eliot Gardiner, dedicated to the performance of the music of Beethoven, Berlioz, and their ilk. Societal trends tend to be mirrored by cultural and artistic developments—never more so dramatically than during the transition of the late eighteenth to early nineteenth centuries. I think Jacques Barzun most accurately describes Romanticism, as a "state of consciousness exhibiting the divisions found in every age. Hence all attempts to define Romanticism are bound to fail. The word 'Puritan' connotes one thing; the word *romantic*, a hundred." Beethoven's life straddles this exciting, albeit confusing time.

Goethe was a friend of Friedrich Schiller, the poet of the "Ode to Joy" that Beethoven used in the Ninth Symphony. Goethe was director of the theater at Weimar, where he produced many of Schiller's plays. During the course of his long and full life, many of Goethe's works were set to music by Mozart and Beethoven, as well as other composers such as Schubert, Berlioz, Schumann, and Wagner. Beethoven championed the idea of a "Faust Symphony," though unlike many composers of the nineteenth century, he did not pursue it.

The music of Goethe's world was conservative, a continuation of what was produced under the Enlightenment (Haydn and Mozart); while he considered Beethoven the greatest living composer, he was not all that enthusiastic about the composer's desire to keep pushing the boundaries. Beethoven held Goethe and his writings in very high esteem and met him in the spa town of Teplitz (now Teplice in the Czech Republic) to discuss the composer's incidental music for the playwright's drama *Egmont*. The famous story of the occasion is the incident of Goethe and Beethoven walking outdoors together, arm-in-arm, passing royalty. Beethoven commented that "they must make way for us, and not us for them!" at which time Goethe broke away from the composer in order to bow to the sovereigns. Beethoven continued to walk forward with his hands in his pockets, ignoring the sovereigns altogether. Very Beethoven.

During my school years (and immediately thereafter), I had only read sections of Goethe's *Faust*. I was, of course, familiar with the musical versions by Berlioz, Liszt, Gounod, and even a musical on the subject by Randy Newman. Recently, I read Goethe's work from start to finish and was overwhelmed by its magnitude and imagination—and by the beauty of the English translation by Walter Arndt. It epitomizes what the Romantic Period is all about—tragedy, the supernatural, scandal, mysticism, eroticism, morality, and a fascination for antiquity and legend.

The story of Faust has numerous sources, though they are all very alike. Faust is a scholar who lusts after knowledge. He prefers the pleasures of earth to those of heaven, and enlists the help of the devil's representative, Mephistopheles, to achieve ultimate knowledge and pleasure—selling his soul in the bargain. Mephistopheles takes advantage of situation for fun, helping Faust seduce the young maiden Gretchen in the process. She loses her life but her soul is saved in the end because of her innocence. She enters heaven, whereas Faust enters hell for his vanity and wrongdoings. The difference of Goethe's version is the ending of the story. In his version, Faust indeed dies, but his soul is redeemed. Goethe's Part One of *Faust* was published in 1808, the year of Beethoven's Fifth Symphony. Twenty-five years later, Goethe revised Part One, and in 1831, completed Part Two.

Berlioz was captivated with the symphonies of Beethoven. To him, they represented the ultimate form of musical achievement. He wanted to devote his own creativity to keeping this spirit alive, to further advance Beethoven's style of poetry. Doing so, he took the technical requirements to a higher, nearly impossible level. Berlioz's passion was music and he couldn't live without it. His emotional life was the Romantic ideal—falling in love early (and often)—and having relationships that were unrealistic. He loved Shakespeare, especially Romeo and Juliet's amorously hopeless story, and was consumed with the idea of tragic love. He wrote about topics such as the supernatural, nature, and travel. His belief in fantasy drove the philosophy behind his tremendous musical risks.

As an orchestra musician, I have played selections from Berlioz's *The Damnation of Faust*, most notably the *Hungarian March*. A staging of *Faust* is extraordinarily difficult, and I never expected to see a production of it in my lifetime. I've now seen two—one at the Salzburg Festival and the other with Achim Freyer's version at the Los Angeles Opera.

Berlioz completed his "légende dramatique" *La damnation de Faust* in 1845 from sketches he began in 1829; it was performed the next year. He alters Goethe's version of the story—Faust indeed goes to hell. Marguerite (Gretchen) goes to heaven. It is another work with very big shoulders, calling for five cast members, a chorus, and a hundred-piece orchestra.

Franz Liszt's *Faust* Symphony is concerned with the characters rather than the story. The first movement is a description of Faust himself, written in an advanced approach, presaging Richard Strauss and Alban Berg. It is some of Liszt's best orchestral music. There are, of course, the influences of Berlioz and Wagner. With all of the bravura, twists, and turns, perhaps Liszt was writing about himself more than about Faust, the character. The Romantic Period, above all else, was about the ego. This makes sense, being that the second movement is about Gretchen and the third movement about Mephistopheles; they describe not the characters directly, but how they are viewed through Faust's (or Liszt's) ego.

Franz Liszt was one of the nineteenth century's two rock stars (the other being violinist Niccolò Paganini). He changed the way that the piano was played for all time. For his many performances, he transcribed the music of other great composers, giving the opportunity for many people to hear this music for the very first time. There were relatively few local performances (opera and orchestra) at the time, so most people had little or no access to popular music. Of course, there were no iPods or classical radio stations, so this was the most effective way to transmit his work. Liszt transcribed all of the symphonies of Beethoven for piano—they are still in print today and available on recording. The Sixth Symphony, recorded by Glenn Gould, is exceptionally nice.

A Beethoven disciple, Liszt raised the money to erect a statue of the composer in Bonn, Germany (Beethoven's birthplace). Liszt met him at eleven years of age, being introduced to the master by his teacher, Carl Czerny (who was a former pupil of Beethoven). After listening to the young musician play the first movement of the master's first piano concerto, Beethoven held the young boy's cheeks and said to him, "…You will give happiness and joy to many other people. There is nothing better or greater than that."

Liszt was a wild romantic. He had an affair with a married countess in Paris; the two cavorted around Switzerland and Italy where they had three children outside of wedlock. The second child was a daughter named Cosima. Liszt recounted these travels in his massive set of piano pieces, *Années de pèlerinage*. As a young woman, Cosima married the very busy Hans von Bülow, a conductor of Richard Wagner operas. She was left alone a good deal of the time and, of course, she and Wagner began an affair and later married in 1870. This kind of drama was the signature of the Romantic Period.

The art world was even crazier. The momentum of over-the-top creativity was at full speed during the time that Beethoven completed his

Hammerklavier Sonata; simultaneously, Mary Shelley was writing *Frankenstein* (1818). Meanwhile, the definitive composer of the time was, of course, Richard Wagner. His *Ring Cycle* was the most ambitious musical undertaking in modern memory, and he was known, absolutely, as the supreme ego of the period. While Liszt thought of himself as Faust, Wagner considered himself to be Wotan, god of the gods. Deems Taylor wrote that Wagner thought the world owed him a living. Wagner was probably right. He thought bigger than anyone else and made music that was outrageous, boisterous, and extremely long. To this day, he is both loved and hated. Mark Twain traveled to Bayreuth to hear *Parsifal* with hour-long intermissions. He wrote, "Seven hours at $5 a ticket is almost too much for the money."

Wagner was a Beethoven disciple and prolific writer. In one story, he concocted an imaginary tale about a journey on foot to Vienna with the idea of meeting Beethoven. After some difficulty he manages to do so; Beethoven complains that so many visitors want to look at him as a type of novelty attraction, but not in appreciation for the music he creates. The two composers hit it off. At the time, young Wagner was primarily a composer of dance music, not yet the great opera composer he aspired to be. Beethoven grumbled about the mixed response to his opera *Fidelio*, stating that maybe he would be better off writing dance tunes as well. Beethoven goes on to say, "There isn't a single theatre in the world for which I'd willingly write another opera. Were I to make an opera after my own heart, everyone would run away from it." Wagner, of course, took this to mean that he had the endorsement from Beethoven to fulfill his own destiny. Certainly, the exchange fueled Wagner's confidence and gave him a feeling of superiority. Ludwig threw Richard a few so-called "Hail Mary" passes—and he turned them all into touchdowns. Did I mention the ego?

The epitome of the literary Romantic age was George Gordon "Lord" Byron. Born in London in 1788, he died from the treatment of a fever in Missolonghi (western Greece) in the fight for the country's independence. This was a month before the premiere of Beethoven's Ninth Symphony. How romantic! Earlier that year, he had written the prophetic poem, "On this day I complete my Thirty-sixth Year." It contains these lines:

> If thou regret'st thy Youth, *why live?*
> The land of honorable Death
> Is here:—up to the Field, and give
> Away thy breath!

Clearly, the great poet wasn't feeling as optimistic as the rest of the artistic crowd.

To most contemporary classical music audiences, a piece from of the Romantic Period is most appealing. It speaks to the heart, implying that it has deep meaning and is full of melodies that you can hum by memory on your way out the door. Audiences generally want to know what they can expect before they enter the concert hall. This is what sells a ticket in the first place. Names on the bill such as Beethoven, Brahms, Tchaikovsky, and Rachmaninoff, to name a few, signify that the concert will be most enjoyable, comfortable, and easy to understand. As the aforementioned composers experienced in their own day, modern composers seem to have a rough go. They are too close to our reality, expressing feelings that we may not be ready to face, much less understand. Will these composers someday be as beloved by future audiences as their Romantic and Classical predecessors? Only time will tell. It's not impossible. Every piece of music was, at one time, a new piece of music.

Variation 19

THE ESTERHAZYS

IT WAS EVA Schneider's idea first. She came up with it during a meeting of the Philharmonic Society's Fundraising Committee, during my first year. The subject was a delicate matter, concerning the amount of money we would ask for when soliciting some substantial contributions from generous prospects, as these requests would be far above normal giving levels. How much? And how would we thank them? What would we call these donors? "Esterhazy Patrons!" Eva exclaimed. I knew who the Esterházys were, that they were deeply important to the success of Franz Josef Haydn—but that was about it. I began to see that this was a pretty great idea. However, the rest of the group was befuddled. "Ester who?"

Eva was a livewire volunteer for the Society, and is still a loyal friend and supporter. She has led our volunteer Committees and chaired our Board of Directors. Eva is Hungarian, had lived in Vienna, and is married to Fred, an Austrian. They are both steeped in Old World arts and are known as an exotic couple among our collection of Southern Californian "culture vultures." Eva told the group about the Esterházy family. It would be a great name for the new major donor giving level as it recalled how that family's largesse had made possible an entire history of classical music. She talked about what our new Esterhazy Patrons could do to secure the future of high quality classical music performances right here in Orange County, California. Richard Reinsch, our incoming board chairman, stepped forward and became our first Esterhazy Patron.

It was certain that no other local non-profit music group in Orange County had used or would try to use this name. It seemed perfect, with a built-in exclusivity. The fundraising committee decided that an individual (family, couple, foundation, etc.) could become an Esterhazy Patron of the Philharmonic Society with a $50,000 (now $60,000) contribution, which could be paid off over three years. The donor would receive recognition and benefits for a lifetime, and would receive the Esterhazy Medal that we designed, showing the Esterházy Palace and a portrait of Haydn on the reverse. It is very satisfying to see recipients proudly display their medals at some of our special gatherings.

We scheduled annual dinners for Esterhazy Patrons, and invited them to hear special exclusive announcements—such as when we first confirmed the Orange County debut of the Vienna Philharmonic. To celebrate the contract (in 1995), we called our Esterhazy Patron families to gather at the office; then-president (now called chairman) of the board, Fritz Westerhout, brought in a couple of bottles of Veuve Clicquot champagne to share. Our dreams were beginning to come true.

Our first group pilgrimage to the Esterházy Palace in Eisenstadt, Austria, happened in the summer of 1996, as a part of the Society's first summer festival group trip. These annual excursions have continued ever since. We had eighteen people with us, including many of our new and future Esterhazy Patrons. Following a week at the Salzburg Festival, we departed for Vienna; we left right after taking in a morning performance of the Bruckner Eighth Symphony performed by the Vienna Philharmonic, conducted by Zubin Mehta. Afterwards, we boarded our bus, leaving Salzburg for Vienna. The first stop on the itinerary was the magnificent basilica in St. Florian, where we were given a private organ recital on the same organ that Bruckner had played for ten years.

I had arranged for this organ recital a year earlier, after experiencing the basilica on my own. On my first visit, the church was completely empty, and I was awed by the overwhelming Baroque architecture. I humbly walked down the aisle toward the altar, until something crunched under my shoe; I assumed that I had stepped on a large beetle, though it would be completely incongruous in regards to my surroundings. I looked down and realized I had stepped on a dried rose on the floor. I was greatly moved to discover it had been placed on the tomb of Anton Bruckner himself. I backed away quickly, after realizing that I was standing directly on his grave. I located some church officials and began the conversation about bringing a group here for a recital a year later, when the restoration of the organ would be complete.

While enjoying the recital with the rest of the group, I came to realize that most of Bruckner's symphonies could be thought of as gigantic orchestrated organ pieces. It was a thrill to hear Bruckner's world of sound. That day ranks as one of my greatest musical memories, having the combination of his Eighth Symphony in the morning with the Vienna Philharmonic and then hearing his organ later that day. A few years before, I had played horn in Bruckner's Eighth Symphony with the Dallas Symphony, conducted by Günther Herbig. During rehearsal, he stopped the orchestra to tell the brass section that we were making our entrances "far too precisely," that they needed to be more like the sound of Bruckner's organ in the St. Florian basilica, more "wet," like you would hear in a reverberant church. I now knew exactly what he was talking about. After the recital, we went to Melk, toured the abbey, had lunch, and continued on to Vienna.

The next day, we traveled an hour south to Eisenstadt and attended a Haydn concert at Schloss Esterházy, in the same venue where much of his music was performed originally. It is called Haydnsaal, which was also the Esterházy dining hall. In Haydn's time, large flat wooden beams had been placed on the floor, so as to deaden the echo produced by live performances. The same beams were still being used. It was dreadfully hot, but the room is spectacular—historically, musically, and emotionally worth a visit.

The Esterházy family, as we know it, commenced in the Middle Ages, taking its name from the original village in northern Hungary, which no longer exists. In the seventeenth century, the family amassed its fortune from land ownership, much of it acquired from Protestants during the Counter-Reformation. The family was the largest landowner in the Hapsburg Empire. But while supporting both the Empire and the Roman Catholic Church, the family greatly valued its independence.

The two Esterházy estates that can be visited today are the Schloss Esterházy in Eisenstadt, Austria, and Esterháza in Fertöd, Hungary. The latter, built close to Lake Neusiedler, was where Haydn composed many symphonies and operas, as it was the home of Nikolaus Esterházy, his principal employer. The court theatre and puppet theatre at Esterháza gave almost 100 performances a year. Sadly, it was destroyed by fire in 1779.

Haydn's operas are not commonly performed for us today. His most popular is *Armida*, which was originally performed at the Esterháza Court Theatre. I have had the opportunity to play horn in the orchestra and to produce his *L'infedeltà delusa* ("Deceit Outwitted"). It is extremely funny, with enchanting music, and must be given attention.

The Schloss Esterházy estate in Eisenstadt is where Haydn wrote his first symphonies; these pieces began the long development of this musical form through his 104th symphony, known as the *London*, written after he had completed his long career in Eisenstadt and had sailed to England to thrill new audiences. By this time, he was considered Europe's greatest composer. He had taught Mozart, Beethoven and the concertmaster of the Esterházy Orchestra, Johann Nepomuk Hummel—the musical connections go on and on. Adam Liszt, father of the composer Franz, was a cellist in Haydn's orchestra in Eisenstadt and later a clerk for the Esterházy family.

With the death of Haydn in 1809, Hummel became the new *Kapellmeister* for the estate. He was dismissed two years later by the Prince for neglecting his duties. Though he started as a rival of Beethoven, the two became good friends; he also had a close relationship with Goethe. He brought the young composer Ferdinand Hiller when visiting Beethoven's deathbed; both Hiller and Haydn each clipped a lock of Beethoven's hair. I discuss this more thoroughly in my variation "Little Faith."

The 200th anniversary of Haydn's death was in 2009. The Philharmonic Society chose that occasion to commemorate his legacy with two concerts featuring his music as well as that of three other composers whose music was influenced by the Esterházy *Kapellmeister*—Mozart, Beethoven and Schubert. We presented the Salzburg Mozarteum Orchestra, conducted by its chief conductor, Ivor Bolton. These musicians had previously helped us open the new Renée and Henry Segerstrom Concert Hall in 2006 with an exciting all-Mozart program to celebrate the composer's 250th birthday.

The benefits of Haydn's long association with the Esterházys allowed him to develop the quintessential classical forms of the piano sonata, piano trio, string quartet, symphony and the mass to near perfection. Without Haydn's creative and technical foundation, the output of Mozart, Beethoven, Schubert and many composers would have been significantly different, even lessened. With this in mind, the purpose of our concerts was to once again demonstrate the debt owed to Haydn by the music world. Furthermore, we hoped to show our gratitude to the Esterházy family, as they made it possible for classical music to develop to the extent that it did. Classical music is vitally important to our culture, and so we hoped to recognize the individuals who deserve full consideration.

The first of the two Haydn concerts featured his Cello Concerto in C major, with soloist Johannes Moser, the Schubert Great C major Symphony, and a brand new work by Kurt Schwertsik, yet another Austrian composer. The new piece, "Mr. K Comes to America," was a part of a commissioning project of the Salzburg Mozarteum Orchestra called Two Orchestras, connecting youth and professional orchestras in performance. It was a thrill to see our own Orange County Youth Symphony Orchestra join forces with the Mozarteum Orchestra to conclude the first concert.

The second concert featured Haydn's Symphony No. 96, Mozart's *Ave verum corpus,* and Beethoven's Ninth Symphony. Soloists Katherine Broderick, Katharine Goeldner, Bryan Griffin, and Ben Weger joined the orchestra, along with the Pacific Chorale.

These concerts were supported by our esteemed Esterhazy Patrons: Donna L. Kendall and Elizabeth and Henry Segerstrom. The programs were great demonstrations of the power of art patronage; we enjoyed the parallel of Esterházy-produced music being presented for our new category of Esterhazy donors. Overall, it proved the importance of collaboration—on an international as well as historical scale. Hearing the result of generosity was a very moving experience.

The Philharmonic Society-sponsored summer festival trips have brought forth a number of patrons that have gone on to become board members; to this day, they make up 28 of the current 54 Philharmonic Society Esterhazy families. This particular giving program has become the Society's most successful. It has been a joy to work with Mitzi Tonai, looking to bring new members to the program. She was so beloved that, last year, an anonymous donor made an Esterhazy gift in her honor, just to make her a member. Now that she is official, she and her husband Yutaka are again planning to travel with us to the Salzburg Festival, in the summer of 2013. As a staff member, she made that first trip in 1996. She was there in St. Florian and for the incredible concert at Schloss Esterházy.

As stressful as it is to try to raise money in the performing arts, it can be a sincerely rewarding experience. Fundamentally, funding keeps the arts going, and allows for the artists to concentrate on performance and creativity. Money keeps things going. I find it an honor to be a sort of catalyst, connecting the support from an individual patron to the music that they love. For me, it is humbling. One of our early Esterhazy Patrons was Winnie Smith. I remember taking her to lunch at the Center Club and asking her to make the commitment as an Esterhazy Patron. She responded that "of course" she would, and was thrilled that I asked her because she had already heard about it. She said she would need a few days to put things in order so that she could obtain the full amount to send to the Society. My gosh, I was thrilled and very moved when, the very next day, I received a thank you note in the mail expressing her deep appreciation for being included. That was a first. But, I have learned, this is how generosity works. Both the benefactor and the beneficiary are excitedly involved and working towards a beautiful goal.

Illustrations

Figure 1. *Ludwig van Beethoven*
(Beethoven © Georgios Kollidas - Fotolia.com)

Figure 2. *Dean Corey and Marino Formenti*
(Photo by Amy Carson Dwyer)

Figure 3. *Detail of the tympanum of the Last Judgement,
Conques, France* (© Fulcanelli - Fotolia.com)

Figure 4. *Dr. William Meredith, Director, Ira F. Brilliant Center for Beethoven Studies, San Jose State University* (Photo by Everett Taasevigen)

Figure 5. *Lock of Beethoven's hair* (Photo by Dr. William Meredith, Director, Beethoven Center, San Jose State University)

Figure 6. *Charles Rosen, John Gingrich (not Brahms) and Dean Corey at the Bar Boulud, New York City* (Photo by Kaly Corey)

Figure 7. *Sound artist, musician, composer, and inventor Trimpin in front of his Sheng High installation* (Photo by Matthew G. Monroe)

Figure 8. *Charles and Jean Schulz in the late 1980s*
(Photo by Giovanni Trimboli courtesy of the Charles M. Schulz
Museum and Research Center)

Figure 9. *Schroeder prepares for the Hammerklavier Sonata* (Detail from
Peanuts, January 15, 1958; PEANUTS ©1953 Peanuts Worldwide, LLC.
Used by permission of Universal Uclick. All rights reserved.)

Figure 10. *Dean Corey and his mother Becky* (Photo by Kaly Corey)

Figure 11. *Sir John Eliot Gardiner and Dean Corey at the Mandarin Oriental Hotel London* (Photo by Kaly Corey)

Figure 12. *Napoleon's Elephant of the Bastille*
(Elephant of the Bastille in Greenwich © KarenDMartin - Fotolia.com)

Figure 13. *Beethoven and Goethe and the Teplitz incident*
(Depicted by Carl Rohling, Beethoven and Goethe meeting the imperial
family, July 1812; The copyright in this work has expired.
This work was published before January 1, 1923 and is in the public
domain in the United States and other countries.)

Figure 14. *Johann Nepomuk Hummel*
(© Georgios Kollidas - Fotolia.com)

Figure 15. *A portion of Beethoven's manuscript draft of the 2nd
movement of String Quartet No. 13, Op. 130*
(Gertrude Clarke Whittall Foundation Collection, Music Division,
Library of Congress, Washington D.C.)

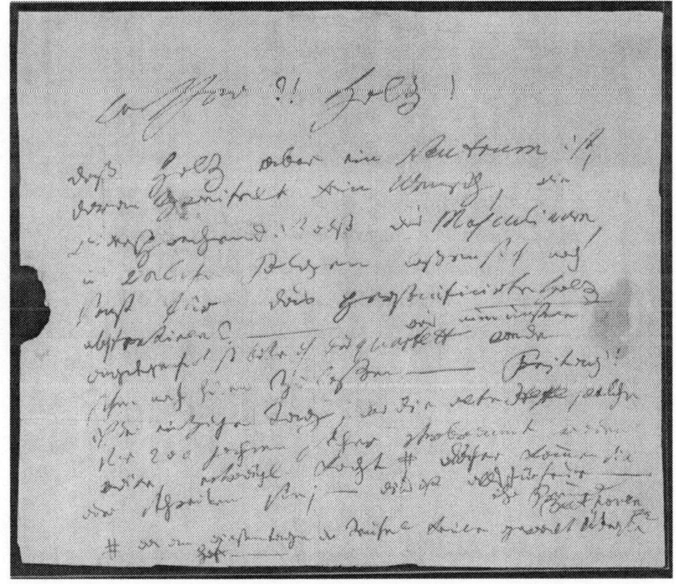

Figure 16. *Beethoven's letter to Karl Holz which accompanied
the 2nd movement of String Quartet No. 13, Op. 130*
(Gertrude Clarke Whittall Foundation Collection, Music Division,
Library of Congress, Washington D.C.)

Figure 17. *Kaly avec ses tournesols*
à « Les Rêves à La Coste » Guizerix, France
(Photo by Fiorenza de la Fuente)

The Music with Big Shoulders

Variation 20

NIMROD

*A President's letter for the February 2013 Segerstrom Center for
the Arts program book for the BBC Concert Orchestra and Itzhak
Perlman performances.*

Dear Friends,

Welcome, and thank you for coming. We are thrilled to present
world-renowned violinist Itzhak Perlman and pianist Rohan De Silva
on our stage as part of the Donna L. Kendall Classical Series. I would
like to acknowledge all of the Rotary International members and families
attending tonight. Twenty-five years ago, Rotary International under-
took the daunting challenge of helping rid the world of polio. Rotary's
End Polio Now campaign has attracted support from famous polio survivors, including Itzhak Perlman. Local Rotarians sold a number of seats
for us to contribute to the cause. I invite you to refer to page 18 of this
program for more information.

It is also a privilege to welcome Keith Lockhart and the BBC Con-
cert Orchestra. They offer us an all-English program recognizing the
Benjamin Britten centenary and two monumental works of Sir Edward
Elgar—the Cello Concerto and the *Enigma Variations.*

The *Enigma Variations* was Elgar's first large orchestra piece—a mighty undertaking. The creative motivation behind the variations on the theme was his friends and their unique characteristics, describing each of them in music. Like many brilliant artists, Elgar fought depression and had trouble staying focused, and work was brought to a grinding halt while writing the variations. At that point, it seemed as though further progress would be impossible, adding this massive unfinished work to the junk pile of disappointing earlier efforts. August Jaeger, Elgar's editor and closest musical friend, suggested they listen to the second movement of Beethoven's *Pathétique* piano sonata for inspiration. Losing patience with his friend, Jaeger said that Beethoven was lonely, ill, and deaf, yet managed to write the greatest music. Jaeger reprimanded the very talented Elgar with near cinematic drama, as did Cher in *Moonstruck* when she slapped Nicholas Cage, yelling, "Snap out of it!" Elgar did, indeed, wake up.

He went on to compose the most beloved variation, titled "Nimrod," after the legendary hunter-king from the Old Testament. This was a play on words on the name Jaeger, the German word for 'hunter.' "Nimrod," then, was dedicated to August Jaeger as a deep expression of thanks. While not exactly like the *Pathétique*, the music captures a similarly deep feeling. It is the product of the type of inspiration that Beethoven's music can engender—the contagious kind that keeps on giving. This is the reason that the *Enigma Variations* are still so popular, much like Rachmaninoff's *Rhapsody on a Theme of Paganini*, where the audience waits with exquisite anticipation for the 18th variation.

I have known "Nimrod" a very long time. My most poignant experience with the music was in Amsterdam in May of 2004. My wife Kaly and I were there for meetings and concerts at the Royal Concertgebouw. We arrived in late April on the Queen's Birthday, a celebration that turns the entire city into one giant party. A few days later, we found a note under our hotel room door that said, "Tomorrow is Remembrance Day, and [that] at 8:00 p.m. the entire country [would] observe two minutes of silence, remembering those citizens who [had] perished in wars since the beginning of World War II." I realized the next day was not going to be like our typical Memorial Day in the U.S., where we are more concerned with discount specials and hot dogs in the backyard. Taking this into consideration, we went to the Dam Square the following day to watch the ceremony in a downpour—along with 5,000 other umbrella-covered spectators. We understood that Queen Beatrix, her family, and dignitaries were attending a service in the Nieuwe Kerk on the Dam Platz. At its conclusion, a procession from the church came into the square, followed by the Queen, who was carrying a large wreath across the square, which she placed on a memorial monument.

This was the moment for "Nimrod," played beautifully by a brass band. It was a very emotional moment. My wife and I both had fathers serve in World War II, and we had lost them both, just recently. There were very few dry eyes in this crowd. It was a moment of great emotion—pride, grief, gratitude, and veneration. Then the clock high on the Royal Palace began to strike the 8 o'clock hour. Afterwards, everyone held complete silence, including the brass band; the only sounds were the ropes flapping on the poles that held the half-mast flags. The sound of "Nimrod" was still playing in my heart. That moment comes back to me every time I hear the piece, as it will again tonight when we enjoy it all together. It is in situations like these that music proves itself as the highest expression, as mere words so often fail to convey life's harmony. Thank you, Herr Beethoven, Herr Jaeger, and to all of you for being here.

Please...enjoy!

Dean Corey
President and Artistic Director
Philharmonic Society of Orange County

Variation 21

Berlioz

*A pre-concert lecture that took place on November 14, 2012,
prior to a performance of Beethoven's Seventh Symphony and
Berlioz's Symphonie Fantastique by the Philharmonia Orchestra
of London, conducted by Esa-Pekka Salonen at the Renée and
Henry Segerstrom Concert Hall, Segerstrom Center for the Arts.*

I'D LIKE TO welcome you all to tonight's performance by the Philharmonia Orchestra, conducted by Esa-Pekka Salonen. It is great to have all of these talented and noteworthy performers play for us, once again. This is a brilliant program—Beethoven's Seventh Symphony and Berlioz's *Symphonie Fantastique.* Why, you may ask, is this program a part of the *Beethoven: The Late Great* project? The Seventh Symphony is not considered a late work. In the interests of our *Late Great* project, the Seventh Symphony is on the same program as the *Symphonie Fantastique* as we regard the connection between the two composers. Being one of the most influential musicians of all time, we most certainly see Beethoven's style and genius reflected in the work of other artists, including Hector Berlioz. This program, so wonderfully conceived by Maestro Salonen, contains the latest symphony of Beethoven (its first performance in

Paris) that Berlioz heard just before he wrote his own first symphony, *Symphonie Fantastique*, a mere two years later.

The Seventh has been my favorite Beethoven symphony—although I must admit that often my favorite Beethoven symphony happens to be whichever one I am listening to at the present moment. I am drawn to the Seventh for several reasons. The first relates to this golden state of California, specifically during my first visit here with my family, when I was eleven years old. It was the great July trip to the West, funded in part by some money left to my dad from a recently deceased aunt in Ohio. This travel marathon lasted about five weeks, moving from one molten locale to another in a non-air-conditioned Chevy that had a propensity for boiling over—miserable. We stayed with old friends along the way. After visiting hot New Mexico and very hot Arizona, Southern California seemed a paradise, despite the very smoggy Los Angeles. Again, we stayed with sets of friends.

The first stopover was in Van Nuys with Joe Fishman and his family. Joe was the second oboe and personnel manager of the Los Angeles Philharmonic, and my dad's army buddy and best man. One morning, I got to tag along to the Hollywood Bowl for a rehearsal. I sat by myself in the middle of the empty Bowl seating, in absolute awe of the immense size. William Steinberg was rehearsing the orchestra in the Respighi transcription of Bach's Toccata and Fugue in D minor, followed by Beethoven's Eighth Symphony. Wow, nice horn duet in the third movement! This was an impressionable experience for me, as I was in the middle of trying to decide which band instrument I wanted to play when starting the next school year—seventh grade. When your dad is a band director and you are eleven, the subject comes up often. I tried to play Joe Fishman's oboe and decided it was going to involve a tremendous amount of effort to get a decent sound out of it. The French horn could be a possibility; besides, it looked cool.

A couple of days later, I found myself in a car with Dad and his friend Mel Best at 4am to go fishing. We spent the entire day working for one lousy mackerel. On the way, Mel, in an effort to be hospitable, tuned the car radio to an all-night local classical station, which happened to be broadcasting the Beethoven Seventh.

I had heard the Seventh many times, since I had been immersing myself in his symphonies since first hearing the Ninth, but it had never been like this. The horns were blaring away, and the overall energy of the piece was intoxicating. I told Mel to turn the volume all the way up. When we arrived at the jetty, still pitch dark, I remained in the backseat of the car until the symphony was finished—a strange scene, for sure, to the puzzled fishermen around us, who were unloading tackle from their cars. In my mind, the matter was settled. I would learn to play the French horn.

A couple of years later, I had a full orchestral score to all nine of the Beethoven symphonies printed in one volume, with four score pages to each page of the collection. Some of you out there know exactly the edition I am talking about. It was cheap—a very thick book with very small print, and it was a tiresome chore to keep it from falling off a flimsy wire music stand. I played the horn part along with my recordings, learning my way in the world of transposing (a skill that would be very useful later), and adjusting as best as I could with the fluctuating pitch of vinyl records. The Seventh Symphony was in the brilliant key of A major, and I had to think and play three notes higher than the printed music. This was not easy at first, but I put in my practice. When I finally got a chance to play the piece for real with an orchestra, I was more than ready. As intoxicating as the symphony is to listen to, playing it was a major rush.

This symphony is also a bargain, a big bang for the buck, the cheapest way for any orchestra you present to "wow" an audience—as long as your orchestra is decent. Why? It's the instrumentation. You can play the piece with a chamber orchestra—strings, winds, in pairs, and timpani. There are no piccolos, E-flat clarinets, English horns, cornets, trombones, tubas, harps, bass drums and chimes—in other words, it lacks all of the extra instruments that Berlioz used in the *Symphonie Fantastique*. This points us to the major connection between Beethoven and Berlioz—one thrilling innovation meeting another thrilling innovation on steroids. Despite the big difference in the size of the orchestras for our two pieces tonight, the excitement level is extreme for both works.

The Seventh Symphony was first sketched in 1811, and was premiered in Vienna in 1814, when Beethoven was 44. Scholars refer to this creative time as his "Heroic Period." It was a most productive time (starting after the writing of the *Heiligenstadt Testament* that I refer to in my welcome letter in tonight's program book). This was in the time of Napoleon. Beethoven was originally supportive of Bonaparte, although this changed when he proclaimed himself Emperor of France. Beethoven's *Eroica* Symphony No. 3 was originally dedicated to him. But soon after, in a fit of anger, the composer scratched the dedication off the title page of the score.

Napoleon was on his way out by the time Beethoven was creating his Seventh Symphony. The allied forces defeated him at the battle of Leipzig and moved on to France. With the fall of Paris, Napoleon was forced to abdicate and was exiled to Elba, an island off of the Tuscan coast. He ran the place for the three hundred days he was there and was given a force of 600 men—a colossal mistake. He returned to France with his men and thus began his famous 100 Days. During this time, the Congress of Vienna had already convened, attempting to sort out Europe after the first fall of Bonaparte. He was finally defeated, most famously, in Belgium at the Battle of Waterloo. Just prior to the Seventh Symphony, Beethoven wrote his very successful and rather dreadful *Wellington's Victory* to capitalize on the occasion. The Bourbon King Louis XVIII was returned to the throne in Paris, and Napoleon was exiled again—this time, to the far away island of Saint Helena in the South Atlantic, where he died in 1821.

Meanwhile, Hector Berlioz was growing up. Having come to Paris seven years before from his native La Côte-Saint-André in the Isère, he was in great conflict with his parents over his pursuit of the Parisian music scene, against their desire that he study medicine. He spent a lot of time at the opera hearing the works of Gluck and Méhul. Berlioz began composing songs in 1822, around the time that Beethoven had begun his late period. The young Berlioz was setting the course for the rest of his life.

In 1812, the year of Napoleon's disastrous Russian campaign, the British poet Lord Byron published his poem *Childe Harold*, a work that would prompt the beginning of the Romantic age and influence a great number of composers—notably Franz Liszt and Hector Berlioz. The poem depicts the pilgrimage of a disenchanted young man in search of something exciting and meaningful among the ashes of war-torn Europe. Byron was able to express his view that "man's greatest tragedy is that he can conceive of a perfection which he cannot attain."

The story is really quite autobiographical, and depicts the adventure of what we know today as the "Byronic Hero." This is the genuine romantic figure that has inspired so many artists, from Berlioz all the way to Hemingway, in my opinion. There is a sense of recklessness in the character—part of his reaction to the horrors of war and its aftermath, which seems to move so many artists. Jean-Paul Sartre and Jack Kérouac also come to mind. Both Beethoven and Berlioz captured the spirit of the "Byronic Hero."

Conductor François Habeneck founded the Orchestre de la Société des concerts du Conservatoire in 1828. He introduced Beethoven's symphonies in Paris during a series of performances. It was in these programs that Hector Berlioz first heard the Beethoven Symphonies played live, One through Seven. He had this to say about the experience:

> In an artist's life one thunderclap sometimes follows swiftly
> on another, as in those outsize storms in which the clouds,
> charge to bursting with electric energy, seem to hurl the
> lightning back and forth and blow the whirlwind.
> I had just had the successive revelations of Shakespeare
> and Weber. Now at another point on the horizon I saw the
> giant form of Beethoven rear up. The shock was almost as great
> as that of Shakespeare had been. Beethoven opened before
> me a new world of music, as Shakespeare had revealed a new
> universe of poetry.

Berlioz was a prolific writer as well as a composer. He wrote a very influential book on orchestration, an interesting memoir, and a book called *À Travers Chants*. The title of this collection of essays is a play on words, described by wonderful Jacques Barzun who recently passed away in San Antonio at the age of 104. Barzun wrote:

> The idiom '*à travers champs*' means walking across the fields, but it suggests also a sense of freedom and a pastoral atmosphere, it is instinct with the nature poetry that is a leading feature of Berlioz's work. By substituting *chants* (songs, music at large), which is pronounced exactly like *champs* [(fields)], Berlioz achieved a happy ambiguity, at once playful and apt, that suited both his critical purpose and his artistic sensibility. The turn of phrase—like music itself—is untranslatable.

Dr. Barzun will be missed. His knowledge of the music of Hector Berlioz is very helpful to understanding this music—especially to modern ears. His reference to the pastoral atmosphere is an important feature to remember when listening to the third movement of the *Symphonie Fantastique*. Beethoven's symphony prior to the Seventh is, of course, the *Pastoral* Symphony. Richard Wagner aptly described the Seventh Symphony as "the apotheosis of dance." It is celebratory. It embodies the vibrant feel of dancing in the country, across the nations of Europe. It is undeniably joyous. He tells us that Europe is on the verge of peace again with the subduing of Napoleon. It is a happy time, albeit brief.

Berlioz again writes about Beethoven giving a description in his *À Travers Chants* of the Seventh Symphony:

> The first movement opens with a broad, majestic introduction, in which the melody, the modulations, and the instrumental design successively vie with one another for attention. It begins with one of those orchestral effects of which Beethoven is unquestionably the inventor. The entire orchestra

strikes a strong staccato chord; in the silence that follows, an oboe is exposed—its entrance was drowned out earlier by the orchestral attack—and it now develops the melody in sustained notes. A more original opening could not be devised…[The] Allegro, whose substantial developments are all based on the same idea, is handled with incredible skill; the changes of tonality are so frequent and so ingenious, and the chords form such new clusters of tonality and progressions, that the movement is over before the fascination and enthusiasm aroused in the listener have lost any of their intensity.

Of the second movement themes, he writes:

These are tears, sobs, entreaties; they express a boundless sorrow, an all-consuming anguish. But after these heartrending strains a glimmer of hope appears: a nebulous melody, pure, simple and sweet, sad, resigned *like patience smiling at grief* [a play on words from Twelfth Night]. The flutes and oboes take up the theme again but in a faint voice, they are too weak to complete it. It is the violins that do so with a few barely audible pizzicato notes, after which the winds, reviving, suddenly like the flame of a dying lamp, breathe a deep sigh over an indecisive harmony and—the rest is silence [more Shakespeare, the last words of Hamlet.]

The theme of the Scherzo [*Presto*] modulates in a new way…[Note] a new kind of crescendo, contrived by means of the second horn in its low register, whispering the two notes A and G-sharp in duple rhythm (though the measure is in triple time) and stressing the G-sharp (though A is the key note). Audiences always seem astounded by this passage.

The finale is at least as rich as the earlier movements in new combinations, piquant modulations, and enchanting flights of fancy…One of his happiest strokes of harmonic boldness is, without doubt, to embellish the great pedal-point on the dominant E by a D-sharp of equal length…One might think this would result in a dreadful dissonance, or at least a harmonic muddle. But nothing of the kind happens, for such is the tonal strength of the dominant that the D-sharp does not adulterate it in any way; one hears only the insistent humming of the E…The coda, ushered in by this menacing pedal-point, is extraordinarily brilliant, a worthy end to this masterpiece of technical skill, taste, imagination, knowledge, and inspiration.

As you can see, Berlioz was a great master with words, as well as notes.

Paris in 1830 was a captivating buzz of crisis and creativity. Charles X abdicated the throne to be replaced by the Duc d'Orleans, who later becomes French King Louis-Philippe. Writers and artists began flocking to the City of Light, making it a capital of philosophy and creativity—a trend that continued well into the twentieth century. Every one of the great composers of this period spent time in Paris. Chopin showed up the next year. Delacroix painted his "Liberty Leading the People," while Berlioz met Liszt and Mendelssohn, who liked Berlioz, the man, but hated his music. Berlioz won the Prix de Rome and composed his *Symphonie Fantastique*.

The actress Harriet Smithson came to Paris in 1828, appearing in Shakespeare plays at the Odeon Theatre. Berlioz saw her there, fell desperately in love, and wrote his *Symphonie Fantastique* about his feelings—having never even met her before. Berlioz, a regular opium user, wrote a symphony that basically described his passion for Harriet under the influence of the drug. It is quite a trip, as you will hear.

Berlioz himself describes the frame for this remarkable music piece. This description is from his own program notes that he included with his five-movement *Symphonie Fantastique*.

A young musician of unhealthy sensitive nature and endowed with vivid imagination has poisoned himself with opium in a paroxysm of lovesick despair. The narcotic dose he had taken was too weak to cause death but it has thrown him into a long sleep accompanied by the most extraordinary visions. In this condition his sensations, his feeling and memories find utterance in his sick brain in the form of musical imagery. Even the beloved one takes the form of melody in his mind, like a fixed idea, which is ever returning, and which he hears everywhere.

1ST MOVEMENT. Visions and Passions.

At first he considers the uneasy and nervous condition of this mind, with the somber longing of depression and joyous elation without any recognizable cause, which he experienced before the beloved one had appeared to him. Then he remembers the ardent love with which she suddenly inspired him; he thinks of his almost insane anxiety of mind, and his raging jealously, of his re-awakening love, of his religious consolation.

2ND MOVEMENT. A Ball.

In a ballroom, amidst the confusion of a brilliant festival, he finds the loved one again.

3RD MOVEMENT. In the Country.

It is a summer evening. He is in the country musing when he hears two shepherd-lads who play the *Ranz des Vaches* (the tune used by the Swiss to call their flocks together) in alternation. This shepherd-duet, the locality, the soft whisperings of the trees stirred by the zephyr-wind and some prospects of hope recently made known to him, all four sensations unite to impart a long unknown repose to his heart and to lend a smiling color to his imagination. And then she appears once more. His heart stops beating, painful forebodings fill his soul. "Should she prove false to him!" One of the shepherds resumes the melody, but the other answers him no more…Sunset…distant rolling of thunder… loneliness…silence.

4ᵀᴴ MOVEMENT. The Procession to the Stake.

He dreams that he had murdered his beloved, is condemned to death, and that he is being led to the stake. A march that is alternately somber and wild, brilliant and solemn, accompanies the procession. The tumultuous outbursts are followed without modulation, by measured steps. At last the fixed idea returns for a moment—a last thought of love is revived—which is cut short by the deathblow.

5ᵀᴴ MOVEMENT. The Witches' Sabbath

Now, he dreams that he is present at a witches' dance, surrounded by the horrible spirits, amidst sorcerers and monsters in many fearful forms—all of whom have come to attend his funeral. He is surrounded by strange sounds, groans, shrill laughter, and distant yells. The beloved melody is heard again, but it has lost its noble and shy character. Now, the theme has become a vulgar kind of grotesque dance. "*She*" comes to attend the witches' meeting, and her arrival is greeted by friendly howls and shouts. She joins the infernal orgy while bells toll for the dead; this is a burlesque parody of the *Dies Irae*. The witches' round-dance and the *Dies Irae* are heard at the same time.

Dies Irae is the medieval hymn from the requiem mass meaning "day of wrath." Berlioz uses the fixed idea, or *idée fixe*, as a reference that provides a unifying method throughout a piece of music—a reoccurring melody, in this case, being his Harriet.

Harriet Smithson discovered that the piece was about her after she heard it in performance. What happens next? The boy does get the girl, and they married in 1832. Berlioz goes on to write a sequel to this piece, called *Lelio*. He also composes a major work for viola and orchestra called *Harold in Italy*, and it is based on Byron's *Childe Harold*, as mentioned earlier. He wrote it for Paganini, who later declined to play it because he felt the viola part had too many measures rest. But after hearing the piece and being much impressed, he was moved to give Berlioz 20,000 francs in appreciation.

Many conductors begin and end their exploration of Berlioz's music with the *Symphonie Fantastique*. It would stand to reason that audiences do the same. This is not the case with Esa-Pekka Salonen or audiences in Los Angeles; in 2003, LA Opera dove deep into music history and produced a rare production of *The Damnation of Faust.* In the organization's continuing celebration of Berlioz's 200th birthday, Salonen led the Los Angeles Philharmonic in a special performance called "Berlioz the Revolutionary: January 2004" in the inaugural season of Walt Disney Concert Hall. Here is the LA Phil's brochure copy:

> To celebrate the 200th birthday of Berlioz, the LA Philharmonic examines the life and work of an artist who personified revolutionary thinking and imagination, which we embrace in this inaugural season of Walt Disney Concert Hall. Berlioz was not only a musical revolutionary but also worked during a time of great political and cultural revolution, and in this context, he redefined the symphony orchestra through his orchestration, his sense of form and his storytelling. This project will be capped by a unique and innovative collaboration with the Theatre de Complicite, which will create an evening of music and theater that captures the life and thoughts of this fascinating musical personality.

It is positively shocking that this piece was written only six years after the Beethoven Ninth. Almost all of the great composers preceding Berlioz were pianists, and some of them legendary. They thought through the piano when writing for the orchestra. But not Berlioz; he dabbled on the flute and played guitar. To him, the orchestral score was a blank canvas, and he applied creative paint directly. This accounts for the long flowing lines, the sudden surprises, unique harmonic shifts, and some really over-the-top instrumental writing.

Berlioz's first composition teacher was Jean-François Le Sueur. Both gentlemen experienced Beethoven symphonies at the Conservatoire. Both were initially impressed. But Berlioz retained his enthusiasm, while Le Sueur later turned away from it. David Cairns, Berlioz's biographer, describes it clearly.

Berlioz dropped the subject, but privately recognized that the time had come to emancipate himself. From now on he would write another kind of music. Le Sueur, he told his mother, belonged musically to the age of Louis XIV. When, two years later, he composed the Fantastic Symphony—the first fruit of the revelation of Beethoven—he did not show his teacher the score.

In a sense, Beethoven threw a "Hail Mary" pass with no intended receiver. In a truly remarkable effort of ingenuity and risk, Hector Berlioz caught the touchdown pass and helped move traditional music in to a new and beautiful age. Working with the inspiration from Beethoven just before him, Berlioz led to the foundation of our modern orchestra and its repertoire.

Thank you, and please…enjoy.

Variation 22

I Am That Which Is

A pre-concert lecture that took place on November 19, 2013, prior to a performance of Beethoven's Missa Solemnis by Sir John Eliot Gardiner and the Orchestre Révolutionnaire et Romantique and Monteverdi Choir.

THE *MISSA SOLEMNIS* may be Beethoven's greatest work. It was controversial when it was written, as it still is today. The piece is a great example of Beethoven's tendency to take the occasional musical risk and produce something way over the top. He arrives at what is impossible, or the seeming edge of impossibility, and pushes us far beyond. The *Missa Solemnis* is a prime example of this dynamic. The same technique is also used with the *Hammerklavier* Sonata, completed in 1818. In the *Missa*, he places great demands on the singers, orchestra, and listeners, wanting everyone included in the presentation. This, of course, makes the piece just as difficult to perform as it is to watch and listen to. Sopranos are especially divided on this piece—they either love it or hate it. The work requires them to sing a number of B-flats, difficult notes that are, at times, sustained without much rest. Furthermore, the soprano solo includes a high C, creating many awkward leaps for the voice. The first trombone has a high D, a semitone higher than the infamous D-flat of which trombonists are so in fear and often miss in Ravel's *Bolero*. There are passages of great complexity and speed—fugue after fugue—tongue-splitting phrases where there is one rapid note per syllable for extended periods at a bright tempo. The work is very big in strength, with large orchestra features for trombones, chorus, and four soloists. Comprehensively, it is a test of both skill and endurance—a very long piece.

The inspiration for the *Missa Solemnis* came in 1819, for the official presentation for the position of Archbishop of Olmütz (in what is now Olomouc, Czech Republic) of Archduke Rudolf, a cellist in the Archduke Trio. Rudolf was a great friend of Beethoven's, as well as his student and benefactor. Beethoven had begun the *Diabelli Variations* in the same year, but would not finish that piece until 1823. He was overly excited, envisioning a giant, solemn mass for the installation ceremony, and missed the *Variations* deadline. This great sacred mass was an over-the-top idea from the start; he was still working on the mass in 1823 while simultaneously writing the Ninth Symphony, having completed the piano sonatas Opp. 110 and 111 in the previous two years. Beethoven fully committed himself to the mass project, and we know this as the most magnificent creative period of his life. All of this work happened before producing his last five string quartets and four years before his death in 1827.

Beethoven was in need of money. After arranging for Anton Diabelli's firm to publish the mass, Beethoven sent copies of the score to each of the crowned heads of Europe, asking 50 ducats from each. This included all of the royal figures except for England's King George IV, who had yet to pay him for *Wellington's Victory*, the greatest piece of musical public relations for nationalism ever devised. Beethoven snubbing a crowned monarch would not surprise anyone. Diabelli was enraged when he found out that Beethoven wanted to delay publication until the dust settled after the royal distribution. Beethoven's other cello-playing patron, Prince Galitzin, who had just returned to Russia, was one of the purchasers of a royal score and is the reason that the mass had its first performance in St. Petersburg. The prince was also miffed when he learned the work was going to be published; he could have waited and bought a score for a few *thalers*.

But it wasn't necessarily all about the money. Beethoven turned down a commission from the Austrian Emperor for another mass because he didn't want to be obligated to the crown. This was a constant dilemma in Beethoven's life—asserting his principles. In publication, the *Missa Solemnis* was going to be a hard sell. A mass in Latin that was more suited to a concert hall than a church was a new and bold idea. It simply was not done.

So money would have to be made from the first performances in Vienna, but it was going to be a very expensive project. The nominally priced Theater-an-der-Wien was the first venue under consideration. Its director, Count Pallfy, even offered his orchestra for free. Beethoven insisted that Ignaz Schuppanzigh, the violinist who would premiere the late quartets, be the leader. But the theater orchestra's leader refused this request, a decision that was backed by all of the musicians. Reaching an impasse, the deal for the orchestra and hall was off the table. This was a pity, for now they would be forced to look at more expensive venues with larger orchestras to pay for.

So, the expensive Court Theater was then booked. The orchestra would number seventy, a large ensemble for its day. Beethoven was, of course, concerned with the financial success of this performance, afraid that the project might be a money loser. The rehearsals got underway with Schuppanzigh as leader and Ignaz Umlauf as conductor, who was bombarded in rehearsal (which Beethoven attended) with complaints from singers as to the difficulty of the piece. He responded by telling them to do the best they could and to leave out the tough parts, but do it convincingly, because the composer couldn't hear them anyway.

Another problem was the church, which would not give permission for a Latin mass to be sung outside the sanctuary in public. Permission from both the crown and the church was needed in those days for public performances of music or theater. The church objected to a mass sung in public and demanded that Latin could not be used. As a compromise for the first Vienna performance, only the *Kyrie, Credo* and *Agnus Dei* were performed, making sure to use inoffensive German text under the title of *Three Grand Hymns*. I might also mention that the other piece on the program was Beethoven's new Ninth Symphony, in its very first performance. It was quite an evening, though the good Archbishop Rudolf couldn't break himself away from his duties in Olmütz to attend.

In modern times, performances of the *Missa Solemnis* are infrequent, at best. I have only heard one live performance and it was with the very same forces, with the exception of the soloists, that you are going to hear tonight. In 1996, the Salzburg Festival presented now *Sir* John Eliot Gardiner, the Orchestre Révolutionnaire et Romantique and the Monteverdi Choir in several performances of Beethoven—the original version of *Fidelio* known as "Lenore" and the *Missa Solemnis*. I was fortunate to secure the last available seat for the *Missa* in the very last row with an obstructed view seat in the Grosses Festspielhaus. The ticket price was reasonable for obvious reasons. I was able to occasionally peek around the corner when the person next me would shift to the left. Still, it was a life-changing experience. I knew the *Missa* from recordings and from a televised performance conducted by Georg Solti in a project for the United Nations. In this live performance in Salzburg, I was taken by the clarity and timbre of the period instruments, the enormous power of the relatively small Monteverdi Choir, and the energy of the performance, but mostly the gigantic impact of the work itself. I savored every note from my hideaway point at the top of the concert hall. It was all of the great moments that Beethoven had ever achieved, rolled into one transcendent, heavenly, and enormous piece of music. The time flew by. I wanted it to go on forever, but was broken from my reverie with the tumultuous applause and cheers from the audience. The loud response was unlike anything I had heard at the festival so far. And the ovation seemed endless, with repeated bows from the conductor and soloists. Even after the stage had cleared, the clapping continued wildly. Finally, a chorus member and a bassoonist appeared on stage, the only ones left backstage, shoved onto the platform by the stagehands and warmly greeted by the still enthusiastically clapping crowd. Barely anyone in the audience was willing to leave, cheering for nearly twenty minutes past the orchestra's last notes. My own hands ached from clapping. And the ovations only continued as I made my way out of the hall to recover.

"God, I love what I do," I thought, as I pledged to myself that this experience would happen in Orange County someday.

Beethoven made a framed little sign for his desk that quoted an ancient Egyptian monument to Isis saying, "I am that which is." He probably got this as a third hand translation, nowhere near the original text. No matter—it was a curious little phrase that struck a chord within him, giving us a clue as to what he believed and felt. In the *Credo*, Beethoven is setting the most sacred text of the Catholic liturgy for a dear friend who was obviously very devout. What does this say about Beethoven's own spiritual beliefs? The toughest part of the mass for the non-or near non-believers is the *Credo*, or *I Believe*. It is a pledge to a very specific and demanding religious creed—parts of which Beethoven felt he could obscure with his music. Despite his personal convictions, he could make a meaningful and beautiful work. I have read that Franz Schubert in his masses would simply not set certain phrases of the *Credo* that he did not like. His genius allowed him to do it so smoothly that no one really noticed. Of course, it is a sensitive subject. I am sure we have an audience here tonight that is divided on the subject. For the believers here, you will hear one of the greatest musical monuments to your faith. For the doubters, secularists, and non-believers, I offer you this couplet—not by the Pope of Rome but poet Alexander Pope of London, who wrote:

…some to church repair
Not for the doctrine but the music there

Now, having covered this background information, we can now enjoy the music together in this concert hall, to which we have now repaired.

"I am that which is." This sums up Beethoven. He was not a churchgoer but he believed that there was a God. He believed God was everywhere, especially in nature and above in the starry canopy. Beethoven was probably the most spiritual and philosophical of the Classical composers. The Beethoven scholar Wilfrid Mellers says Beethoven's God was as "Hegel's Geist through which all things are manifest and to which all things return; most remarkably he reminds us of Beethoven himself." He was an individualist, and believed he had the moral responsibility for all his actions. Beethoven was responsible for doing the best work he was capable of, and giving it back to the society in which he lived—and the world in which the rest of us would make an appearance. And now, we are gathered here tonight, together, about to experience his great gift of the *Missa Solemnis*.

Mozart and later Haydn became Masons. The Masonic influence was very evident in Mozart's late works and also in the *Missa*. Beethoven was not one of the Masons but he was curious about them, their influence being very strong in his day. The opening of the *Kyrie* is a great example. It is a simple text, only six words long—two of which are constantly repeated. We hear *Kyrie eleison, Christe eleison, Kyrie eleison* (Lord have mercy, Christ have mercy, Lord have mercy). Rather than write music that uses all six words or the three phrases as a whole expression, he divides them into three distinct sections, each with a chorus entry followed by the soloists' entry. According to Bramwell Tovey, Beethoven uses this alternating chorus and soloists pattern to "bring out an overwhelming and overwhelmed sense of the Divine glory, with which he invariably and immediately contrasts the nothingness of man." Mellers says that the three sections represent the three knocks on the door of the Masonic lodge, historically symbolizing Beauty, Strength and Wisdom. The opening of the *Kyrie* is, to me, straight out of *The Magic Flute* by Mozart, his hugely Masonic-influenced opera. Beethoven marks that the movement should be performed "Mit Andacht" (with devotion).

The *Gloria* is indeed spectacularly glorious. At this point in Beethoven's creative life, he was inserting fugues whenever possible. Harkening back to his long-time study of the 48 Preludes and Fugues of Bach, he uses all of the same devices—techniques such as making the theme twice as fast, twice as slow, and then turning the theme upside down. Where Bach might tastefully use one device in a fugue, Beethoven would often use them all. The *Gloria* contains some truly great ones. In listening to this music, I think Beethoven was far more interested in Bach's fugues than his preludes.

In the *Gloria*, we now hear the mixture of soloists and chorus beautifully woven together. The Masonic flavor is now replaced with shades of *Fidelio*. Listen for the huge chorus entrance, *quoniam tu solus sanctus,* introduced by a soft timpani roll, then followed by the *tutti* orchestra in octaves in the spirit of the Ninth Symphony's first movement. And then follows a truly exciting fugue on *Gloria Dei Patris.* All of this leads to the final *Amen,* one of the most spectacular moments in all of music. Beethoven exploits the word *Amen* in a fantastically over-the-top way, as I mentioned earlier. Two horns bray a hunting call. The text then reverts back to the beginning *Gloria in excelsis Deo,* not usually done. It remains glorious to the end, when we experience the chorus shouting *Gloria* in the last bar, without the orchestra. Only Beethoven could come up with this kind of dramatic ending. It is pure genius.

We have talked about the *Credo.* Pay special attention to the very rapid, complex and florid *et vitam venturi,* and understand why the Monteverdi Choir is considered to be the greatest in the world.

The *Sanctus* is also marked "Mit Andacht (with devotion)," like the *Kyrie.* The three trombones are featured as if they were playing hymns from a church tower—like they might have done two hundred years ago in Germany, before Beethoven's time. Next, it is now the soloists' chance to shine. Listen for the *Osanna,* where the soprano enters against the violins, playing twice as fast, hitting notes that are often just a step off from what she is singing. This is a modern effect not normally heard in Beethoven's day—again, his dynamic touch, over the top. This is termed heterophony, where a melody is sung and/or played simultaneously with another voice or instrument, but not perfectly in time. We enjoy little clashes here, which add depth to the flavor of sound. This is similar to an ancient technique in Asian music that I am not sure Beethoven was aware of. We are all more familiar with monophonic and polyphonic music. Then, after all of the soloists have had a go at the *Osanna,* an orchestral preludium follows that is right out of *Tristan,* a passage of some of Beethoven's most advanced harmonic writing.

This leads to the wonderful *Benedictus.* The solo violin enters on a heavenly G, at first only hovering, and then is lowered gently by a pair of angelic flutes, gently folded into the arms of two grounded clarinets as the bass section of the chorus enters with *Benedictus qui venit in nomine*

Domini (Blessed is he who comes in the name of the Lord). This lovely violin *obbligato* floats above until the end of the movement. Do we hear Beethoven interjecting a violin concerto into a mass? And is this some sort of final statement? He only wrote one violin concerto. The violin here might be Beethoven's own personal voice. Perhaps we can think of the violin *obbligato* as representing the late composer himself, returning to personally guide us through some of his most beautiful music, an extraordinary and brilliant touch, as if he had returned from his spiritual visit to the canopy of stars so distant from the rest of us and returned to report through music what he experienced. At this late point in his life, unique ideas like this never seemed to fail him.

The *Agnus Dei*, the mass' final prayer, is the most beautifully set portion of this text, even considering other composers. One has only to think of the *Agnus Dei* in the Fauré Requiem as a prime example. Where Fauré's is hopeful, Beethoven's is dark. When he sets *miserere nobis* (have mercy on us), he means it. Notice how the mood is also given with use of the bass soloist and men's chorus. There is a stunning interaction between the soloists and the chorus. Listen next to what Beethoven calls a *Prayer for Inward and Outward Peace—Dona nobis pacem*. A new uplifting fugue emerges; the mood has changed and now we look upwards. We have drums and trumpets as we enter a joyous land of serenity. There is an orchestra interlude like the last fugue in the *Diabelli Variations*. More drums and trumpets. Peace has prevailed, it is now at hand; the drums and trumpets of war have faded away.

The *Missa Solemnis'* intelligence will astound your mind, its power will stir your soul, and the fact that Beethoven never heard it will squeeze your heart to pieces.

The *Missa Solemnis* is Beethoven's greatest work. His other greatest work, the Ninth Symphony, will be heard tomorrow night. Thank you for coming and for your constant support. Please…enjoy.

August 2012
Guizerix, France

Variation 23

YE BILLIONS

*A pre-concert lecture that took place on November 20, 2012,
prior to a performance of Beethoven's Ninth Symphony by
Sir John Eliot Gardiner and the Orchestre Révolutionnaire et
Romantique and Monteverdi Choir.*

IN CLASSICAL MUSIC, we spend most of our time celebrating the music of dead white guys. This imbalance is beginning to change, and 100 years from now, the musical landscape will look significantly different in many areas, not to mention with more gender equality.

The culture of classical music, its support and its survival, and the way it preserves dead white guy music, is largely dependent on the females of our species. The Philharmonic Society's Youth Music Education programs are totally reliant on its female managers and volunteers. Our audiences are two-thirds women. My staff is 70% female. Granted, women outlive men in this country. I am greatly shocked, when visiting places such as Gascony, France, to see so many nonagenarian males in the village markets. They are much healthier than our guys in America who, as a rule, don't usually last that long. We have too much stress, too much driving, not enough red wine, and a severe lack of duck fat.

Women's involvement with music has not gone unnoticed by instrument manufacturers or by their advertisers. The piano is the best example. In the nineteenth century, piano manufacturing rose dramatically, thanks to the steam engine that supplied the energy to make all of the repetitive parts of a piano. Steam engines are inefficient if you have to stop and restart them. Keeping them continually running was a boon to cranking out thousands of pianos at cheap prices. Where once only the nobility could afford harpsichords and early pianos, by mid-century, every household of at least modest means could have a piano. The instruments would be the center of hearth and home. Boys could become soldiers, doctors, farmers, businessmen, composers, and such. They were expected to go out and make a name in the world, to be trained and active. Girls, on the other hand, could sew, cook, and stay at home; this encouraged them to become "accomplished," as they used to say, on the piano. Where would the Jane Austen novels be without the household keyboard? Enter the Victorian-era marketers. They realized that selling a piano was not much different than selling a sewing machine—the target markets being pretty much the same. The two industries banded together, markedly in the United States. Women's magazines were brimming with articles on sewing and needlepoint, with selections for recipes and songs for the piano. All of this was, of course, geared toward the target market of mothers, grandmothers, wives, and daughters. What does this have to do with Beethoven?

An 1882 edition of Boston's *Musical Herald* held articles on sewing machines, fancy needle work, and a piano piece called "Jesus, I My Cross Have Taken" next to Cod Liver Oil ads, and, surprisingly, a "Comprehensive Analysis of Beethoven's Ninth Symphony," by Dr. George Grove, underneath a large ad for corsets. What is surprising is not the juxtaposition of corsets and Beethoven as is the fact that someone was already writing a comprehensive study on the symphony which only had its premiere in New York in 1846, 22 years after its first performance in Vienna. Equally impressive is that the extraordinary power of the work had developed such strong traction in such a short time. It was spreading throughout the western world with great speed and intensity without recordings or the internet, but simply with a few live performances and piano arrangements. As we now know, it would never cease to expand its grasp. It reached thousands, then millions, and now billions. Why is this so? What is so special about Beethoven's Ninth Symphony?

The idea of conceiving a symphony with the addition of a chorus took a number of years to percolate. Beethoven had the idea of setting Schiller's "An die Freude" or "To Joy" as early as 1792, an idea he tossed about for the next twenty years. Parts of his opera *Fidelio* and the Choral Fantasy sound very similar to the "Ode to Joy" theme of the Ninth Symphony. They were a part of the creative development.

The running time of this musical adventure is about an hour. Most of us here tonight have experience with various disc products that contain recorded sound—the 78, 45 and 33 1/3 RPM records, and the compact disc. The CD was transformative in its sound quality and especially in the amount of music it could hold. After much industry argument over what the standard time capacity of a CD should be, it was finally decided that the standard would, at least, be able to contain Beethoven's Ninth Symphony in its entirety, unlike any of the earlier recording media. And so it does.

The Ninth Symphony is truly a standard of excellence. It is a valid measure of what is possible for a musical genius to achieve. It is twice as long as any symphony previously written, is more demanding for players and listeners, has the largest instrumentation (up to that point), and ends with the addition of vocal soloists and chorus. Above all, it reaches deeply into various realms of human expression that no symphony had done before. The Ninth has a message. It was a great point of departure for composers who tried to match or outdo it, with little success, and a point of inspiration for true adventurers like Hector Berlioz, who then influenced Liszt, Fauré, Debussy, Ravel, Satie, Stravinsky, and Messiaen—just to mention the Parisian-based composers alone.

One of Beethoven's guiding principles was that "Liberty ennobles the soul and exalts the spirit." Keeping this in mind, we will consider the work and explore its complexities and wonder. Most of you here tonight have heard this symphony before, many of you a number of times. I invite you to erase your mind and experience and approach it tonight with a fresh point of view. Put yourself in the place of an audience member who was present at the symphony's first performance on May 7, 1824, at the Theater am Kärntnertor in Vienna. This is the same concert where, during the first half, three sections of the *Missa Solemnis* had their first Vienna public premiere. You would probably be shocked by the audacity of a composer to write such difficult and complicated music. But with Beethoven, you already know to expect the unexpected. So what are we about to hear in this next piece—with a chorus standing behind the orchestra?

The symphony begins. Two horns softly sustain a fifth on D and A. We have an outline of the D minor chord without the middle F, and hear the interval of the perfect fifth. This is a Pythagorean fifth, something very ancient, as basic as the earth's rotation. Beethoven has plumbed to such a depth of which even he is unaware. But get there he did, and right away. Skipping strings outline the shape of the fifth, much like a flashlight held by a furtive hand, the light bouncing off the walls of this very dark cave. An oboe enters, then a flute. All crescendo into a unison theme, a serious—even angry—statement with pounding timpani, bringing us into the first full harmony of the first movement. Upon resolution, there is a scurry of violins to take us back to where it all started, to those ancient fifths and bouncing lights, until the theme returns. He gives us a gravitas that we find in the first movement of the familiar Fifth Symphony. Maybe Beethoven needed something solid to cling to, as he moves further into this dark new world he has entered, emboldened by a robust spirit.

A second theme, in a major key, tells that there is hope even though the ground still feels unstable. We are moving deeper and deeper. We can tell that the journey will be long and unlike anything we have undertaken before. The fifths return again and shift to a new area, developing the material we have already heard thus far. A fugue emerges. We have witnessed many of these in this late period of Beethoven. The angry statement and pounding timpani are back, and more furious than ever.

What is this place? There are major-minor shifts, which are concerning, but very appealing. We are enjoying this ride, even though we cannot tell where it will take us. But the ending does not matter right now. We are entranced. It might not end well for us but that does not seem to matter now; we are in too deep. Even when we think we have heard all we can hear, the music continues with relentless energy. Then a horn call with the second theme. Is it a signal to follow? Is it showing us the way out? There are chirping flutes and clarinets. Then we hear a dirge that builds to a coda. The first theme returns with a final burst, and the movement ends. Where are we? We are certainly not in Costa Mesa anymore.

Then the *Scherzo*. The word means "joke," but we are not in the mood for one now—and this certainly is not one, to be sure. Beethoven senses this, and continues with a rather mischievous dance; it starts abruptly by the orchestra and timpani in a brilliant declamation. We are still in D minor. This becomes serious, outrageous rollicking fun, sort of like a guilty pleasure. The impish hopping of the strings suggests what Berlioz wrote in the last movement of the *Symphonie Fantastique*, written three years after Beethoven's death. Berlioz didn't actually encounter the Ninth Symphony until after he wrote the *Symphonie Fantastique*. Strange this. Is Berlioz's spirit lurking around in a corner of this cave? In the trio, cute woodwinds are answered by a gorgeous string response, possibly suggesting the "Ode to Joy" theme that we will later encounter. And there is another horn call, more signs of hope, possibly freedom. Briefly, liberty has ennobled our soul and exalted our spirit. This theme is taken up by the orchestra as a whole; the gorgeous response returns, as well as the horn. The closing version of this theme reminds us of the *Pastoral* Symphony. Beethoven again holds onto something helpful and solid. The dance starts again, in a way that is even more fun than the first time. We are learning the steps, but this is still not a joke. Although we are having fun, it is cautious and feels temporary. It's like the thrill of stealing a car, a rush of excitement that knows something is about to happen. What's next?

Now Beethoven brings us into a late afternoon, as the sun is soon to set behind the trees. We are returning to nature again. It's like a hymn from an old wooden church in the wildwood that I used to imagine from time to time, when I was a boy, sitting through boring sermons. Then this wonderful, gently climbing theme begins, and you want it to go on forever. Then back to the hymn, more elaborate this time. We have clearly left the first two movements behind and, while we still don't know where we are, we like it. We like it a lot. The climbing theme is back, now a vine with opening blooms—very beautiful. Now the hymn again. The horn returns, this time the fourth horn, in a very exposed passage. Beethoven possibly wrote this for the newly-invented valved French horn, because of its difficulty. Tonight you will hear it on the valve-less natural horn, where the player is required to shove his hand deeper in the bell to get some of the notes that are easy on a horn with valves. The main theme continues with a flowing violin obbligato. As listeners, we really like this place. Does there have to be a last movement? Rumor has it that there is a chorus. I can see them on the stage, but I am happy where I am, and satisfied to stay right here for the rest of the evening. But, alas, the composer has other things in mind. On to the last movement.

Ludwig, OMG! What kind of chord is that? Are we going back to that dark, scary cave? We found a happy place in the third movement—for which we are grateful. But now we need some sort of explanation. We have come this far with you; you owe us that. The cellos and basses are talking through their notes, trying to tell us something, and it sounds urgent. A touch of the first movement, more talking, the second movement, more talking, the third movement, more talking. Ah, and now a new theme! Is that it? It is very simple and beautiful, we really like it. It sounds like an answer. It repeats, this time with a bassoon *obbligato*. Oh, to be that bassoonist—such a sublime responsibility. Then the heavenly strings take it up, and now the winds are added. I think we will like this better than anything we've heard yet. What does this mean? Ah, that OMG music again. What are you trying to tell us? We need some real words, please, Mr. Composer.

And then they come.

The bass intones:

> *O Freunde, nicht diese Töne!*
> *Sondern Lasst uns angenehmere anstimmen*
> *Und Freudenvollere!*

> O friends, no more these sounds!
> Let us sing more cheerful songs,
> More full of joy!

He summons help and is joined for the start of the moment we have been waiting for:

> *Freude, schöner Götterfunken,*
> *Tochter aus Elysium?*
> *Wie betreten feuertrunken,*
> *Himmlische, dein Heiligtum!*
> *Deine Zauber binden wieder,*
> *Was die Mode streng geteilt;*
> *Alle Menschen werden Brüder,*
> *Wo dein sanfter Flügel weilt.*

> Joy, bright spark of divinity,
> Daughter of Elysium,
> Fire-inspired we tread
> Thy sanctuary.
> The magic power re-unites
> All that custom has divided,
> All men become brothers
> Under the sway of thy gentle wings.

The soprano, mezzo-soprano, and tenor join the bass as the soloists sing, "Join in our song of praise."

The chorus returns, then the soloists again, in male and female pairs, answered by the chorus. We now seem to have a set of variations on this *Hymn to Joy* on our hands. All transition to the loudest F major chord in music—then silence. Is this a new key, the relative major of D minor? If this is what you expect, our late-period Beethoven will not give it to you, of course. Instead, he gives us a little Turkish Band marching toward us in the key of B-flat major, another joyful variation on the joyous theme. What must the first listeners of the Ninth have thought when they heard this, even though Turkish culture and fashion were all the rage at the time? Listen for the piccolo, a new arrival to the symphony orchestra since the Fifth. The tenor sings, "Brother, you should run your race, as a hero going to conquest."

A brisk fugue follows using the angular rhythm of the Turkish march as a subject, as fleet of foot as the second movement *Scherzo*. Now it is a happy joke, and we are in the mood for one now. A joyous return to the first verse then follows with all joining in. The trombones lead the unison chorus as they sing, "You millions, I embrace you…Brothers, above the starry canopy there must dwell a loving Father…above the stars must He dwell."

The Ninth Symphony has one of the most exhilarating endings of any piece of music ever conceived. It is purely breathtaking. At the first performance, Beethoven was on the stage with his score facing the chorus and orchestra. Unable to hear the proceedings, he followed along in the score of the piece that was going on inside his head. Even when the singers and musicians finished, Beethoven was still deep in the music. One of the soloists had to turn him towards the audience so that he could see the tumultuous ovation; the standing audience was thrilled with this new and joyful work.

This symphony is the apex of classical repertoire, and Beethoven knew it would be important. Is it the simplicity of the *Hymn to Joy* tune? Certainly, the text has something to do with it. But it may not be as much as we would like to think. The tune has been used many times with and without the original text. As the Anthem of Europe and because of the many languages involved, only the melody is needed. At First Methodist Church in Arlington, Texas, we sang it as the hymn *Joyful, Joyful, We Adore Thee.* I would smugly mutter to my Sunday school classmates, "This is not really how it is supposed to go," to which they responded by rolling their eyes.

Filmmaker Kerry Candaele is completing a great project that fits perfectly with our *Beethoven: The Late Great* project. This documentary, called *Following the Ninth,* will be premiered in Orange County in April 2014, and we are helping him with the funding to finish it. Your help with this would be greatly appreciated. Here is what Kerry says about this amazing film:

> I have been filming *Following the Ninth: in the Footsteps of Beethoven's Final Symphony* for four years. Filmed on five continents and in 12 countries, *Following The Ninth* tracks the stories of four people whose lives have been transformed, repaired and healed by the Ninth's message: "*Alle Menschen werden Brüder.*" (All Men Will Be Brothers). All people are connected by this hymn to freedom and transcendence. At Tiananmen Square in 1989, students played the Ninth Symphony over loudspeakers as the army came in to crush their protests for freedom. In Chile, women under the Pinochet dictatorship sang the Ninth at torture prisons, and those inside took hope when they heard the music. In England, the cherished singer/songwriter Billy Bragg has rewritten the words of the most powerful piece of art ever created by a man who was completely deaf and could not hear his own music to the "Ode To Joy" for a new era, and has had his version of the Ninth performed before the Queen. Throughout Japan each December, the Ninth is performed like no place else, often with 10,000 people singing in the chorus. It's a symphony of hope, of profound beauty, and one of the most powerful pieces of art ever, created by a man who was completely deaf and could not hear his own music.

Beethoven continues to inspire.

Finally, I think I can demonstrate the power of the Ninth Symphony with a little story.

A very lonely man is adrift in the middle of the Pacific Ocean, there through no one else's fault but his own. His personal life is in complete and seemingly irreparable shambles. His poor preparation for this voyage has resulted in a snapped mast, a broken radio, and an almost exhausted supply of fuel, food, and water. He lays on the deck of his boat in the black of night, in a state of near exhaustion and dissolution of spirit. The man stares blankly into the night sky, but is suddenly aroused by the brilliant streak of a meteor. In that moment, he realizes that he is not alone. There are millions—no, billions—of stars. Each star represents even more distant galaxies, representing billions of more stars. These are all the same apparent size—the size of a light on a distant shore, or perhaps the size of a rescue boat that he has little expectation of ever seeing, or the same size as the dim flashlight of his boat at a distance. And yet, he takes comfort. He realizes that no matter how insignificant he is, he matters as a part of the much greater whole. He is a star on board his own decrepit vessel, on this vast ocean, on this speck of light that is his planet, among all the other planetary specks, orbiting the sun, yet another more brilliant speck. He is a brother of all people, living as specks beneath the same giant sky. How many millions of other people were, in this same moment, staring up at the stars? How many will stare into the heavens in the future, or who are also adrift somewhere in the vast oceans? These stars are overlooking all of them, himself and the people of both the past and the present. He realizes that, no matter what happens to him, he was a part of all of this, no more or less important than anyone or anything else. He is grateful for being a part of it—for being able to experience this moment of wonder. It is a source of inner joy and strength, and gives him hope. He experiences joy, and feels that he is free. We are his brothers and sisters of Elysium. Liberty ennobles our souls, and exalts our spirit, as well.

Seid umschlungen, Millionen, nein, Milliarden!
Embrace each other now, you millions, no billions!

Diesen Kuss der ganzen Welt!
The kiss is for the whole wide world!

Tonight, Sir John Eliot, the orchestra, and the chorus open with a ten minute work by Beethoven called *Calm Sea and Prosperous Voyage,* with the text by Goethe. I will leave you with his words:

The fog is torn,
The sky is bright,
And Aeolus releases
The fearful bindings.
The winds whisper,
The sailor begins to move.
Swiftly! Swiftly!
The waves divide,
The distance nears;
Already, I see land!

Bon voyage, and please…enjoy.

Two Poems

Variation 24

A Christmas Eve

I wrote this poem in Guizerix, France, December 2012, anticipating the arrival of Christmas Eve and contemplating what it would be like for the families of Newtown, Connecticut.

> A score of angels, freshly winged
> From felled tots taken by trembling hand,
> Try and explain to me this thing
> That rages on throughout the land.
>
> I'm far away from wails and cries,
> Frustration paramount, and jaws agape,
> The quaking horror and squirting eyes,
> That's screaming in whirling schoolscape.
>
> I am out here with the world around,
> Shaking our heads in disbelief.
> Constant media's sight and sound,
> Blast silly solutions without relief.

Rage on against the wee ones' flight!
Rage on against their siblings' fright!
Rage on this holy, lonely night!

Again this hell gives no rest.
This time's the worst, please no more.
What's its home? Where's its nest?
It's time to end it at its core.

We shine best when we're down for the count.
We are brothers and sisters, quite a team.
The sum of our parts is an enormous amount
To honor these Children of Elysium.

But what of those so close at hand,
Of dear ones, those left unhealed,
Over dreams and hopes so abandoned
Now that dreams and hopes were killed?

Rage on against the wee ones' flight!
Rage on against their siblings' fright!
Rage on this holy, lonely night!

This is a time that should come no more.
The solutions are there, as clear as the sun.
We must do more than bellow and roar.
We must rethink our mankind's gun.

There are those in need who do such deeds
For whom we must care, for all our sakes
With compassion for their nightmarish needs,
To prevent return of such dreadful mistakes.

Rave on, rave on with all of our might!
Rave on, rave on for an end in sight!
Rave on beyond this hollow night!

Variation 25

LES TOURNESOLS

Les Tournesols, they're called in France,
Growing in ranks and files as one,
Looking ahead, nary one askance
Together staring at the sun.

Sunflowers like millions, nay, billions of stars
Undulating on hills in French countryside,
Swaying together as gusty wind roars,
The temptation to break their trance defied.

They are as one people with a common desire
To uphold a faith, to worship the crest.
It must be this Apollo they require
As they follow him daily from east to west.

They are a joy to behold, when standing in front,
With the sun at your back, they are all yours.
At the rear of the field you are without regard,
To them you're not there, the field ignores.

Very much as humans they seem in their way,
Not thinking of why they do what they do.
They move faithfully as one the course of the day
Thoughtlessly snubbing what they should eschew.

They have no thoughts of France, why they are here,
Imported from lands across the seas,
Their humble existence allowed only a year
To give us seed's oil in Trie-sur-Baïse.

The scene shifts from France to La Porte, Indiana,
Where the Sunflower Fair had a noteworthy drama.
A young lad's bloom was given the prize
That inspired so many with tears in their eyes.

One of his sunflowers stood out from the rest.
In all categories it was clearly best.
Enough to win the ribbon and win it with ease,
An enormous seed head, free of disease.

That young lad Wyatt Wilkie went ill to bed
With a sore throat and a feverish head.
His sunflower had been blown down
But managed to survive its collapse to the ground.

Hours before the fair, Wyatt got sicker and sicker.
His chance of survival became bleaker and bleaker.
He could not, would not miss the big day.
It wouldn't be right to have him taken away.

But pass away he did, seven years on this earth.
His parents and siblings celebrated his birth
With no thought such a thing might ever happen.
How could an act of God be so brazen?

The next morning his sunflower sat on a chair.
Did everyone forget about it and the fair?
They gathered it up and drove to La Porte,
Seemed the right thing to do, no one would exhort.

Neither mother nor father can even remember
Which accepted the ribbon that day in September.
Wyatt's sunflower entered the contest and won.
What an extraordinary way to honor their son!

At the fair no one knew what had actually happened.
It did later explain why the family was saddened.
Plans were then made to continue this example
Of how passion and bravery can come from the fragile.

The Sunflower Contest was named in his memory.
The seeds from his sunflower kept as its progeny.
Kids started a garden at their school in his honor
As a reminder one can always try harder.

And back in France I often think of this story,
How all of us are really the same,
Especially when sunflowers have reached their glory
And brighter to me since I've learned Wyatt's name.

At night, the sunflowers are in a kerfuffle.
The old ones turn east, waiting for dawn.
Which way to turn, right, left or middle,
Into such arguments the young ones are drawn.

Les tournesols, my wife and our neighbors
Are awakened by roosters' sonic melée,
Still stiff and sore from yesterday's labors,
Together as we welcome the break of day.

THE LAST FIVE QUARTETS

Variation 26

Opus 127

*A pre-concert lecture that took place on Sunday, April 21, 2013,
prior to a performance by the St. Lawrence String Quartet at the
Irvine Barclay Theatre.*

Good evening, ladies and gentlemen, and welcome to this afternoon's
performance by the St. Lawrence String Quartet. This concert is another
installment in our *Beethoven: The Late Great* project. Today you will hear
the first of the five so-called late Beethoven quartets, the Quartet No. 12
in E-Flat, Op. 127.

To open the program, we hear Franz Josef Haydn's String Quartet in
D major, Op. 71, No. 2, followed by Osvaldo Golijov's *Qohelet*.

Haydn was incredibly instrumental (pardon the pun) in preparing
the way for composers yet to come, such as Mozart and Beethoven. He
firmly established the forms of the piano sonata, the string quartet, piano
trio, and symphony, and made it easier for these latter two composers
to develop these forms to the degrees that they did. Haydn provided
the creative oxygen these two composers used to breathe life into their
music, reaching levels that had not yet been achieved up to that point in
music history. This Op. 71, No. 2, Quartet was a hit with London audiences and enhanced the reputation (and pocketbook) of Haydn's London

sponsor violinist, Johann Peter Salomon—so much so that it caused great envy among local musicians. Their response was to form a group called the Philharmonic Society (100 years later becoming the Royal Philharmonic Society) to champion new music of continental composers. Their first beneficiary was Ludwig van Beethoven, whom they commissioned to write the Ninth Symphony. We celebrate this piece next spring, in the 2013-14 season, along with the Royal Philharmonic Society's 200th anniversary and the Philharmonic Society of Orange County's 60th anniversary.

Orange County audiences first encountered live performances of Osvaldo Golijov's music in 2002, when the Philharmonic Society presented the Southern California premiere of his *La Pasión según San Marcos* at our Eclectic Orange Festival. A few seasons later, we presented *Ayre,* a song cycle performed by soprano Dawn Upshaw and an ensemble comprised of members of eighth blackbird and others. Tonight's St. Lawrence String Quartet has had an artistic relationship with Golijov for more than 20 years. It is from that affiliation that *Qohelet* was derived, their first collaboration being *Yiddishbbuk*. The work *Qohelet* is a meditation inspired by the Biblical book of Ecclesiastes. Qohelet is the narrator (or teacher) of this autobiographical scripture. Many find the text to be negative, while others are inspired by its sparse ideas. It's the most humanistic book of the Bible, and is probably the most popular part of the Old Testament among the general population. Partial credit should go to the Byrds singing Pete Seeger and George Aber's adaptation of the text in the song "Turn, Turn, Turn:"

> A time to be born, a time to die;
> A time to plant, a time to reap.
> A time to kill, a time to heal;
> A time to laugh, a time to weep.

To talk about the late style of any creative artist implies that nothing will come after. Late style is ended either by the cessation of creative activity or by death itself. For any artist, there is nothing after the "late."

The word becomes ambiguous, whether followed by the word "style," or as it appears in our project title *Beethoven: The <u>Late</u> Great*. In Beethoven's case, he undoubtedly embraced a late style that was recognized, if not entirely appreciated, in his lifetime. In the time following his death, the notes on the page stayed the same, but the way we perceive them has had its own journey. We have the perspective of many changes in musical creation in the 186 years after his death to now be able to reflect back on his later works; discovering the metamorphosis that music in general has undergone is somewhat parallel to that of Beethoven in his final years. Knowing way too much now about so very little may obscure our vantage point. In our modern point of view, his late period has become the most intriguing of them all. But this appreciation happened gradually. In the first 25 years after his death, records show that there were only around seven performances of these late quartets in Vienna; in the next 50 years, there were only around 1,000 done worldwide. Today, these late quartets stand side by side with contemporary music, oftentimes contrasting the latter in pale comparison to the former. Of the *Grosse Fuge,* Op. 133, Igor Stravinsky said the work was an "absolutely contemporary piece of music that will be contemporary forever."

There was a 12-year gap between the Op. 95 F minor Quartet, the so-called "*Quartetto Serioso*," and the Op. 127, the first of the late five that is on this afternoon's program. Why such a space in time, and why would Beethoven select the string quartet format to finish out his late period (before he became, literally, the Late Great)?

The last string quartet Beethoven wrote before the one we are enjoying this afternoon was the Quartet in F minor, Op. 95, "*Quartetto Serioso*." It is important to speak of this quartet before we begin the exploration of the next one, Op. 127, which is the gateway to the last transcendent path of Beethoven's work, the five late quartets.

The first movement of the "*Quartetto Serioso*" is marked *Allegro con brio* (fast with fire). It is more impetuous than anything else—nervous hyper-energy, propelled by frustration that shoots out in all directions. It is exciting but somewhat uncomfortable. The second movement appears to be a fugue with the cello leading the way, but it goes in another direction. It is marked *Allegro ma non troppo* (moderately fast but not too much), and connects to the third movement with a bit of a shock. The third movement is marked *Allegro assai vivace ma serioso,* and it is easy to understand where the quartet gets its name. The same sense of spirited frustration from the first movement returns. The fourth movement is marked *Larghetto espressivo-Allegretto agitato-Allegro.* This is episodic and dramatic, marking the middle period of his work, when Beethoven's deafness was becoming more pronounced. It was during the time of his so-called heroic pieces, most notably the *Eroica* Symphony, as well as the Fifth Symphony (his most famous work), the *Pastoral* Symphony, the *Appassionata* Sonata and a number of string quartets. This "*Serioso*" Quartet, while written at the end of this period, gives a strong impression that he had much more to say.

What happened during the gap? After the death of his brother Kaspar, Beethoven managed to win sole custody of his nephew Karl, after a protracted court battle. This, along with illness, greatly hampered his creative energy, dramatically slowing down his output. He did, however, manage to complete two massive projects: the *Missa Solemnis* and the Ninth Symphony. The works that link the middle period with the late period are the last piano sonatas. The uses of the fugue, theme and variations and multitudinous trills appear and stay with his work until the end. One other explanation for why he wrote the *Diabelli Variations* is that maybe he was not finished with this form after the variations in the Piano Sonata, Op. 111. He seems to have been in a special place where variations kept flowing; he was a variation machine.

In 1823, Beethoven returns to the string quartet. He was very busy working on the *Missa Solemnis,* the Ninth Symphony, and had just wrapped up the *Diabelli Variations.* His friend and benefactor Prince Galitzin commissioned Beethoven to write a piano quartet in 1822. Beethoven now had the string quartet format in his head and took off in that direction. Prince Galitzin didn't exactly specify how many works he was expecting, which, of course, turned out to be five late quartets. About this time, Beethoven's favorite quartet violinist, Ignaz Schuppanzigh, returned to Vienna, setting the stage for the creation of the Op. 127.

Let's investigate the Op. 127, movement by movement.

The first movement is very amiable. Opening *tutti* chords are like hearty handshakes welcoming Beethoven back to the string quartet. With a lyrical embrace, the affectionately flowing first violin leads into a room full of old friends, Beethoven's muses. We can tell that he feels at home, as old emotions and skills return with a great sense of relief. There is a pleasant striving, like that used so much later by Brahms trying to sound like Beethoven. He is welcomed warmly, with generous reception; the main themes are developed. He expresses contentment and then makes a graceful exit.

In all of the late quartets, there are precursor shades of Mahler—patches of beauty and articulation that Mahler purloined and incorporated into his later symphonies. In his 1973 Norton Lectures at Harvard, musician Leonard Bernstein likened the final pages of the last movement of Mahler's Ninth Symphony to that of a dying spider whose web is becoming slowly detached; it happens one strand at a time until the last one gives way, allowing a perishing spider to pass into oblivion. Mahler is, of course, alluding to his own mortality, a topic which always seemed to be underscored in his compositions.

We can clearly see the "Mahler" treatment in the second movement of the Op. 127. Rather than the dying spider losing the filaments one by one, Beethoven's happy spider—we'll call her "Charlotte"—sends out the first strand, then the second, the third, and more and more, as she begins her morning stroll over an ever-expanding home. The slow development of the opening gives us a clue that this is going to be a lengthy movement, and it is, clocking in at more than 14 minutes. One thinks back to the *Hammerklavier* Piano Sonata, with its 20-minute slow movement. This one is a theme and six variations, a form that Beethoven calls upon numerous times in his late works. It is a movement to get lost in. The time passes faster than you want it to. We would be happy if it went on forever.

The third movement, *scherzando vivace*, has a fanfare akin to the one that opened the first movement, only this time it is short and hushed with pizzicato strings. What follows is a rollicking "quasi-fugal" treatment.

The middle section is an energetic scramble that makes a brief reemergence before the end, much in the same manner of the *Scherzo* in the Ninth Symphony.

The Finale is in a duple rhythm, in contrast to the first three movements that are mostly in a triple or a derivative thereof. After another brief fanfare, we hear a melody with a drone, like a hurdy-gurdy. This hearkens back to the Bagatelles, Op. 126, an earlier set of pieces in this same late period. In this movement, listen for the stomps, as if to depict a sort of rustic dance. Nature and country life always had a deep fascination for Beethoven; this treatment is most notably used in his Sixth Symphony, the *Pastoral*. There is something pleasing and universal about its appeal—we never tire of listening to it. A false ending followed by a brief dizzy return to the main theme, before three final chords close the entire quartet.

So there you have it, the first of the five late quartets by Ludwig van Beethoven—the String Quartet No. 12 in E-flat major, Op. 127. He also made sketches of additional movements to be inserted among the four—this was a revolutionary idea. Such a thing was simply not done at the time. Even more, he managed to do it in his next few quartets, only returning to the four-movement layout with the final one, Op. 135.

Beethoven knew he had more to say and that the string quartet would be the appropriate avenue. The Op. 127 is a happy piece of music by a composer who was very satisfied with it despite his severe physical afflictions. He wrote it with us, the listeners, in mind. I think this little passage from Ecclesiastes sums it up very well:

Wherefore I perceive that there is nothing better, than that a man should rejoice in his own portion of works: for who shall bring him to see what shall be after him?

Variation 27

HEILIGER DANKGESANG

A pre-concert lecture to be delivered prior to a performance by the Mandelring Quartet on February 23, 2014, at the Irvine Barclay Theatre.

"For God, time absolutely does not exist."

BEETHOVEN WROTE THIS statement in one of his *Tagebuchs* and was most assuredly contemplating this concept when he approached writing the third movement of his Op. 132 Quartet. He had recently recovered from a severe illness that halted his usual working pattern. This was debilitating to his productivity, as well as to his energy and his spirit. Through the strict approach of his doctor, the composer regained his strength and was able to mitigate his pain. His growing sense of relief was so profound that he found this third movement as the perfect vehicle to express his powerful feelings.

Communication is a very complicated and often difficult part of human nature. Each of us, in our own life journey, may or may not experience true personal connections, and will greatly struggle with the notion of vulnerability. But intimate expression is what makes life most satisfying, most meaningful, and most beneficial. It takes great effort to communicate, especially on an intimate level—and by intimate, I am referring to the kind of connection that is timeless and without ego. Words are used to bare the soul, exposing one's opinions, fears, and personal reflection.

But not all people are good with words and there are certain times that are beyond the reach of verbal expression. Beethoven, in his own way, went beyond the boundaries of communication by way of his music. This third movement is possibly the most personal piece of music ever written. The composer is allowing us, the listeners, to grow closer to him in ways that mere words could not afford. And, by way of the timelessness of his music, we still feel close to him, almost two hundred years later. With the millions of people who have heard this music after all of this time, it is still a one-on-one experience.

His pain was tremendous, and music was a safe place, a sort of escape where he could recover. And he articulated a profound gratitude for this process, as writing helped him reengage in real life. Grief, depression, and frustration are all in the music—emotions that are surprisingly honest for a man who was otherwise guarded. Of course, his music, until that time, had been very descriptive and dynamic, complete with feelings of joy, tragic loss, glory, passion and religious transformation. But all of this music is written in the third person, as it were. Beethoven has created this third movement from a first person point of view; he shares his most thoughtful personal feelings directly with you.

He called this movement *Heiliger Dankgesang eines Genesenen an die Gottheit, in der lydischen Tonart* (A Convalescent's Holy Song of Thanksgiving to the Divinity, in the Lydian Mode). Beethoven underscores feelings of gratitude with this most unconventional title. Before we examine the movement as a whole, it would be a good idea to focus on this Lydian mode that he mentioned. The Lydian is one of several modes (or scales) that were used in Gregorian Chant from the Middle Ages. Originally derived from ancient Greek modes, they can be more easily understood when we think in terms of the white keys on a piano. In modern usage, we think of terms of major and minor scales. If you play eight notes starting on middle C, ascending up the keyboard, it forms the Aeolian mode, or major scale as we know it today. Starting with D and going up 8 notes, you have the Dorian mode; going up the keyboard, starting with E, is the Phrygian mode (very exotic sounding). When you play the same eight notes, beginning with F, you have the Lydian mode. Its intervallic relationships are a flip-flop of the Aeolian mode, or major scale—two whole steps, a half-step, three whole steps, a half-step versus three whole steps, half-step, two whole steps, half-step for the Lydian. To change the Lydian mode, starting with F to an F major scale (having the right intervallic relationship), we have to lower the fourth note B a half-step to a B-flat. This is why the key of F major has a B-flat in the key signature.

For Beethoven to write in the Lydian mode, he had to make the note in the key of F—but he did not put a B-flat in the key signature. This is complicated to think about but very easy to understand. In an episode of the TV show *All in the Family*, Edith Bunker is rehearsing with her daughter Gloria and soon-to-be son-in-law Michael for their upcoming wedding. She is playing the Wagner wedding march on her out-of-tune parlor piano in the key of F major, inadvertently ignoring the B-flat that is in the key signature. This jarring B-natural sounds horrid on one the hand, but is extremely funny on the other—which is the point of the bit. She was playing in the Lydian mode, of which, I am sure, she had not a clue. The wonderful late Jean Stapleton who portrayed Edith Bunker was, of course, completely aware. She may have been the mind behind this funny musical bit.

Let us contemplate the medical significance behind this movement. The first, and most obvious, is Beethoven's appreciation for his recovery. But there is also the question of healing. Was Beethoven, in fact, healed by his own music? Was he revived and strengthened with the inspiration of creating this movement? Did he feel better as his writing progressed? When listening to this movement, can we, too, be healed? These days, there is much attention being paid to the therapeutic power of music. Is there really something to all of this? What are the relationships between brain, body, and music? Time will tell, and probably sooner rather than later.

Let's take a careful look at Beethoven's String Quartet No. 15 in A minor, Op. 132, movement by movement.

The piece will have been performed three times during my tenure with the Philharmonic Society. The first time was in 1998 by the Brentano Quartet.

I am generally a pretty mild-mannered guy. The small temper I do have can easily be kept in check (after a number years of working at it). One of the few things that can turn me from Bruce Banner into the Incredible Hulk is a rude audience member. Their actions can make me crazy and send me into a rage. I once loudly whispered, "Y'all hush!" to a yakkety couple seated close by. Shut up they did, immediately. Kaly gently whispered in my ear, "You, of course, know the philanthropic foundation they have, don't you?" It did not matter to me at that moment—respect for the music and performers was my sole concern. I must add that we are still without support from their particular foundation. I will leave this situation to my successor.

The opening measures of the Op. 132 first movement are incredibly soft. At the Brentano Quartet performance, a woman seated directly across the aisle from me chose this very delicate moment to remove a crinkly wrapper from a piece of candy (after noisily digging in her purse to retrieve it). The sound immediately took me back to my childhood, when I was awakened one time by neighbors who were tearing down a shed at the crack of dawn. They were in the process of removing the sheet metal roof, using crowbars to slowly and raucously remove rusted spikes that had held the roof down for decades. The unencumbered roof crashed to the ground—what a clamor! "What is this candy wrapper made of," I wondered, "sheet metal?" I turned purple (on the way to Hulk green). But before my shirt sleeves could begin to split, my new bride Kaly gently patted my arm and I recovered control over myself. In similar ways, she has been saving me from these circumstances for fifteen years—to her, I am lovingly grateful.

All of this is to say that this first movement begins very quietly (my seated neighbors tonight, be forewarned). Regarding the first movement, Maynard Solomon writes, "[Beethoven] wants us to join him in overhearing events as they are already ongoing: he is the brooding observer, inviting us to share what he had seen to let the music enter us, unresisting." This is an accurate, though strange, notion. It seems rather Zen, akin to "pre-boarding" an aircraft—whatever that inane avionic term actually means. You feel as though you have just walked into the room where the piece being played is in progress. In your imagination, you can indeed see the frowning Beethoven leaning against the wall in the back of the room. The music is marked *Allegro-sostenuto-allegro,* or fast, sustained and just plain fast, indicating that the second *Allegro* is more *marcato,* or marked. The movement is rather brooding, such as the image of the composer leaning against the far wall. The mood is a little ambiguous. Is it the players, or is it the composer? The movement is highly enjoyable, nonetheless. This quartet is called No. 15, the next to last of the final five quartets. It was published that way. It is actually the second written of the last five. Except for the third movement and the little march following, it lacks some of innovations that follow in Opp. 130 and 131.

The second movement is marked *Allegro ma non tanto,* meaning fast, but not overly so.

We are now in the key of A major. The motive of a half note, followed by four eighth-notes, a quarter note and quarter rest, is the stitch that holds the first section together. The second section, corresponding to a trio (in the normal sense), relies on the hurdy-gurdy drone idea that frequents so many similar pieces of the late period. It offers an easy contrast to the first section. This part is essentially comprised of running *legato* eighth-notes over *staccato* quarter notes. There is a brief stormy break in the flowing proceedings, which ushers in the end of the section and the *da capo* return to the beginning.

And now we come to the *Heiliger Dankgesang eines Genesenen an die Gottheit, in der lydischen Tonart"*—the immortal third movement. It is marked *molto adagio,* or very slow. Samuel Barber's *Adagio for Strings* is also marked *molto adagio*—its pulse is the quarter note. In the Beethoven, the pulse is primarily given to the half note; it is very slow. The first three lines of music take almost three minutes to play—that is the length of the entire *Stars and Stripes Forever* by John Philip Sousa. For God, time absolutely does not exist. For someone like Beethoven, who is able to step back from death's door, time is a restored luxury that should be savored as long as possible. Because of the extremely slow tempo, it is hard to pick out the melody that is handed from instrument to instrument. But the melody is not as important as the overall effect; Beethoven uses this constant theme to keep things organized. We don't need to know how it is put together, this melody that only Beethoven and God can pick out. In the last bar of this section, the second violinist plays a C-sharp, making an A major seventh chord with his other colleagues—the dominant of the key of D major, which comes next.

We have now left the Lydian mode and have moved on to the second section marked *Andante* (a walking tempo) and *Neue Kraft fuhlend* or "with renewed strength." The second violin has the melody with the first violin trilling overhead, after which they join together. Beethoven is indeed feeling much better here—he is optimistic. The composer makes no type of broad statement that would develop the themes into an extended section. The writing becomes more florid. All the players enjoy a turn at the lead, and it works wonderfully together. The section ends gently, and we find the return of the *Heiliger Dankgesang* material back the Lydian mode, again, *molto adagio*. The second violin returns to the slow fugue, only, now with a slight touch of renewed strength, characterized by the syncopated eighth note. Again, the tempo is markedly slow. We now understand Beethoven's changing energy, hence the return to the "renewed strength" music marked *Andante* this time in D major—ending deftly as before.

Then the *Heiliger Dankgesang* hymn returns for a third time and final time. The emotion is a bit more fervent. As always, the second violin is first to enter in a way that is reminiscent of the "with renewed strength" section. The viola is next, followed by the cello, and finally the first violin. Each of their entrances is marked "with great sentiment;" the movement ends as quietly as it began.

Beethoven is feeling better now, and so are we—let's celebrate! Obviously with music, but with what music? Shall we march around triumphantly for a couple of minutes? And so we have it, marked *Alla Marcia, assai vivace* in the key of A major. Then we have a quick and moody transition into the final fifth movement (in A minor), marked *Allegro appassionato.* The blood is flowing again; we are waking up. This is a terrific movement—Beethoven is back.

So there you have it—a string quartet in five movements (instead of the usual four), phenomenally enhanced by a difficult time of personal recovery. Beethoven would go on to write his next two string quartets in the "extra-movement" format. In the final fifth quartet, he returns to the four-movement norm, bookending the quartets with the first of the five, Op. 127, also in four movements. But after completing these late five quartets, the same illness that had plagued him in Vienna returned with a vengeance. He passed away a few months after completing the Op. 132. Time and health are realities that we cannot escape.

Variation 28

OPUS 130

A pre-concert lecture that took place on February 11, 2012, prior to a performance by the Brentano String Quartet at the Irvine Barclay Theatre.

GOOD EVENING AND welcome to another concert in our *Beethoven: The Late Great* series. We are surveying the late quartets as well as the major works, the *Missa Solemnis* and the most famous of all—the Ninth Symphony—over the next couple of seasons. The quartets will be coming to you out of order, so tonight we have the Op. 130. On March 20, the Takács Quartet performs the Op. 131, along with Garrick Ohlsson joining in for the G minor Piano Quintet by Shostakovich. I look forward to introducing that program to you as well.

For tonight's concert, the Brentano Quartet will open with the second quartet of Ferruccio Busoni. He was an amazing talent who lived at the turn of the twentieth century (born in Tuscany in 1866 and died in Berlin in 1924). This was an extraordinary time to be a composer or any kind of artist. The old world was colliding with the new, both through innovation and tragedy, as referenced in *Downton Abbey*. A great example would be two of Busoni's later-to-be-very-famous students, Percy Grainger and Edgard Varèse, who could not have been more different from each another. During Busoni's lifetime, Berlioz, Liszt, Brahms, Bruckner, Mahler, Sibelius, Strauss, Ravel, Schoenberg, Stravinsky, Gershwin, Copland, and Shostakovich were alive—some of the most extraordinary musical composers in near history. I haven't even mentioned the writers or visual artists.

Busoni was a composer, a formidable pianist, conductor, teacher, writer, and editor. He is best known for his transcriptions of Bach organ pieces for piano; these are often referred to as by Bach-Busoni, so well-known that his wife was once introduced at a party as Mrs. Bach-Busoni. He went on to write an extremely difficult and lengthy piano concerto, which has famously been recorded by a number of pianists, including Garrick Ohlsson, who comes to you next month with the Takács Quartet. He recorded it with the Cleveland Orchestra that will be performing for us on April 17.

I asked Mark Steinberg of the Brentano Quartet why they selected the Busoni second quartet for the first half of the program that contains the Beethoven Op. 130. He responded:

> We are looking forward to coming to play for you! We are
> really loving the Busoni Quartet—I think it's a wonderful piece!
> Like you, I have a sense that it's a good choice as a first half
> before the Op. 130 but in all honesty, it's a completely intuitive
> pairing. There's a richness of invention and a contrapuntal bent
> in the Busoni which it shares with Beethoven and there seems
> to be some influence, but I can't explain more clearly than that,
> I'm afraid. We did this program a couple of times in Europe
> in the last few weeks and it is very nicely balanced and seems
> right, somehow.

Sometimes, planning goes by intuition. And this just feels right. In 1924, Busoni wrote the following in a journal publication:

> A composer seems to me to be like a gardener who is given
> a plot of land of smaller or larger size to cultivate. He has the

task of picking what grows on his land, at least of ordering it, of forming it into a bouquet, at most of making it into a garden. It befits this gardener to grab and to shape what is within reach of his eyes, of his arms (his distinctiveness).

This music of the beyond, what he called *Tonkunst,* he found unattainable, as did Beethoven. But they found reaching for it worthwhile.

The second quartet is comprised of four movements. The first *Allegro energico* begins with accented chords, followed by the opening themes interwoven with contrapuntal figures. It concludes with a return of the opening chords that serve as an introduction to the second theme. There are elements of the writing that are dependent on the ancestral style found in the Beethoven quartets. The second movement, *Andante con moto,* is a moody, waltz-like piece. It is very expressive—a period piece of its time. The third movement, *Vivace assai,* is a true *scherzo,* as one would expect in a string quartet. It is very different from the upcoming Beethoven Op. 130. The final movement, marked *Andantino-Allegro con brio,* brings us a happy *Allegro* in contrast to the gloomy tinges so attendant in the first three movements.

Busoni's philosophy was that "Music was born free; and to win freedom is its destiny." To me, this is the great link between his Second Quartet and Beethoven's later works, especially tonight's Op. 130.

I love the Op. 130 quartet. Of the five late quartets, this is the third, and the first to seriously stray from the four-movement norm. These five quartets were published out of order. The first three, Opp. 127, 132 and 130, were commissioned by Prince Nicholas Galitzin. The final two are Op. 131 (played next month) and the Op. 135 (played next year, along with Op. 127). We'll get to the Op. 132 in the 2013-14 season with the Mandelring Quartet.

Prince Galitzin, a patron of Beethoven and a cellist, was from an important Russian family. He fought in the Battle of 1812—the Russian War of 1812, not the one in the States with Colonel Jackson. He spent some of his youth in Vienna, where he became a great fan of Beethoven, and asked the composer to write a few string quartets. Galitzin was a member of the St. Petersburg Philharmonic Society and was very influential in arranging for the Society to give the premiere of Beethoven's *Missa Solemnis* in 1824. Incidentally, Galitzin died the year Busoni was born.

Beethoven communicated to others during this period of his most profound deafness by means of conversation books, beginning in 1818. Interlocutors would write down what they wanted to say or ask the composer, and he would answer either through direct speech or in writing. In the 137 sheets of the conversation books that exist today, he referred to the Op. 130 as his *Leibquartett*. There has always been a bit of confusion in his meaning for this term. Literally, it can be translated to "body quartet, belly quartet," or "torso quartet." Some scholars translate it to mean "love quartet"—*Liebequartett* rather than *Leibquartett*. An old college mate of mine, Theodore Albrecht at the University of North Texas, is now a much respected Beethoven musicologist at Kent State. I ran across a reference to this subject in a paper that Jeff Mistri, the Society's artistic administrator, was able to unearth or more accurately "un-ether" from the internet for me. The explanation is quite simple and brilliant.

Dr. Albrecht, or Teddy, as we knew him, had a way of getting to the crux of a matter, an important trait for a future musicologist. The two of us, along with our fellow music nerds, would spend weekends in discussion while listening to the complete symphonies of Mahler and Shostakovich, or the total *Ring Cycle*. Teddy had a pet cactus that he named *Der Führer*, which we all thought was hilarious. There was obviously some beer involved on those weekends. Teddy, in his paper "Beethoven's So-Called *Leibquartett*, Op. 130: A Case of Mistaken Identity," states that many of Beethoven's pieces had nicknames originated by the composer himself such as *Eroica, Pathétique* or *Pastoral*. Others are associated with their commissioners or dedicatees—such Kreutzer, Rasumovsky or Archduke (Rudolph, the younger brother of the Emperor of Austria). Some names were attached by friends, like *Tempest,* or publishers for marketing purposes, such as *Moonlight, Appassionata,* or *Ghost Trio.* All of these names make some kind of sense. On the other hand, *Leibquartett* as the belly quartet, bowel quartet or womb quartet, certainly does not. The distinguished Beethoven scholar William Kinderman refers to the term as denoting Beethoven's favorite quartet, substituting the meaning of *Liebquartett,* or beloved quartet, for the actual term *Leibquartett,* a glossy way out of the puzzle without really solving it. Albrecht claims, and I believe him, that the meaning of Beethoven's reference was mixed up in translation. Beethoven coined this term *Leibquartett,* not referring to his Op. 130, but to the actual quartet of musicians performing it—namely Ignaz Schuppanzigh, Carl Holz, Franz Weiss and Joseph Linke—his *Leib quartett* or his "personal" quartet, a group of guys to whom he was close. This group organized to perform what would be Beethoven's last works, and was the very first professional string quartet. Prior to the advent of the Beethoven quartets, especially the last ones, professional musicians and talented amateurs could play most string quartets with just a few rehearsals. Schuppanzigh, a violin teacher of Beethoven, formed his group to tackle the difficulties of the Beethoven quartets. They went on to perform Schubert and other composers as well. Schuppanzigh became extremely corpulent later in life, so much so that Beethoven wrote a choral ditty poking fun at him, called "*Lob auf den Dicken*" or "Praise to the Fat One." Nice.

Of the Op. 130 itself, its six movements, while retaining some cohesiveness, are individual souls—like a pack of creatures, the alpha movement of the group being the final great fugue. This grouping of characteristic individuals carries over from the concept of the *Diabelli Variations,* and the Bagatelles, Op. 126, again presages the romantic idea of separate ideas pulled together in spite of themselves, as we see later in the works of Schumann and Chopin. Beethoven is having a good time.

The first five movements are delightful, with an exhilarating, if somewhat disturbing, final sixth. The first movement marked *Adagio ma non troppo—Allegro* meaning "slowly, but not too much—and then fast," is somewhat deceiving. I would say it is more like slow-then-fast, then not-too-slow, then fast again, then hold on a second, then slow and fast at the same time, and so on. It is not your garden-variety slow introduction and then fast movement string quartet written up to this point. Beethoven builds the whole movement on a series of cadences interspersed with rapid sixteenth note figures. A cadence is a device used by composers to close a phrase or end entire piece with a single chord—or a few chords moving towards a key that brings the passage to rest. Beethoven, in this case, weaves the cadences and the rapid passage into a cohesive fabric with an unpredictable direction, keeping the audience pleasantly off guard. It all makes for some fascinating listening. I feel it is best to treat the music like a clever short story, taking care to relax and enjoy the twists and turns. It all seems to work out beautifully. You can almost hear Beethoven's creative process at work, the joy of taking the road less traveled. We are all having fun along with him on this sojourn. The genius of it is how much he can do with only two ideas—the cadences and the rapid sixteenths.

And the second movement? It's a *bagatelle*, a trifling two minutes long. This piece is a lively sorbet—a cleansing of your musical palette, as it were. Again, it is not something that you would expect in a quartet, especially one from any composer's late period. Curious, towards the end, are the downward chromatic violin *cadenzas* followed by the punchy *tutti* chords that lead back to the opening material briefly—and then out. It is a lively little dance that is suddenly here and then suddenly and completely gone.

Schuppanzigh and company were asked to repeat this one at the first performance. It is addictive in a way, leaving you wanting more. And Beethoven knew this. He made it very attractive, even cute—but not long enough for you to get your fill, the secret for any successful dinner party.

The third movement is seven minutes long, marked *Andante con moto ma non troppo, Poco scherzozo*. After a few rather melancholy opening bars, a lovely melody ensues, suggestive of upward steps and probing questions, followed by a descending passage of answers that foretell the future Dvořák. This movement begs to be choreographed as other movements of this quartet have been. It is elegant. Towards the end of the movement, we hear a chromatically descending sequence with tri-tone skips and an accompanying *ostinato* that is extremely intriguing. This is another example of the late-period Beethoven peeking into realms to which we mere mortals have no access. He goes to new heights and then returns to us, describing what he has seen. Maynard Solomon astutely writes, "With the Quartet in B-flat, Op.130, Beethoven perhaps (almost certainly) had tried to carry his audience with him into a realm which their training and sensibility would not permit them to enter." We are just now really beginning to get it.

The fourth movement is marked *Alla danza tedesca* which is what it really is—a lovely German dance. One can picture couples gliding gracefully across a dance floor in a great manor house. It is bittersweet in the sense that Beethoven was never a part of such a couple. Having a family of his own eluded him his entire life. Now, as he is growing in years, this delightful movement is all the more poignant. Added to this is the crisis with his nephew Karl that I will discuss in a moment. This piece is also short, less than 4 minutes, sort of a bookend pairing with the *bagatelle* supporting the *en pointe* movement. This cleans the slate for the powerfully beautiful penultimate movement—the fifth, *Cavatina: adagio molto espressivo*.

This is the movement that has been described as otherworldly. Figuratively, the deep personal expression seems born of that style that was so rich in Beethoven's late period. His vision and understanding seem somehow transported beyond our sphere, into a good place that he is able portray in this music. Literally, a recording of the *Cavatina* by the Budapest String Quartet is traveling at this moment through the Kuiper Belt on the far edge of our solar system aboard the Voyager 7 launched in 1977. I think this was Carl Sagan's idea.

A *cavatina* is a short, simple song. Beethoven's, though simple and kind of short (six minutes), probes our innermost feelings, connecting his with ours. It is a meditation, almost Mahleresque. Beethoven himself said that the *Cavatina* cost him tears, both in the writing of it and merely reviving it in his thoughts afterwards.

The second section features a violin solo marked as *beklemmt* or "anguished," which probes furtively, somewhat painfully upward in melodic development of the *Cavatina* then is joined again by the repeat of the theme, quietly ending the movement. In earlier times, Beethoven would have further developed this *beklemmt* solo, but his compositions are now in a final phase of transcendence—not so much exploring as probing. As his slower movements go, this *cavatina* does not dominate the entire quartet as do those in earlier quartets. This gives us a premonition that something very powerful is around the corner, which indeed it is. We are on the doorstep of the greatest explosion of Beethoven's extraordinary vision and imagination—the *Grosse Fuge* or "great fugue," the final and sixth movement.

The *Grosse Fuge* is Beethoven's most controversial piece of music. To quote Joseph Kerman on this subject, of which he is the great expert, "The finale worried everybody: the players, the elite audience, Beethoven's friends, very definitely the publisher, and by implication the composer himself." One review called the *Grosse Fuge* "incomprehensible, a sort of Chinese puzzle." The violinist Schuppanzigh found it troubling. Beethoven's not-always-to-be-trusted biographer Anton Schindler calls it *Monstrum aller Quartett-musik* (the monster of all quartet music), an honest statement on his part. Paul Bekker wrote, "Each movement is merely episodic inasmuch as it prepares for the finale."

The Philharmonic Society's 1995-96 concert season is still my favorite, as it was the first one where I had a clean slate for securing new attractions. I remember it as the first time I could really strut my stuff. On that season, I scheduled the Arditti Quartet from London on the very series that tonight's program is a part of. The Arditti is arguably the most outstanding modern string quartet for contemporary chamber music, and I wanted our audience to experience them firsthand. Knowing that some (as it turned out many) would object to the absence of familiar composer names on the program, I suggested to Irving Arditti, the quartet's founder and first violinist, that it might be a good idea to include a piece by one well-known classical composer that would fit it with the more *avant-garde* music on the program. The choice was obvious—Beethoven's *Grosse Fuge*. It worked to a degree. At the intermission, Irving commented to me backstage, "Dean, that's a tough crowd." I responded, "Yes, they can be but the most important thing is that they are troopers, still in the hall and want to hear what you have on the second half." There was a mixed reaction to the overall program—the subscribers seated in the best seats offered tepid applause while those in the marginal seats, the single-ticket buyer enthusiasts went wild. We are still heavily involved in the programming for the *Grosse Fuge*. The Brentano played the fugue alone the last time they were here.

The fugue is the alpha leader of the previous five movements, clocking in at 15 minutes long. The opening is in your face; some may find it a bit brash or downright rude. The counter-subject to the fugue theme is jerky, often angular. Even the harmonies push the edge of tonality. It has a rollicking energy that propels the movement along. The inventions, twists, and turns seem to cascade endlessly—but certainly not effortlessly. It is obvious that Beethoven worked very hard on this movement. Suddenly, there is a more serene treatment of the counterpoint. It still has that now-familiar probing feel, trying carefully to find its way in the dark. Like a horror movie, tensions have calmed now, but you cannot help but have the suspicion that the monster will be back. What a shock to the sensibility of the early nineteenth-century audience! We are lulled, then surprised again, finally nearing what seems to be some closing material. Is it going to end? Of course not, this is Beethoven—and late Beethoven at that. We are back into the fugue, followed by a flurry of trills. The harmonies are unstable, continually shifting. The dotted rhythms of the counter subject are further explored. We come to a stop with a clear cadence or two (like the first movement) and then hear what sounds like a coda. It's happy and almost reminiscent—then come closing chords. The fugue theme once again returns, in octaves that try to dominate the proceedings. The counter-subject, amid more trills, brings the movement to a more normal and final close.

The Op. 130 was completed in 1825 with the fugue. It was published in June 1827, after Beethoven's death, by publisher Matthias Artaria. He had previously asked Beethoven for a replacement movement for the fugue, telling the composer that sales of the published work with the fugue would be difficult seeing as how no amateur group could play it, much less understand it. Beethoven unexpectedly agreed, seeing that his income could increase—especially when Artaria also agreed to publish the fugue separately. The quartet, with the replacement, was published as

Op. 130 and the *Grosse Fuge* as Op. 133. When Beethoven submitted the manuscript to Artaria, he attached a note that said, "Put together from pilferings and one thing and another." When the publisher protested in a panic, the composer said, "The note was a joke. It's brand-new."

Holz, one of the quartet violinists, remarked to Beethoven that the B-flat was the greatest of the first three final quartets (Opps. 127, 130, and 131). The composer replied, "Each in its way. Art demands of us that we shall not stand still. You will find a new manner of voice treatment and thank God there is less lack of fancy than ever before."

A few words about the nephew Karl:

He was born in 1806, the only child of the three Beethoven brothers. At the death of his brother Kaspar, Beethoven fought for and gained the guardianship of his nephew, in an effort to rescue him from his mother, Johanna. Beethoven thought that she was immoral, though I think he was secretly in love with her. He thought of his nephew Karl as his own son, a carrying-out of his family romance fantasy, extremely sad.

All of this drama took an emotional toll on the young Karl, especially during court proceedings when he had to testify. Beethoven took custody and for a time forced Karl to study music, but to no avail. The boy had no talent for it, in contrast to Beethoven, whose father *beat* music into him, a boy who *was* greatly talented. During the time period that Beethoven was composing his Op. 130, the despondent 15-year-old Karl loaded two pistols, put one to his temple, and fired, only to have the bullet graze the side of his head. So Karl was sent for military service, returning to Vienna only after his uncle had died, never seeing him again.

Karl later married. His only son immigrated to Detroit, where he worked for the Michigan Central Railroad. His son's only son died childless, ending the Beethoven name.

The composer Beethoven, though deaf, extremely ill, and caught in the turmoil of emotional family episodes, managed to provide us all with some of the most sublime creations of human endeavor. I can think of no better example to follow. No matter how you feel, always take the best of yourself and give it back to the rest of us. We will all try to do the same for you.

Variation 29

Opus 131

A pre-concert lecture that took place on March 20, 2012, prior to a performance by the Takács Quartet and Garrick Ohlsson at the Irvine Barclay Theatre.

It's my pleasure to welcome you all to our latest installment of *Beethoven: The Late Great*. Tonight we have the String Quartet in C-sharp minor, Op. 131. In October, we continue with the Parker String Quartet performing the Op. 135 and Sir John Eliot Gardiner, the Orchestre Révolutionnaire et Romantique, and the Monteverdi Choir in performances of the *Missa Solemnis* and the Ninth Symphony. We continue with further performances and a special Beethoven exhibit at the Bowers Museum that will bring some very special surprises. I am delighted to announce that The Segerstrom Foundation has given the Philharmonic Society a $175,000 challenge grant that we must match, dollar for dollar. We greatly appreciate help, and you can do so by earmarking your annual contribution to the Philharmonic Society of Orange County for our project *Beethoven: The Late Great*.

But first, a few words on the Shostakovich Piano Quintet in G minor. Dmitri Shostakovich has come to be regarded as one of the principal twentieth century composers. Working in all the traditional genres, he was particularly prodigious with his monumental cycles of 15 symphonies and 15 string quartets. Despite his early modernist tendencies and a distinctively contemporary and personal sound, Shostakovich primarily worked with traditional forms within a largely tonal harmonic vocabulary. This sense of modern voice within an unbroken traditional lineage is nowhere more apparent than with his glorious piano quintet of 1940. Impressed with the composer's first string quartet, the Moscow-based Beethoven Quartet asked Shostakovich to write a quintet that would feature him at the piano. The result was an immense success, earning Shostakovich the Stalin Prize and a cash award of 100,000 rubles—often cited as the largest sum ever commanded by a chamber music work. An early entry in his chamber music catalog, Shostakovich's quintet is one of his most popular works, destined to join the small pantheon of singular piano quintets from the likes of Schumann, Brahms, and Franck.

Traditional forms and modes of expression pervade the entire quintet. The first two movements supply a massive prelude and fugue in the finest Bachian sense. Shostakovich was a skillful and artistic contrapuntist, with masterful fugues all throughout his *oeuvre*. Directly inspired by Bach's *Well-Tempered Clavier*, Shostakovich wrote his own substantial set of 24 preludes and fugues for piano—again a modern voice within an ancient tradition. Here, the prelude and fugue acquire an extra dimension, due to the fact that the piano quintet naturally divides between strings and piano, each capable of multi-part textures on their own as well as combining for a unified ensemble. The fugue engages in a variety of traditional techniques including a prominent countersubject.

The third movement is a fantastic *scherzo* and trio, a highpoint of the work. In startling contrast to the poise and grandeur of the prelude and fugue, the *scherzo* dances with a rustic, wild abandon, veering towards the colorful parody and dark sarcasm so typical of Shostakovich. Less traditional is a second slow movement, a cumbersome *intermezzo* placed between the *scherzo* and finale. Here is another one of Shostakovich's vivid themes: an intimate sorrow that rises to a peak of anguish, with a plodding sense of fate underlying a poignant song. But it is only a glimpse, which quickly fades into the relaxed tone of a breezy, uplifting conclusion. The finale has a clearly articulated classical sonata form with distinctive themes and a development section. A march-like feel lies just beneath the surface, occasionally swelling with grand gestures while, in between, a brief recollection of the *intermezzo* temporarily clouds an otherwise sunny ending. Throughout the quintet, Shostakovich maintains a remarkable clarity of texture, avoiding the dense or quasi-orchestral grandiosity towards which piano quintets tend. This is due, in particular, to a relatively restrained piano part and a fluid, dynamic ensemble where all five instruments are rarely played at the same time.

And now to Beethoven's Op. 131. The philosopher Kant said that man is "the single being upon earth that possesses…a capacity for setting before himself ends of his deliberate choice." The artist should "multiply…the symbols of perfection, till appearance triumphs over reality, and art over nature." In this spirit, Maynard Solomon writes that these late works "keep alive mankind's hope and sustain faith in the possibilities of human renewal." And, of course, Schiller has the final word: "To arrive at a solution even in the political problem, the road of aesthetics must be pursued, because it is through beauty that we arrive at freedom." Beethoven felt that he had more artistic license before the advent of Napoleon; however, after the Bourbon Restoration, he entered his late phase, as one of the first avant-gardists now writing music with an audience in mind. He cared how his music was received; it was important that his audiences got it.

The English composer Sir Hubert Parry says, "[Beethoven had by now found] the accepted scheme of organization which he himself had brought to perfection too constraining and restrictive to the impulse of his thought, and therefore endeavored to find new types of form and to revive sundry earlier types of organization and combine them in various ways which departed from the essential principles upon which composers had been working for generations."

Tonight, we sonically join this late transcendence of the greatest composer ever known in his favorite quartet—perhaps the greatest quartet of all time—the Op. 131 in C-sharp minor. Sir Donald Tovey (from his essays) recalls, "All art involves conflict…the normal solutions of all conflicts will be mutual service, and here alone we find perfect freedom."

The C-sharp minor quartet is the most deeply integrated of all of Beethoven's quartets. Rather than offering a first movement in *sonata allegro* form with two principle keys, as would be the norm, he begins with a fugue with six key changes related to the C-sharp tonic, preparing us for the seven-movement journey through six distinct keys and 31 changes of tempo before ending back in C-sharp minor in the finale with a quote from the first movement fugue.

This Quartet is a very significant piece of art. It is Beethoven in the extreme. He abandoned the traditional four-movement layout in the Op. 130 that we discussed last time. The first movement of the Op. 131 is a beautiful, melancholy fugue marked *Adagio, ma non troppo e molto espressivo* (not too expressive). Early on, Beethoven would normally eschew fugues, feeling that they were a waste of his time—too mathematical—and many of his attempts at writing them were not as top notch as they would be in the future. In his later works, this sentiment changed dramatically, most notably the fugue in the *Hammerklavier* and Op. 106 Piano Sonata, the two in the *Diabelli Variations*, the Ninth Symphony, the *Grosse Fuge,* and, of course, this particular quartet. This opening movement of the quartet is worthy of Bach, again recalling his early training in Bonn. The main difference is how the voices line up vertically—the result is Beethoven's harmonic language, a very new sense of a musical dialect, to be sure. In the fugue subject from the beginning, there is a curious *crescendo* and *sforzando* each time on the fourth note, characteristic of Beethoven's style in all of his creative periods. His idea of great fun was catching the audience off-guard. Masterfully playful, he bounces from sequence to sequence, from key to key. He gives us a valley followed by plateau, leading us curve after curve, and this is one of the greatest joys of this work. Taking a soaring glide over a melancholy landscape makes a kind of a private listening experience—the listener feels as if it were written entirely for him.

An interesting way to approach this fugue is to consider it as a conversation between four close friends (two violins, a viola, and a cello), mutually consoling each other over the loss of a dear friend. Sometimes they echo one another's sentiments; other times, they try to be more supportive by moving to more positive expression through changes in key and tonality. In this scenario, it is difficult to know if Beethoven is one of these friends, the actual object of affection, or if he is merely using the whole exercise to further obfuscate his own feelings. In any case, please empty your mind and take the ride, adding whatever subtext that comes to your mind; simply let the music flow over you, as if it were the waves and breeze of the surf on a cloudy afternoon.

Joseph Kerman says that, at the ending of the fugue, "the great machine comes to a perfect rest on bearings that are frictionless, but only a feather stroke is required to reactivate the modulatory momentum." The movement ends with all the instruments on C-sharp, slurring up an octave to a fermata. The second movement begins with the same device on a D. In contrast to the fugue, this movement is a sonata without a development section, somewhat in perpetual motion. I think the movement evokes a sense of *Gemütlichkeit,* as so much of the music of the period was written. The time between the Congress of Vienna and the 1848 revolutions, occurring in several countries at once, is referred to as the *Biedermeier* era. There were strict rules for public gatherings in Vienna, making public concerts a problem. Friends and families gathered in homes as an obvious alternative. This is the age of Schubert, Mendelssohn, of the art song and, of course, of chamber music. Thus, it becomes more evident why Beethoven would focus on writing string quartets at the end of his creative time. *Biedermeier* culture, including music, art, literature, and especially furniture design, expressed a sense of comfort, close relationships, domestic harmony, and a fondness for tradition. It was very middle class and, above all, was much protected from the outside world. The music of this period is about all of these things. Once again, we are reminded how much Beethoven relished the domestic life of others. You can hear how he understood the definition of happiness in such things by listening to his music—and it is somewhat bittersweet, I think.

The third movement is rather like a narrative. Declamatory chords are followed by sentimental, apologetic entrances by each instrument. The whole thing is only a little more than 50 seconds in length. It is a connecter, holding the quartet together, moving it forward.

The fourth movement, in the key of A major and marked *Andante, ma non troppo e molto cantabile* (like walking but not too fast, and very singable), hints at Mozart—elegant and urbane. It's a wonderful theme and variations, a format that Beethoven excelled and called upon in his late period. As the *Grosse Fuge* was the central organizing force of the Op. 130 quartet, this set of variations is the central rock of the Op. 131 quartet, the longest movement. Beethoven is on comfortable ground. Having made great exploration of the late works of Beethoven, can we believe that the variations are tongue in cheek? The rather obvious *pizzicato* notes, are they little jokes? Who are they poking fun at? It presents a rather lovely mystery. Of course, it may be nothing at all. And yet, it does not matter; let us not worry ourselves with the questions, but sit back and enjoy the experience as it is, with no investigation.

The fifth movement, in the key of E major, is marked *Presto*. The opening is light and fun (which, of course, makes me suspicious on first hearing). A small, brash fanfare runs down and up a triad, serving as the overall organizing device for the whole movement. A second theme sounds like a hurdy-gurdy piece. Maybe this movement suggests a country village stroll or a nature walk, some of Beethoven's favorite things. The last time we hear this theme, it is played *sul ponticello*, or "bowed closed to the bridge," producing a glassy, unreal, and rather magical sound. It, again, presages Mendelssohn, with elfin darts and dashes. And the ending is wonderful, full of *pizzicato* nonsense; this all connects with the next movement, in the key of G-sharp minor. No. 5 ends with three sharply accented notes. No. 6 begins with three accented notes. Joseph Kerman describes this as "a deaf man's harsh peremptory shout—commanding an end to this and a new beginning."

This *Adagio quasi un poco Andante* (*adagio* almost a little *andante*) movement serves a serious recitative style introduction to the finale. The seventh movement is a full gallop in contrast to the lyrical second theme. This movement has no grand fugues, but brings a real finale, in the traditional sense.

So there you have it, the Op. 131. The organization of the seven movements is very interesting; the first and last movements are about the same length, while movements two, three, five, and six are in the pattern of short introductions to movements, all about the same length.

The fourth movement, the theme and variations, is the anchor of the entire work, the longest of all at about thirteen minutes. Beethoven covers a tremendous range of styles and techniques—fugue, suite, recitative, variation, scherzo, aria and sonata. It makes for a luxurious listen.

The Op. 131 was never given a public performance during Beethoven's lifetime. In 1828, Franz Schubert heard it in a private performance, five days before he died. It is said that he was ecstatically enthusiastic.

This is the penultimate of the late quartets. In 1822, Prince Nicholas Galitzin, a cellist and adoring fan of Beethoven, asked him to write several quartets. The composer agreed a year later, and commenced work on them two years after the *Missa Solemnis*, the *Diabelli Variations* and the Ninth Symphony.

They were published out of order, and only the Op. 127 was printed during his lifetime, in 1826; the rest were published posthumously, in 1827.

They were written in this order.

Op. 127: February 1825, which we will hear next spring by the
        St. Lawrence Quartet.
Op. 132: July 1825.
Op. 130: July-November 1825.
Op. 131: July 1826.
Op. 135: 1826.

This defines the so-called late period of Beethoven. Throughout his life, the composer knew that he was especially gifted, and felt he had a responsibility to use his gift in service to society. While always a somewhat rebellious sort of composer, he was now stretching the limits of musical forms and performance limits in length, volume and technique. Theodor Adorno called Beethoven's late period both subjective and objective. He says, "Objective is the fractured landscape, subjective is the light in which—alone—it glows into life. He does not bring about their harmonious synthesis. As the power of dissociation, he tears them apart in time, in order, perhaps, to preserve them for the eternal."

Franz Grillparzer, the great Austrian dramatist, captured the value of Beethoven when he gave a somewhat maudlin eulogy at the composer's funeral. He wrote in part:

> He was an artist, and who shall stand beside him? As the behemoth sweeps through the seas, he swept across the boundaries of his art, from the subtlest interweaving of willful artifices to that awesome point at which the fabric presses over into the lawlessness of clashing natural forces—he traversed all, comprehended everything.

Herr Grillparzer expresses a sentiment that is right on point, if a little overdone. He says that Beethoven "remained alone, because he found no second self. But until his death he preserved a human heart for all men, a father's heart for his own people, the whole world."

Basically, Beethoven was really no different from you and me. He suffered afflictions, loss, loneliness, and fear just as we all have—just as we all will. He also experienced, on occasion, the incredible joys that life can surprise us with. Beethoven was often both foolish and courageous. He is the everyman, taking from the highest highs and lowest lows. The magnificent difference was that he could brilliantly articulate these feelings in a musical language like no one else, and we have been able to appreciate this talent for decades. His musical gift was indeed passed on, and has lasted through the ages. Life, good and bad, in its truest form, should be shared.

That is what we are here for. For no matter our vocation, no matter our skills—whether it be a cable guy, a U.S. President, or a lowly arts administrator—our purpose is to do the best we can with what we have and to share our efforts with others. Connection, interaction, inspiration—these are the human building blocks that forge a society and make a civilization. And it can be a great civilization, if we are honest and dedicated.

Thank you and please…enjoy.

Variation 30

THE LAST WORD

*A pre-concert lecture that took place on October 20, 2012, prior
to a performance by the Parker String Quartet at the Irvine
Barclay Theatre.*

GOOD EVENING, LADIES and gentlemen, and welcome to the first concert
of the Philharmonic Society's 2012-13 season, and the first program in
our Laguna Chamber Music Series. I have prepared my remarks for this
evening in the form of an essay that I will read to you. This is my four-
teenth such reading. I am currently in the process of compiling a book
that entails 33 such essays of mine; this special publication will be given
to each subscriber household in January 2014. I am calling it *Beethoven:
The Late Great—Thirty-Three Personal Variations.* Having come up with
this idea more than a year ago, I have enjoyed reflecting back on my
career, and selected the number thirty-three because it is the same number as the *Diabelli Variations.* As for the composer, I don't think there
was a specified plan; Beethoven just kept writing the variations, one after
the other, and ended up with thirty-three. This number now seems a bit
daunting to me at times, but I have mapped the entire project on a time-
line. I will get there and you will get your book on time.

The Parker Quartet is offering us three works on tonight's program.

They conclude with Beethoven String Quartet No. 16 in F major, Op. 135, making this concert a part of the Society's *Beethoven: The Late Great* project. I will be happy to take a few questions at the end.

They open with *Fratres* by Estonian composer Arvo Pärt. Originally written for string quartet in 1977, the composer has since rearranged it for a number of instrumental combinations. The *Fratres* comes from the Latin word for "brothers," and it stands as a prime example of Pärt's so-called compositional style of *tintinnabuli*, or bells, using triad chords that are very suggestive of bells. The technique is derived from the writer's attitude, as Pärt explains:

> *Tintinnabulation* is an area I sometimes wander into when I am searching for answers—in my life, my music, my work. In my dark hours, I have the certain feeling that everything outside this one thing has no meaning. The complex and many-faceted only confuses me, and I must search for unity. What is it, this one thing, and how do I find my way to it? Traces of this perfect thing appear in many guises—and everything that is unimportant falls away. *Tintinnabulation* is like this.

Fratres is hauntingly beautiful, often used to open serious concerts, recitals, and chamber music as an appealing way of incorporating a new piece of music into a traditional program. It has a way of separating the listener from the reality that he or she entered the concert hall with, entering into a new realm within the music to be heard. Pärt writes a good deal of religious music, much of it choral. His minimalist style is well suited to reflective, meditative music. If you appreciate his sound, I suggest that you check out his work *Litany* for chorus and orchestra, as it is also quite beautiful. Like everything else, it can be found on Amazon.com. We presented that very piece on this stage during our Eclectic Orange Festival, more than ten years ago.

The second work on tonight's program is Benjamin Britten's Second String Quartet, written when the composer was 32 years old, and composed as an homage to Henry Purcell on the 250th anniversary of the great musician's birthday. And while it is already an emotional piece, it was further enhanced in its first performance by the fact that the pianist Britten and violinist Yehudi Menuhin had been touring the concentration camps after the end of the war, performing for the survivors. Britten's own hundredth anniversary comes up next year. It is said that, since the time of Purcell, he was England's greatest native-born composer.

This string quartet holds significant ranking in the twentieth century, along with the likes of those by Bartók and Shostakovich. Although he was English through and through, Britten's music was influenced by continental composers such as Mahler, Stravinsky, and Prokofiev. He had a unique voice that was quite different from other British composers, such as Elgar and Vaughan Williams.

The first movement, *allegro calmo senza rigore* (cheerful, calm without rigor), is in *sonata allegro* form. You can hear in it the influence of the aforementioned composers. The second movement, marked *vivace* (lively), has the exotic sound of a middle-European gypsy camp. The last movement, the true homage to Purcell, is a *Chacony*, a form used by Purcell where a repeated theme is treated by a number of variations. This is the most powerful movement of the quartet, and reminds us of the *Fratres*, a sort of a *chacony* itself, smartly programmed for performance by the Parker Quartet.

The String Quartet, Op. 135—Beethoven's last major work—premiered after his death. Knowing this influences how we accept the piece now, how we approach it.

I, for one, and I am sure I am not alone, read much into the decisions the composer has made. Is there symbolism, deeply coded messages of ideas, or something secret about its genesis? Probably not, but we can never know for sure. It is simply Beethoven going about his work in the usual late period style that we have been exploring. If he was indeed working in another sphere, as he seemed to demonstrate in the works following the *Diabelli Variations*, then we should accept it as such and simply enjoy it.

This quartet is in the normal four-movement setting, as was the Op. 127, the first of these so-called five late quartets that we will hear after the first of the year.

Beethoven chose to return to the standard four-movement format after having produced massive scale multi-movement creations that had allowed him to explore new creative paths that had been brewing for quite a while. This quartet is a bookend to the Op. 127, holding up the massive Op. 130 (including the *Grosse Fuge*), and Opp. 131 and 132. There are, again, sets of quirky ideas to be found in this one as are found in the other late quartets. We feel the presaging of things to come, of composers to be, which so often shows in a writer's later works; such a trend is clearly abundant in this quartet.

We know that this quartet is a part of Beethoven's later patterns by clues found in the very beginning of the first movement. The opening phrase seems more like the ending of a piece, rather than an introduction. It is as if Beethoven is musically clearing up an existing idea, as opposed to starting a new one. He is actually taking up a new musical exploration. Counterpoint flows freely. The "ending-like" beginning seems to lean against everything that follows, urging it gently onward to make us more anticipatory of a genuine conclusion. We follow every path put before us, knowing that we are safely on our way to a valid, meaningful somewhere. We are conscious of the road we are taking, and it is a delightful journey. There is no anger or strife. It is joyous without being overwhelmingly so. There is no particular message, just pleasure.

The second movement is like a mechanism of sorts. It works its gears in a merry way, seemingly pre-designed with just the trip of a switch to set it in motion. Beethoven uses a device from some of his past works, notably in the last movements of the Eighth and Ninth symphonies. He gives us an obliterating blast that stops or abruptly changes the motion of harmony, rhythm and volume. Its purpose is to allow the composer to go forward in whatever direction he chooses. It saves the time and hassle of progressing toward a change of key, mood, tempo, etc. It takes one big blast and, after the dust settles, the composer has free reign, in a manner very much like Stravinsky. This is an excellent example of the tail wagging the dog, a quite invigorating Beethoven in his over-the-top very best.

In the last movement of the Ninth, he employs an enormous F major chord blast as the culmination of a rather intricate passage of modulation and development. Is this chord the beginning of a new key, the relative major of the symphony's main key of D minor? Or is it something else completely? This is late Beethoven after all, so, of course, it is something else. It turns out to be a dominant chord. After the big choral and orchestral blast—this, the biggest in all of Beethoven's music—things calm and we now have a little Turkish band marching toward us in B-flat major. This brings yet another variation of the *Hymn to Joy*, a truly clever moment. What a completely wacky idea! Filmmaker Stanley Kubrick loved the Turkish march very much and used it in his film *A Clockwork Orange*. This was a controversial film of 1970 (still a little tough today) from the same man who brought us *2001: A Space Odyssey*. Come hear this blast on November 20, at our presentation of the Ninth Symphony in the grand Renée and Henry Segerstrom Concert Hall.

In the second movement of the Op. 135 quartet, a much smaller-scaled blast comes abruptly, seemingly halting the forward motion—but not really. The beat stays steady; the blast is really an exaggerated bit of syncopation. It represents the steel that the mechanism is made of, showing how the craftsman Beethoven saw great possibilities in such solid raw material.

Would there have been a Gustav Mahler without the influence of Beethoven? Doubtful. Mahler owed much to this man. The great expression of pathos that Mahler excelled in, the probing of the inner self—Beethoven was there first, nowhere more so than in the third movement of this quartet. Generally, one movement in each of these late quartets serves as the center, a sort of anchor. In the Op. 135, I believe it is this third movement. This "Mahler" effect is found throughout Beethoven's works, in many other immortal moments. But this is the last time that it happens. I'm not sure if Beethoven was aware of this at the time. There is a rather valedictory sense of melancholy that lingers in this movement, a farewell to the string quartet, to all forms of music or to life itself; this is something Mahler did over and over.

While this quartet, at times, seems a throwback to Haydn, Beethoven is in his full late period "enigmatic mood" in the final fourth movement. In the manuscript score, he titles this movement *Der schwer gefasste*

Entschluss, or "the difficult decision." To add to the mystery, in the manuscript over the slow introduction, Beethoven wrote the question, "Muss est sein?" (Must it be?), to which he answers in the ensuing allegro, "Est muss sein!" (It must be!) He reflects the question/answer idea in the music also—a three-note theme for the question and the answer in a three-note inversion of the question theme. Was he inserting the words to remind himself what to write later or is there something deeper?

The question is rather foreboding—dark and unsettled. It is repeated, as if Beethoven was ruminating its meaning, probing for an answer. The response, when it does come, is affirmative. It comes with an immense sense of relief. The "must it be?" question returns again, this time in a passage that could be drawn directly from Dmitri Shostakovich (who composed his foreboding, dark and unsettled music more than a century later, at the same time as Britten). After a transition, we return again to the "it must be" answer. A *pizzicato* passage, so characteristic of these late quartets, alerts us that a joyful ending is around the corner, much to our relief. While he did have plans and sketches for compositions beyond this quartet (including the replacement movement that he wrote for the *Grosse Fuge* published version of the Op. 130 quartet), it is interesting to think that he was summarizing his life and his work together in the last movement of the Op. 135, with the use of a question that he directly answers. In a voice that is similar to Hamlet's "To be or not to be," there is no "Conscience making cowards of us all," but rather a firmer answer saying that *this has all been worth it and he has done his best,* a fitting position to take looking back on one's life and accomplishments. Must it be? It must be! Beethoven, indeed, has the last word.

Please…enjoy.

CODA

Variation 31

Little Faith

Our rental car glided north toward the French Aveyron through cold December air. Dry specks of snowflakes flurried across the windshield, catching on the trees that arched over the highway. As she drove, Kaly paid close attention to the road ahead, watching carefully for black ice. Meanwhile, my anticipation of arriving at the village of Conques and visiting the abbey-church grew with each gentle curve. Passing Rodez, with its beautiful Notre Dame cathedral, I was disappointed that we couldn't take the time to stop. But we had to get to Conques before the church and its treasure were closed for the night. The next day, we were scheduled to make a "forced march" to Lalbenque to get in line at the black truffle market. This is another example of time being a precious commodity— or perhaps I just try to cram too much into twenty-four hours.

The French countryside changed dramatically as we drove. Entering the narrow canyon of the Ouche River, I noticed the water rushing along the left side of the highway. The village of Conques appeared in the mist, seemingly growing out of the cliffs. The Ouche had carved this spectacular site, wearing down the impenetrable rocks that blocked its way over thousands of years. Its coursing destiny continues to pound away, widening its path towards the Burgundy canal. We arrived at the Auberge St. Jacques, noting that we were the only guests. The village was deserted. Being that it was a few days away from Christmas, I assumed the town would be buzzing with excitement, but we had it to ourselves. Our first activity was a visit to the reliquary, which contains a portion of little Sainte Foy's skull in the museum vault—it is regarded as a dear treasure. It is a gold statue about three feet high, encrusted with precious jewels brought by pilgrims over the centuries to honor the Sainte. There was unbreakable glass around the statue. It was eerie for the two of us to be alone in the presence of an object that meant so much to multitudes through the centuries. We were in a special place. I was struck with a desire to write about Sainte Foy, learning about her miracles, and curious as to how her story parallels that of Beethoven.

Why am I so attracted to this place? I wasn't raised Catholic, rather a failed Methodist. I have always been intrigued with the saints, at first as a mocking Protestant, but now with greater understanding and empathy. Because Kaly and I would be living full time in France in the coming years, I read as much as I could about the Midi-Pyrénées, the place we now have a second home. I came across and read the book "Little Saint" by Hannah Green. In a combination travelogue and hagiography, Green movingly describes the village, the church, and the treasury that contains the reliquary of Sainte Foy. I was fascinated with the author's loving devotion to this Sainte and the resting place of her relics. Green's language, at times, is a little maudlin, but certainly her affection is heartfelt and very moving.

I have always questioned the power attributed to relics, as it goes against general logic. And my opinion is not unusual—many people have the same opinion—yet, in the same way, we treasure the remains of our own families and friends. Funeral services in the United States are a big business, an industry that has no economic downturn. We have cemeteries, mausoleums, memorial plaques and statues, ashes on mantles, personal bits and pieces in frames—drawers and boxes of lives lived and left behind. It must be because of our innate fear of the end, our panicked desire to hold on to one another, not to lose contact or be isolated at the final moments our lives. The lives of saints, contrasted, are stories of often painful sacrifice and ghastly violence. Perhaps, when contemplating our own ends, remembering the saints who had a much worse time of it gives us some consolation. As odd as it seems, their misery served a purpose. Every life, despite the drama or comedy, has fantastic meaning. Another common ground of saints is also their fame and the attributed ability to perform miracles for those who tend their remains and earnestly pray to them. Sainte Foy is a perfect and an early example. Her story is a dramatic one.

By the early fourth century, the Western Roman Empire was nearing complete downfall. In the next 150 years, the power would self-destruct. Rome was ruled by Diocletian, an emperor dedicated to eradicating Christians from the realm. By this time, Christianity was widely popular, having spread all across the European areas as we know them today; this included the French town of Agen. In this region, the proconsul was the very cruel Dacien, who ruthlessly carried out the pogrom mandated by Diocletian (coincidentally, Diocletian is the same emperor whose anti-Christian sentiments resulted in the persecution of the princess Theodora and her Christian-converted Roman lover Didymus in Handel's opera *Theodora*, which we'll be presenting at a future date). In October 303, Dacien arrived in Agen with his soldiers with the purpose of rooting Christians from the populace. The choice given to Christians was to honor the pagan goddess Diana or be tortured and killed. Men and women of all social ranks fled to the forests and mountains, including the wealthy parents of a twelve-year-old girl called Foy, or "Faith." They assumed that, because she was so young, she would be left alone. She stayed behind with a housekeeper.

Everyone who remained in the village, including Foy, was brought before a tribunal and questioned. When it was Foy's turn, Dacien was struck by her fairness and beauty, and he offered a rather simple passage out of the unfortunate fate that awaited the others. He told her that she would be let free if she would simply touch the crystals of incense that were used to be burned in honor of the goddess Diana. She replied, "There is but one God—He who came down from heaven for us." This greatly angered Dacien. He ordered Foy stripped and shackled on a brazier that was set over brightly glowing coals. But she suffered without a scream. The story goes that a white dove covered her nakedness with a cloud and made rain to put out the fire. Still not willing to recant her faith, and refusing to simply touch the crystals, she was beheaded with a swift gleaming sword—along with some sympathetic bystanders. This tragedy, from the distant mists of time, still reverberates in the hearts of those of have passed down the extraordinary story.

Again, what does this have to do with Beethoven? There is a corresponding story here that exemplifies martyrdom and the sacrifice for others and their future. Both of these stories concern miracles. Beethoven's end-of-life story is an equally dramatic one.

Blood is thicker than the rushing water of the Ouche River, but not a force powerful enough to overcome the cirrhotic scarring in the human liver left by abuse in the early nineteenth century. Because the blood cannot pass through these impenetrable wounds, the liver cannot filter toxins—especially those that contain lead. Such was the course of physically debilitating events that would haunt our esteemed composer, and there was no turning back. Many other calamities would then await Beethoven the invalid—most being extremely painful—that would ultimately lead to his death. This is a tragic journey that, once begun, cannot be managed or halted; the advice and care of a physician can, at a certain point, only do so much. There comes a time when the recommendations of a doctor are no longer applicable.

Beethoven's long experience with spirits brought adverse physical complications; his physician prescribed frozen alcoholic fruit punch to relieve his symptoms, which seemed to work for a while. He was then able to sleep and perspire, which he was told he needed to do. He felt better for a few days, but was again plagued with the return of pains of the head, the throat and irritability of the bowels. The doctor reconsidered his decision and, fearing Beethoven might revert to overindulging (as if it mattered at that point), he ordered the frozen fruit punch regimen to be stopped. The composer wept at the news.

After having his abdomen "tapped" four times in an effort to relieve his terrible edema, the doctors concluded that saving Beethoven would be impossible. During his last stage of painful melancholy, Beethoven was gifted a print of Haydn's birthplace in Rohrau by his friend and publisher Anton Diabelli. This brought him some happiness. The composer enjoyed showing it to visitors, saying it was the first house of the great composer. He also managed to send the Philharmonic Society in London the metronome markings of the Ninth Symphony that they had commissioned. He informed them by letter that he was composing a tenth symphony, the sketches of which were on his unorganized work desk. Meanwhile, he was in agony from unsuccessful medical treatments and very depressed. He said, "My days' work is finished." Referring to a physician who he imagined could soon relieve his suffering, he said, "His name shall be called 'Wonderful.'" This line was probably inspired from the works of Handel, whose scores Beethoven had received as a gift, just a short time before.

Five hundred years after Sainte Foy's incredible demise, the hermit Dadon formed a Benedictine community of monks in the valley where Conques is today, after receiving a bequest from Louis the Pious, the son of Charlemagne. With this new fortune, the community grew rapidly, and there was keen interest in the possibility of acquiring holy relics; these would attract pilgrims, walking on the Way of St. James. Sainte Foy's relics were stolen (or "discreetly transferred") by some monks coming from Conques, who carefully arranged to be guardians of the relics, which were secretly buried at the basilica outside of Agen, on the site of her execution. They embedded themselves into the community and waited ten years before they stole the relics. What followed was a harum-scarum attempt, directed by the bishop of Agen, to recover the relics that had found their way to Conques. Eventually, the objective was accomplished—moving the pilgrim action from Agen to Conques, seemingly unchallenged by the Agen bishop (a circumstance rather hard to believe). The bishop may have been ashamed of his and his cohort's ineptitude at losing possession of the relics in the first place, hoping that the loss would be obscured in the passage of time. But that would not be the case.

Anton Hüttenbrenner, an Austrian composer, was present the moment Beethoven died. He relates how, during a raging thunderstorm, Beethoven raised an angrily clenched fist for several seconds and then gave out his last breath. Hüttenbrenner wrote, "The genius of the great master of tones fled from this world of delusion into the realm of truth."

The most famous relic of Beethoven is a lock of his hair, clipped from his head by the prodigious 15-year-old composer Ferdinand Hiller. This lock had an adventurous travel experience, as once did Ste. Foy's skull fragments. The young Hiller arrived in Vienna with his teacher and one-time rival of Beethoven, Johann Nepomuk Hummel, who was Haydn's successor at the Esterházy estates. The pair had traveled from Weimar when they heard that Beethoven was in his final struggle. They were eager to speak with him; Hummel believed that such a meeting would further inspire the *Le Savant Hiller*, which of course it did. They made several visits to the composer's deathbed, and returned again the day after Beethoven died. Hiller asked for, and was granted, permission to take a lock of Beethoven's hair. He had brought a pair of scissors and a small oval locket frame for the occasion, anticipating the approval. Others had clipped samples of his hair, as was a common practice of the time.

Hiller moved to Paris the following year, and became a great friend of another passionate Beethoven devotee, Hector Berlioz, who was astounded that Hiller had actually spoken with Beethoven and, of course, was overwhelmed by the fact that he had a locket containing the master's hair. I write about more about Berlioz's Beethoven enthusiasm in another of my variations, "Berlioz." Hiller was involved in a social group of young composers that not only included Berlioz, but also Liszt, Mendelssohn, and Chopin.

The clipped lock of hair traveled with its custodian far more extensively than Beethoven the man ever did while living—Frankfurt, Weimar, Leipzig, Paris, Florence, Rome, Dresden, and finally Cologne. And that was only the beginning of its journeys.

Ferdinand Hiller became a well-known composer in the nineteenth century—also known as an organizer and a respected teacher. But his compositions were rarely played in the twentieth century, limited to just a few student pieces. Despite his excellent start, he didn't have the lasting genius for the time-honored music compositions of his friends. Before his death, Hiller gave the hair to his son Paul on his 30th birthday; Paul then settled in Cologne and had a successful music career.

Paul died in 1934, a time of growing unrest for Jews in Germany. Members of the Jewish Hiller family likely moved to Denmark, as did a number of North German Jewish families. Even though the story becomes hazy at this point, it is for certain that the Beethoven locket made it to the northern Danish port village of Gilleleje, the end of the line for Danish trains traveling north on the island of Zealand.

The Nazis were not in conflict with the government of Denmark, and life went on there as normal during the first years of the war—even for the Jews. When the fortunes of Germany began to change—defeat in Russia, Africa, and failed attempts in bombing Britain into submission, life took a change for the Jewish people in Denmark. On the morning of September 30, 1943, Rabbi Marcus Melchior made a chilling announcement to the congregation at the Copenhagen Synagogue:

Last night I received word that tomorrow the Germans plan to raid Jewish homes throughout Copenhagen to arrest all the Danish Jews for shipment to concentration camps. They know that tomorrow is Rosh Hashanah and our families will be home. You must pass the word to all that are Jewish. Speak to your Christian friends and tell them to warn the Jews. You must do this immediately, within the next few minutes, so that two or three hours from now everyone will know what is happening. By nightfall tonight, we must all be in hiding.

The Danes are a great people. They went to great lengths to hide their Jewish neighbors in attics, country houses, and hospitals, in case the Gestapo ever decided to look for them. Sadly, the Germans came right away, responding to the reports of large transit activity, with Jews fleeing the country. Speculation began as a large, mysterious transport ship appeared in the harbor; the Danes quickly made underground plans to move the Jews the short distance across the water to Sweden, a neutral country in the conflict. 8,000 Jews were saved—an astonishing and unprecedented effort.

One thing is certain—the lock of hair made it to Denmark—but by what means, it is still unclear. A certain Dr. Kay Fremming was very active in moving the Jews to Sweden, as well as tending to those within the country who were ill. Prior to the Gestapo's capturing of the remaining Jews, someone gave the locket to Dr. Fremming before boarding a boat in Gilleleje that departed for Sweden. According to his wife Marta, it was given in appreciation for the doctor's courage, and in deep appreciation for the lives that he spared. Due to the grave danger of the times, names were withheld for security reasons. The identities of those who gave him the locket will probably never be known. After Dr. Fremming's death in 1969, Martha gave the locket to their adopted daughter Michelle, who then learned about the locket for the first time.

While the locket had spent its years with the Fremmings in a locked desk drawer, Michelle displayed it on the wall—not as an homage to Beethoven, but to her deceased father, Dr. Kay Fremming, and his courage during one of Denmark's most critical times. While the doctor was an amateur flautist and avid record collector, music was not Michelle's thing. After the death of her mother, Michelle and her younger son, Thomas, decided it might be a good idea to sell the locket—the extra money was much needed. Michelle was a widow and times were tough, and she hoped that the locket might go to someone who cared about its musical legacy. After sending it to Sotheby's in London, she designated that if it did not go for the £1,800 minimum auction price she specified, she would happily return it to her wall. In December of 1994, it was sold to an American party; enter Mr. Ira F. Brilliant, and another interesting story.

In August 1996, I was in Salzburg with a number of our Philharmonic Society patrons on our first of many annual pilgrimages to summer festivals in Europe. I was also on the lookout for outstanding music attractions to bring to Orange County, as it was a perfect showcase of talent. In particular, I wanted to experience conductor John Eliot Gardiner and the Orchestre Révolutionnaire et Romantique and his

Monteverdi Choir. The previous year, they had issued a stunning set of recordings of the complete nine Beethoven symphonies, performed on period instruments. This was a great opportunity for one to hear the symphonies in the timbre, pitch, and *tempi* that Beethoven intended. Being the Beethoven nut that I am, I was determined to figure out a way to bring John Eliot and his musicians to the West Coast (for the first time)—the only question was *how*. But they were without artistic representation in the United States, which would be a necessity for a project this enormous. From Salzburg, I phoned Neil Benson at what is now Opus 3 Artists in New York, saying I needed an agent. He was shocked, because it is usually the reverse. Agents are always hounding me, wanting gigs for their artist roster.

I would have to formulate a careful approach to the Orchestre Révolutionnaire et Romantique/Monteverdi organization. The rehearsals at the Salzburg Festival are closed to the public, and, in 1996, I was unknown to the festival. The only contact I had was the festival director, Gerard Mortier. He was quite busy, and I wouldn't be seeing him for a number of days, so I was afraid that John Eliot and troops would be packed and on their way home to London by that time.

One afternoon, I was sitting in Triangel, a local watering hole. It was a relaxed scene, me writing postcards while enjoying sausage and beer. I overheard a conversation in English a few tables away, and noticed two gentlemen, one who had a distinctive Northern Irish accent. They were talking about trumpets, enjoying the same sausage and beer. I assumed that they had to be the trumpet section of the ORR, and thought it was a perfect opportunity. The Irish gentleman, Michael Harrison, remains a wonderful friend to this day. Being a fellow brass player, it was easy to enter into the conversation—even more helpful that I offered to buy their meals. Soon enough, I was walking with them past the festival security, right into the rehearsal.

This set in motion their visit to Orange County in May of 1999, where they performed all nine of Beethoven's symphonies on period instruments over five performances. We organized an exhibit of Beethoven-era documents and instruments at the Bowers Museum, on loan from the

Beethoven Center at San Jose State University and America's Shrine to Music at the University of South Dakota. Two people made this exhibit possible: the first was Marge Rawlins (a graduate of University of South Dakota and a native of Vermillion, the university's home). She had made major gifts to America's Shrine to Music, where they had amassed a major collection of historical instruments, especially those of Beethoven's time. Andre Larson was their director and a tremendous asset to this project. I was connected with the Beethoven Center in San Jose through our major project sponsor, the Leo Freedman Foundation, and its trustee, Sharon Lesk. Her mother was an Arizona neighbor of real estate investor Ira F. Brilliant, who was a passionate collector of Beethoven goods and first editions. He and a Dr. Che Guevara (not the revolutionary) had purchased the lock of Beethoven's hair at the Sotheby auction. Through Sharon, I met both Ira and Bill Meredith, director of the Beethoven Center, where the lock is now kept. The hair caused quite a sensation, and Martin Russell wrote a book that also spawned a wonderful documentary. The peak of excitement was having the hair sample DNA tested.

Two lessons were learned. First, it was authentic—the DNA matched samples of Beethoven's skull taken in 1888 when his body was moved to the *Zentralfriedhof* (Central Cemetery) in Vienna. To me, the most significant, was the second finding, the fact that Beethoven's system was free of the narcotic laudanum when he died. Laudanum, an opiate, was administered to terminal patients in the nineteenth century to relieve pain, as morphine is used today. It was commonly given by physicians of the time, who were very limited in what they could do to improve the condition of a patient and, at best, provide comfort. The drug also clouded the senses, a condition that would have made it impossible for Beethoven to work, much less create such late life masterpieces. This meant that he rejected taking laudanum, choosing a clear head over unbearable physical pain. This was truly a heroic act, and civilization is much better for it. Beethoven's late great creative transcendence is miracle enough. Now with the knowledge that was gained from analyzing his hair, his story is now beyond remarkable, completely inspirational.

The theme of this essay is *making choices*. This is part of the human experience for us all, and decision-making can be extremely difficult. Sometimes we choose wisely, other times poorly—sometimes very poorly. And for whom—others, ourselves, those we love, those we do not know? I always believe in taking the high road. But how high? Believing in something is one thing; doing something about it is yet another. Sainte Foy had little time to consider her choice, and was without the depth of real life experience. Was she doing the right thing for herself, alone? For her family? Did she understand her faith and the ramifications that deeply? She was very young, so I imagine she thought, "How bad could this really get?" And, "Where are my parents anyway?"—she was a pre-teen, after all. But make a choice she did, with probably no thought to how we might regard her or her decision 1,700 years later—if at all.

Beethoven made choices as well. Certainly his circumstances at the time were nowhere near that of Foy's. His terrible dilemma was that he had to decide how to suffer through the end of his lifetime: to decide whether to exist in a peaceful cloud or battle on with a clear creative spirit, even in the last hours when he knew he could work no longer. Unlike Foy, he *was* thinking about his legacy on the world, and he had something very important to say. As with Foy, it came down to a moral choice. It somehow makes it slightly easier for us when others have bravely met and prevailed in such challenges before we have to. A little faith in one's moral impulses can make all the difference.

December 2011
Guizerix, France

Variation 32

A Tale of A Thousand and One Nights (and Weekends)

*En te levant le matin, rappel-toi combien précieux est le privilege
de vivre, de respirer, d'être heureux.*
—Marc Aurèle, *Pensées pour moi-même*

I am beginning a new transition. My life is about to go from third gear
to fourth, with hopes for a much later fifth; if I'm lucky, I'll have a sixth
before I have to park, long term. I don't look at this period as retirement
so much as an era of doing *what I want to do when I want to do it*. I'll have
time to enjoy my marriage, entertain family and friends, travel, garden,
swim, cook, read, write, improve my miserable French, learn Beethoven's
Hammerklavier Sonata, hike the Pyrénées, and keep my mind open for
any new adventures. Henry David Thoreau's advice to "Go confidently
in the direction of your dreams. Live the life you've imagined" is my new
mantra, along with Marcus Aurelius' guidance, written above. He says,
"When you get up in the morning, remind yourself how valuable is the
privilege to live, to breathe, to be happy."

For the greater part of the past 42 years, I have been in the music
business—both on the stage as a horn player and on an administrative staff, with some teaching on the side. 80% of horn playing in an
orchestra is fairly boring, with the remaining 20% being extraordinarily

wonderful—both challenging and extremely worthwhile. Of course, any job takes time and commitment. The difference in the music industry is the actual time obligation. Working hours take place when everyone else is at leisure; you work weekends, holidays, evenings, early morning, and straight through meals. The end of your day can be quite late, with activities often painfully early the next morning. You work many nights and weekends, when everyone else is off.

In this line of work, you often miss birthdays, anniversaries, and on the rare occasion, your daughter's dance recital. One season in Fort Worth, the orchestra was preparing an all-Wagner concert that we were about to take to the San Antonio Festival. I was the orchestra manager, as well as one of the horn players. Our conductor was the late Horst Stein, a brilliant—and often cranky—conductor from Germany. He had been hired by the San Antonio Festival to lead us in a program of *Prelude to Die Meistersinger*, selected arias, and *Die Walküre* (Act I) on the second half. Among the singers were sopranos Janis Martin and Karan Armstrong, with tenor Siegfried Jerusalem—an incredible collection of singers. Not too shabby. I think Maestro Stein was dreading working with us Texans, assuming that we were far below the standards of the Bayreuth Festival Orchestra that he was used to. Ultimately, we proved ourselves well-qualified for the task. Nevertheless, the rehearsals were tense. He even had an assistant who would stand behind any orchestra member who seemed to be having trouble with their part. Furthermore, the assistant obsessively watched over the harp section, which was very unnerving for them as they aren't the most secure beings even under the best circumstances.

The orchestra size for the hour-long first act of *Die Walküre* is gargantuan. It requires oodles of woodwinds and a huge brass section, including eight horns—four of which double on Wagner tubas. It was difficult enough to play horn, and even more so to manage the rehearsal timing because of the vast amount of musicians involved and the looming possibility of overtime (which, with that size orchestra, could be a financial disaster). You didn't want the extras to sit around waiting to rehearse (not playing) and being paid for it. The schedules must be strictly adhered to. In this instance, I had to be very firm. Unfortunately,

Maestro Stein and I did not get off to a great start. One of our extra clarinets was a student and she couldn't make a particular morning rehearsal due to her college finals. Her part was small and simple, so I didn't think it would be a big deal. But when I approached the Maestro with this information, he had a conniption and accused me of "trying to take over." He went so far so to call me Joseph Stalin. *Wow!* I've been called a lot of names in my life, but never a tyrannical Russian dictator.

Stein went to his dressing room, stating if we didn't have the clarinetist at the rehearsal, he would cancel the entire engagement. Imagine the amount of grief that would cause, not to mention that I would likely be out of a job. The Maestro spent a half hour pacing back and forth, steaming mad in his private room (after a very dramatic door-slamming). There was no way to get the girl to the rehearsal. Personnel Manager Don Thomas got on the phone and located a last-minute substitute player. We were lucky the college girl had left her music on the stand, or disaster would have ensued. With timing that could have not been possibly worse, I had purposely placed myself as the eighth horn in the section to be more inconspicuous, because I was planning on taking off the next night's rehearsal to attend my nine-year-old daughter Courtney's dance recital. Naturally, I had not shared this with the Maestro. After having emerged from his dressing room (not unlike the dragon Fafner in *Siegfried*), I told him we had a substitute clarinetist but stated that since we now had to pay two players, we would let him choose the one he wanted. There was more rage, but reluctantly he gave in to Stalin's request. The thought of asking permission for time off for myself was clearly out of the question—you pick your battles, I guess. Courtney forgave her daddy and has been in dozens and dozens of shows since; I have made a conscious effort to make as many as possible.

Woody Allen says that 90% of success is just showing up. In the music business, showing up 100% of the time is a minimum requirement—and this means having your music and instrument in hand. The devil lurks in the details and is always ready to make an entrance—along with his sidekick, "La Catastrophe." In my first season running the Chattanooga Symphony and Opera Association I hired a young lady to be our production manager. She was already our prop person for the opera and was extremely reliable, which is very important. You don't want a character on stage lunging forth with a knife to the sound of a gunshot. I told her the biggest rule of all was to *never assume anything*. You can probably see where this is going.

The symphony orchestra had a run-out (when you don't stay the night) to McMinnville, Tennessee, which was in the Central Time Zone, as opposed to Eastern Time, in Chattanooga. We had a guest conductor for the concerts that week. My parents were visiting from Texas, so Dad rode along with the conductor and me as we drove to McMinnville. We had left early because I had a new production manager (NPM) and I wanted to see how she was doing. Dad wanted to see his son in action as an executive director of an orchestra—my first such gig.

Upon arrival, we were greeted by a collection of miserable people— two musicians, the orchestra librarian, and my NPM. Seeing as how the latter two were in tears, I went first to the musicians. One had dented his car; I asked him how he was and he said he was fine, so I moved on to take care of the next problem. The other musician had something caught in his teeth. I gave him the toothpick from my Swiss Army knife and told him I wanted it back clean. Next? I dealt with the remaining two young ladies. Meanwhile, my dad was loving all of this drama. He saw the makings of a story he would tell for the rest of his life (which he did).

It seems when the equipment truck was loaded back at the rehearsal hall in Chattanooga, a green trunk was not included. This trunk is usually where we put music for the next pops concert. Our NPM assumed we wouldn't need it, thinking it would be unnecessary to bring parts we were not going to use anyway and risk the possibility of losing them. What she did not know is that the librarian put all of the trumpet, trombone, tuba, and percussion folders in this trunk because they wouldn't fit with the music in other trunk. Now, when one of the pieces on the program is Respighi's *Pines of Rome* (which extensively features the brass section) and you have no music, you have a very big problem on your hands.

What to do? While trying to find a solution, I asked the conductor and the soprano soloist (we were also doing Barber's *Knoxville: Summer*

1915 and Strauss' *Four Last Songs*) to do a pre-concert talk to the sold-out audience of more than a thousand—who would be arriving shortly. This would kill some time and the folks would love it. I desperately needed to buy more time. One of the violinists had the music to the Franck violin sonata and one of the orchestra members was her pianist. That would buy us some more quality time. One of the clarinetists said he and other orchestra members regularly played Dixieland. That idea might do, except that it was out of line with the overall presentation and might confuse or frustrate the audience. I didn't know the cultural scene in McMinnville very well.

I could temporarily halt disaster but had no idea how to control the situation. I knew that I would have to bring the presenter into the conversation, and I was dreading it. The big question: how would I locate the music we needed? I could call my secretary Linda Morris, who lived with her husband Hal on Lookout Mountain, which overlooks Chattanooga. She could go to the office, get the rehearsal hall key, and go downtown to find the music. That would work, if only I could get her on the phone. Meanwhile, the orchestra members were hanging out in the band hall. There were no cell phones in those days, so I prayed I could get a long distance line on the band director's office phone line. Fortunately, I was able to, but had no idea how to explain it all to Linda on the other end. What would I tell her? It was 6pm here and 7pm there. The concert was at 8pm. Driving here would take two hours. The plan could work but it was beginning to pour down rain. It would be awfully dangerous and a lot to ask. The road was treacherous, going up and down hill at a 12 degree grade in some places. My imagination ran wild with options—maybe the Tennessee Highway Patrol could pick up the trunk and speed it to McMinnville. Of course, if they were called because of an accident (very likely in this weather), they would have to respond and our trunk might not get here in time. Then another idea came to mind: what if the trunk flew here?

I rummaged through the band director's desk (thankfully he was not there) and found a white pages book. I called the McMinnville Airport and was connected to a guy who was in charge. He was not only the air controller, but also managed operations (including manning the snack bar and sweeping up). He was there by himself and was about to leave for the evening. "Ain't much going on here tonight with this rain," he said. I explained our desperate situation as calmly as I could; he responded, "I might could put out a radio call and see if anybody is flying this way who hadn't passed Chattanooga yet, but it's gonna cost ya." "How much?" I asked. He replied, "I reckon around $200." "Done! Please call me back if you find someone," I countered. Trembling, I hung up the phone. He called a few minutes later, "I got an old boy who can be at the Chattanooga airport in ten minutes." A miracle! I said, "Tell him we will have the cargo at the airport 20 minutes from now." This plan just might work!

I got Linda back on the phone. She and Hal were already wired to take part in this potentially disastrous adventure. I told her to call me when she arrived at the rehearsal hall, and noted, "Let's make sure each folder that we need is there. Don't worry about the parts for the pops concert. Leave them in there. Take the whole trunk." She called back and confirmed.

They were at the airport looking for the pilot when they heard someone call out, "Hal?" Someone there was walking by and recognized Hal. Her husband Hal was Mr. Chattanooga, a well-known and very passionate member of the Chamber of Commerce. He was deeply loved in the community and he knew everybody—including this fellow—at the airport. Hal asked, "What are you doing here?" The fellow responded, "I was flying from Atlanta and some guy in McMinnville asked if I would land here and pick up a trunk." Hal and Linda were astounded. Hal went on to explain that they had been cozily relaxing in front the fire at their [great] home on the side of Lookout Mountain, enjoying the rain, when the Symphony's new executive director phoned. Hal and his friend starting catching up on old times, when Linda nudged her husband to make it snappy. What are the odds that you could reach up into the stormy ether in the southeastern United States and pluck a plane out of the sky that had a pilot that Hal knew? The trunk was put on the plane but a new flight plan had to be filed—yet another delay.

Meanwhile, back at the McMinnville High School Auditorium, I ask

Dad to go talk to the presenter to see if they could locate a few teenage guys to go with him to the airport to get the trunk. "They will know how to get there, here are the keys. Be careful—and thanks."

Now I was really starting to get worried. Yes, we had a plane, and we were waiting on news from the airport. The Dixieland band was playing "When The Saints Go Marching In" for the umpteenth time. I had made my public apologies to the audience. Now, standing at the backstage door looking across the parking lot through the downpour, I thought, *Dad, I need you and that music here now!*

And then they arrived, soaking wet. The presenter called off the Dixieland music (much to the relief of the players and the audience), announcing that the symphony concert would begin momentarily after a brief intermission. I met with the conductor and we agreed to cut the *Four Last Songs* of Strauss. Undoubtedly, it would have been a McMinnville premiere, but these people had been sitting for a long time, and it was already 9:15pm. The "second half" would be Egmont, the Barber, and *The Pines,* straight through.

(Dad was really having fun now, adding to his growing story.)

I had noticed, when in front of the audience explaining the situation earlier, that there were a couple of empty seats in the middle of the first row. By the time we got to *The Pines of Rome* they were occupied by an elderly couple, seats saved for them by their children. The orchestra played the brilliant pines of the Villa Borghese, segueing with the pines near a catacomb. The pines of the *Janiculum* came next, which blends into the pines of the Appian Way. A Roman legion is approaching from the distance through the fog getting closer and closer. We hear the drums and fanfares growing louder and louder and know this is going to have a big ending. Respighi is a spectacular orchestrator, and this is his best moment.

I also noticed that, while the music was about to reach its climax, the elderly couple got up from their seats and began a slow move towards the exit. The moment was surreal. Here, as the legions are arriving at Rome's Capitoline Hill in triumph with the full orchestra blaring, it all seemed to be perfectly and dramatically choreographed for the exit of this man with his cane and delicate wife. Couldn't they have waited? Didn't they understand what we had just been through?

So Dad had his story and, to my knowledge, the Chattanooga Symphony has not been invited back to McMinnville. I have many such stories and it is good to finally write some of them down so I won't have to keep repeating them. The lesson I learned from this experience was my own—*never assume anything*! I should have been at the rehearsal hall helping my NPM to pack the trunks, showing her the ropes first hand.

Do I have some regrets as a presenter for the Philharmonic Society? One is that we never got to have the Boston Symphony. Despite my best efforts, it never worked out to have Sir Mark Elder and the Hallé Orchestra. Pianist Maurizio Pollini almost made it here. My holy grail was to bring conductor Nicholas Harnoncourt, despite the fact that he hates to travel. When you think about it, why should he? He has his own early music ensemble and regularly conducts the Vienna Philharmonic and at the Salzburg Festival. Why leave Austria? I did hear him in Amsterdam conducting the Concertgebouw, where I asked him to consider coming to California. He responded, "Why don't you bring your patrons to Salzburg this summer?" I assured him that we already had, and would continue to do so. No further luck.

What will I miss, aside from the near catastrophes, union and artist negotiations, budget writing, rubber chicken dinners, cocktail parties, speeches, a few deficits, cash flow crunches, and late meetings—along with the exhausting nights and weekends? It's too soon to tell. It will be nice not to have the year divided into "the season" and "off-season," which is pretty much the way it has been organized most of my life. I look forward to there being *four* seasons ushered in by weather, birds, sunlight, crops, and the animals. These days, I don't even have to wear a watch—but, of course, I am still addicted to the reminder calendar on my iPhone. I want to tell the time of day by observing which birds show up. You can do it and it's very cool. There will be so much more to discover from here on that I can't imagine. And I want the option to do nothing—or everything.

Variation 33

BOWS

Managing is getting paid for home runs someone else hits.
—CASEY STENGEL

PART OF MY horn-playing career I spent in the orchestra pit of Casa Mañana summer musicals in Fort Worth, Texas. It got to be kind of a drag, especially when you had a multi-week run of a show that was boring to play, such as *The Sound of Music*—too many nuns and kids, as well as too many sustained whole notes for the horn. To relieve the monotony in the pit, we quietly substituted new lyrics such as doe, a deer, a blank-blank deer—or worse. This was good for a lot of laughs (we didn't include the conductor). The guys in orchestra were fun and we looked forward to our after-show beers together (including the conductor). At least we all had a steady gig.

After you play a bunch of these musicals, their pattern of construction begins to emerge. Successful shows were successful for a reason—they were all the same. There was always the strong first-half closer, and my favorite part was the Exit Music, especially if the show was boring to play. When the audience was finally out the door, we were out the stage door.

The penultimate number in every show is called "Bows." This is when all the cast members come out on stage in reverse order of importance to the evening's proceedings. They accept the audience's roaring approval. It is always a happy moment, no matter how things go in the previous two-and-a-half hours. This process is carefully choreographed and rehearsed. It is made to look spontaneous to match the audience's applause and cheers, which are supposed to be spontaneous. Because the Casa Mañana stage was in the round, the exuberant hand-in-hand bowing of the entire cast was more like a rotating version of Winslow Homer's *Snap the Whip*. And yes, there was the occasional tumbling chorus member.

I have chosen the title "Bows" for the final thirty-third personal variation as opposed to the standard "Acknowledgements." I am certainly acknowledging all of the people who made this book possible, as well as those who were integral to the Philharmonic Society's *Beethoven: The Late Great* project. Unlike the normal bow routine, I am thanking people in groups of activities. I first want to sincerely thank those individuals who helped make all of this possible, whose names I have failed to recognize below. Thanks, and sorry!

I will continue with those who were part of getting this idea going. The first person would be David Lieberman, a highly respected performing arts manager who lives in Costa Mesa. David and I have worked together for years. He is always tempting me with fascinating artists and projects that he knows appeal to my weakness for eclectic performance and interesting stuff. A few years ago, he was working on a deal to tour a Broadway show he thought I might be interested in. It was a play by Moisés Kaufman called *33 Variations,* starring Jane Fonda. David and I attended a performance together in New York. He thought it might be appropriate for the Philharmonic Society to present the play because of the connection to Beethoven.

While watching the play, my mind went further. Certainly it would be great to present this play—our folks would love it—but what would *really* be great would be to present the play along with the major late works of Beethoven, starting with the 33 *Diabelli Variations* all the way through to the late quartets, over a period of months. After the show, I met Jane Fonda, congratulated her on her performance, and told her my idea. She liked it. Whether she did or didn't, I was already committed in my heart to make such a project happen.

As it turned out, we didn't have to present *33 Variations* because it had a run at the Ahmanson Theatre in Los Angeles. Another friend, agent Adam Friedson, introduced me to Moisés Kaufman himself, who was directing the Los Angeles production of his play. He was inspiring. We had a terrific conversation. Heather Cromleigh from the Philharmonic Society staff arranged for a bus to take many of our patrons to a matinée performance of the play. We were off and running. Thanks to all thus far.

If you are planning to present the late works of Ludwig van Beethoven, you must do the last five string quartets. They can be scheduled over five programs that contain additional works, or they can each be played by a different string quartet and spread over a couple seasons. The Philharmonic Society has a chamber music subscription series, so this is not a problem. The critical pieces of late Beethoven that you have to do are the *Missa Solemnis* and the Ninth Symphony—those are the big ones. We could have used local groups; however, I had another idea. I thought it might be possible and fitting to schedule the same musicians who performed the complete nine symphonies for us in 1999. It was, and we did.

I would like to thank Sir John Eliot Gardiner and his wife, Isabella, the Orchestre Révolutionnaire et Romantic, the Monteverdi Choir and soloists Elisabeth Meister, soprano; Jennifer Johnson, mezzo-soprano; Michael Spyres, tenor; and Matthew Rose, bass; for splendid performances of these two key works, as well as colleagues Clive Gillinson of Carnegie Hall and Emil Kang of the University of North Carolina at Chapel Hill. The participation of Clive and Emil as presenters was critical to making this tour work. I would also like to thank David Foster and his team at Opus 3 Artists in New York, and Terry Dwyer, President of Segerstrom Center for the Arts, for respectively arranging for the artists and providing a world-class concert hall for these concerts. Another London ensemble, the Philharmonia Orchestra conducted by Esa-Pekka Salonen, performed a fabulous Beethoven/Berlioz program as a part of our project. Thanks to them as well. Special thanks must go to Warren Coy, Vice Chairman for Concerts on our Board of Directors. He led the Concerts Committee and arranged for the board to approve the project.

Thanks to Jonathan Marriott, Allison Heinrichs, and Randy Polevoi for selling all of the tickets, and thanks to our Director of Finance, Chau Schwendimann, and her associates, Roan Alombro and Patrick Le, for keeping the money straight.

I asked pianist Marino Formenti to learn the *Diabelli Variations.* He did and gave his first public performance of this masterpiece for us. Thank you, Marino, for your cooperation, brilliance, and sheer guts.

Those five string quartet ensembles we needed were the Takács, St. Lawrence, Parker, Brentano, and (after this book is published) the Mandelring. Each ensemble had to alter its planned touring repertoire to accommodate us, for which we are most grateful. I especially appreciate the artist managers, Seldy Cramer, David Rose, Pat Winter, and Susan Endrizzi, for their cooperation. All of the scheduling and producing of all related programs was handled by our artistic administrator, Jeff Mistri, who has now left us to do the same work for the Fort Worth Symphony. We send him best wishes.

All of the late quartets were performed at the Irvine Barclay Theatre. Its president, Doug Rankin, has run a very high-quality operation there for more than twenty years. It is the perfect venue for chamber music as well as theater, dance, film and the occasional opera. I am grateful for The Barclay and what it means to our cultural community.

To complete our survey of late, great Beethoven from the *Diabelli Variations* onward, we included the Bagatelles, Op. 126, for piano. They are wonderful but not that difficult, easy enough for me to play, which I did for a number of meetings of our twenty-three volunteer Committees scattered around Orange County. I talked about the pieces and late Beethoven as you have read in personal variation number six. The ladies of the Philharmonic Committees raise the money and organize youth programs that reach more than 150,000 children a year. They are extraordinary and can never be thanked enough. Along with Heather Cromleigh, Madeline Fields of our staff gives them great administrative support.

One of the annual presentations organized by The Committees is called Concerts for Fifth Graders. These programs have been going on so long that we are now performing for children whose grandparents came to our first Concerts for Fifth Graders. As we do every year, the Orange County Youth Symphony Orchestra, conducted by Daniel Alfred Wachs, performs eight concerts to 1,800 fifth graders at a time. The objective is to make sure the kids get an understanding of the orchestral families of instruments. We always include an appearance by the Anaheim Ballet with directors Lawrence and Sarma Rosenberg. This season, the kids will get a large dose of Beethoven as well. South Coast Repertory actor John-David Keller will be on stage portraying Ludwig van Beethoven, and the fifth graders get to sing the final "Ode to Joy" from Beethoven's Ninth with the live orchestra. We have done this before. It is truly a joy to behold, witnessing the transfer of culture from one generation to another. The fifth graders sing in an English adaption of the German by one of our super volunteers, Marilynn Mandershied. It goes as follows:

> Sing of joy that fills the heavens, bright as stars and warm as
>   sun…
> Magically beneath its gentle wings our voices sing as one.
> We can all be friends to each other, freedom for all the world
>   we sing.
> Look for good above the stars and find the joy that goodness
>   brings.

Pretty cool, eh? Our education director Rita Major and a slew of our volunteers put this all together. A bevy of accolades to all!

To do all that is described above you might think would be enough. But no! One must engage as much of the community as one can when dealing with the late, great Beethoven and keeping his legacy alive for generations. Others before us handed down his legacy and it is our obligation to pass it on. Beethoven would approve.

In addition to the concerts, we will offer two exhibitions, a film, an art installation and, of course, this book.

When you are endeavoring to hit it out of the park, you must be patient and wait for a good pitch. Be ever on the lookout for serendipity and take full advantage of it when it comes along. A couple of years ago at one of my annual Saturday Texas Barbecues, my friend Peter Conlon was at the house. He told me that he suddenly took early retirement from the County Superior Court when he realized he would be better off retired than still continuing to work. He was a financial analyst administrator and a great planner. He wondered if we needed any volunteers in the Philharmonic Society office—Peter was willing to stuff envelopes or whatever we needed doing. An idea suddenly hit me, and I told him to come in and see me on Monday.

I needed someone to coordinate our *Beethoven: The Late Great* ideas and to make them happen. Peter Conlon was the man for the job. Thanks to his efforts, we have an exhibition opening at the Bowers Museum. We always appreciate the continuing Bowers partnerships with visionary Peter Keller and his staff. It will contain a lock of Beethoven's hair, Beethoven first editions, and other items from the Ira F. Brilliant Center for Beethoven Studies. I want to give special thanks to its director, William Meredith, and curator Patricia Stroh. Peter Conlon also arranged for us to have some manuscripts for the exhibit, on loan from the Library of Congress. We would like to thank Rachel Waldron and Ray White from that esteemed institution.

In addition to the Bowers exhibit, we are presenting an exhibition of cartoons by Charles Schulz we are calling "Beethoven and Schroeder." Peter Conlon arranged all of this, along with scheduling an interview for me with Jean Schulz, Charles's widow. The Charles Schulz Museum is a must-see if you are in the Bay area. Randy Polevoi is playing the first movement of the Hammerklavier Sonata to be loaded into a Disklavier to accompany the exhibition. Thanks to Randy, Yamaha, and the Charles Schulz Museum.

Peter also coordinated our Beethoven post-dinner concert at Britta's Cafe after the St. Lawrence String Quartet performance. Many thanks to Britta Pulliam.

Peter was instrumental in tracking down film director Kerry Candaele, whose documentary *Following the Ninth: In the Footsteps of Beethoven's Final Symphony* will be a part of *Beethoven: The Late Great* and also an entry in the 2014 Newport Beach Film Festival. Prior to this, I had found Kerry's website for the film, on which he was trying to complete the documentary's funding. With the generosity of Phil and Mary Lyons, we were able to help him finish his masterpiece, which will be available for all to see in April 2014. Thanks Phil, Mary, and Kerry. A special acknowledgement goes to Gregg Schwenk, Todd Quartararo, Amanda Salazar, and the Orange County Film Society for their splendid cooperation. Kerry's film has since had its very successful premiere in New York City. Journalist Bill Moyers discussed it lovingly on his PBS program. He made the following statement directly to Kerry about the film:

> If millions could experience its affirming and incandescent message, we might turn around the destructive dynamics that are overwhelming the earth.
> Thank you for making it.

After much searching, Peter, along with our Vice President of Marketing, Chantel Uchida, was able to secure South Coast Plaza as a venue for a sound/visual installation by the artist Trimpin. He has created a piece called *Red Hot* that plays the "Ode to Joy" theme when interacted with by someone standing nearby. The installation is essentially an upturned red grand piano without a keyboard, suspended in a large tripod. The strings are activated by a number of mechanical devices that help to produce a sound. His work symbolizes the universality of Beethoven's theme and its accessibility to all mankind.

To wrap up the *Beethoven: The Late Great* project is a grand concert on Thursday, May 15, 2014. This idea began a number of years ago when I was having some refreshments in New York with my friend and colleague Graham Sheffield, who was at the time chairman of the Royal Philharmonic Society of London and director of the Barbican Centre. With important anniversaries of the Royal Philharmonic Society and the Philharmonic Society of Orange County—200 and 60 years, respectively—coming up, we thought it might be a good idea to do something together because of our organizations' similar names, and primarily because we were about to embark on a celebration of Beethoven's late works and the Royal Philharmonic Society's first musical commission was Beethoven's Ninth Symphony.

This past August, the National Youth Orchestra of England performed the Royal Philharmonic Society's 200th anniversary concert at Royal Albert Hall as a part of the BBC Proms. There was a commissioned work called *Frieze* by Mark-Anthony Turnage based on Gustav Klimt's homage to Beethoven and, of course, the Ninth Symphony with a combined collegiate chorus. Members of the Orange County Youth Symphony Orchestra and their conductor, Daniel Alfred Wachs, were in attendance. This performance gave them a chance to hear the very same program that they would perform in May 2014 as the finale to our season and to the *Beethoven: The Late Great* project. I would like to thank Daniel Wachs for his participation in this project. He was in on it from the beginning, as was Jeff Mistri. Jeff was the man behind the scenes who handled the production details behind all of the performances of *Beethoven: The Late Great*. He also worked closely with Rosemary Johnson, Executive Director of the Royal Philharmonic Society, on the joint anniversary project. Jeff's successor Sean Samimi will handle the upcoming Beethoven events in the spring. I thank Jeff for what he has done and Sean for what he is about to do. Our industry is fortunate to have such fine young talents. I also want to recognize our soloists for the May 15, 2014, Beethoven finale: Jessica Rivera, soprano; Renee Tatum, mezzo-soprano; Nicholas Phan, tenor; Craig Colclough, bass; and Marc Yu, piano.

Orange County Register music critic Timothy Mangan and his wife Margaret were in London with us because their son Spencer is a violinist in the Orange County Youth Symphony Orchestra. Earlier in the day, Tim, Daniel, Kaly, and I were at the unveiling of a plaque on the wall of a NatWest Bank building in Westminster, London. It recognized this site as being that of the Argyle Rooms where the Ninth Symphony was given its London premiere. While the Argyle Rooms are no more, the Argyle Pub in the back—where the musicians of that first performance hung out after the show—is still up and running. Tim and I each had a pint in honor of Beethoven and everything he has meant to us. I want to thank Tim for his support and excellent music journalism through the years and for writing the foreword to this book.

The many springtime events take a lot of planning and money. I give thanks to Bonnie Hall, Halim Kim, and Allison Heinrichs for keeping on top of it.

It was my dear friend Doug Smith who asked me, "Dean, why don't you write a book?" He may have said that to get me to stop talking, but I took his suggestion to heart. This is my first book and I am planning on it *not* being my last. Publishing a book takes a lot more work than just writing it. I am very grateful to a number of people who made this happen. Firstly, my Philharmonic Society Board Chairmen, Alan Beimfohr, Sabra Bordas, and Noel Hamilton, whose dedication to the cause of the Society was inspiration enough. Chantel Uchida and her marketing staff have put this book together. Jean Hsu kept everything in order, supervising the editing process. Marie Songco-Torres worked directly with the layout designer Dotti Albertine and printers, and arranged for the illustrations. Staff interns Elizabeth Rosenberg, Francesca de la Fuente, and Kenza Tikito were great proofreaders. The overall read-through was done by Rita Major, the Philharmonic Society's director of education. She's picky, one of her many needed talents. Peter's wife Debbie Shaw, Karen Evarts, and Kaly provided some wonderful photos. Catherine Holland from Knobbe Martens is dealing with copyright issues. Thanks to all of these wonderful ladies.

I am thrilled to have Michael Levin as the editor of *Beethoven: The Late Great—Thirty-Three Personal Variations*. He is the founder of BusinessGhost, Inc., a company that is the world's highest quality provider of writing services for visionary individuals and organizations. While my book is certainly not ghostwritten, I asked Michael if he would edit it for me. He graciously said yes. I was introduced to Michael by our mutual friend and Philharmonic Society board member David Rosenberg. I was very fortunate. Michael, besides being a very talented and empathetic human being, is also a music lover—the perfect combination for editing my book. We completely hit it off.

In the same interview format I used in earlier variations, I asked Michael how he got started and some questions about his business.

MICHAEL: I was a Columbia Law School graduate. Didn't want to practice law. Kept failing the bar. I was unemployable in the legal profession. I had sold three novels to Simon & Schuster at that point. I was a starving writer below the poverty line. I met a man who had a business that offered writing classes. I rented space in a church to teach them. That led to people saying, "Why don't you consult with me?" which led to, "Why don't you write my book for me?"

DEAN: What started you writing in the first place?

MICHAEL: When my Dad read me the book *Ask Mister Bear* when I was four years old, I thought I wanted to write books. Later in school, when I saw a film strip of an author holding his galleys, I thought, "That's it."

DEAN: That's great. You knew what you wanted to be. The whole history of music is that of fathers wanting their sons to be lawyers instead of the great composers they were destined to be. These sons all tried it, but they had this music thing they simply had to do. I don't know any stories of a father wanting his son to become a musician only to have the son follow his own dream and become a lawyer.

MICHAEL: I remember telling a Russian lit professor in college that I wanted to write. He responded, "Look, your grandfather is a lawyer, your father is a lawyer." It was like a medieval guild. You couldn't get out of it if you wanted to.

DEAN: That's very funny. What was your first book?

MICHAEL: It was a non-fiction book about religion. The crux of it being that my family and friends thought that I had flipped out and joined a cult, and I wrote the book to show them that was not the case. After that I wrote my first three novels.

DEAN: Simon & Schuster, that's a big deal. How did you get that to happen?

MICHAEL: My mother had been engaged to a guy who was the number three man at Simon & Schuster. Before she ended the engagement, I came to him with my novel. He said he liked it and turned it over to an editor, and told me it was going to be his call. It took eleven months for that editor to make his decision.

DEAN: What did you get—a letter, a phone call?

MICHAEL: I got a phone call. I would get a letter or a phone call every two months telling me to hang in there. That last call was on a Friday and he said, "We are going to have a meeting next Thursday." During that time, I died a thousand deaths. This was in 1986 before call waiting or answering machines. On Thursday I went out, got a muffin and a coffee, and returned home to wait by the phone. I checked the mail that day and I got a rejection letter from the last of five agents I had contacted about my book. Two hours later, the man at Simon & Schuster called and he didn't have that undertaker's tone in his voice. He said, "We like your novel and we are going to offer you $7,500 for it."

DEAN: For 1986, that's really good.

MICHAEL: I had been told that, whatever they offer you, try to negotiate. I tried with my friend there, even though he advised me against it. "I wouldn't do that if I were you," he said.

DEAN: Of course—because then he would have to go to somebody! With technology today, the drama of the phone call is pretty minimalized.

MICHAEL: People don't use the phone today. I think people are more isolated now than ever. I'm now so provincial that when I get a phone call and the area code is 212, I go, "Wow, New York is calling!"

DEAN: Now you are writing books for people. What was the first book you ghostwrote?

MICHAEL: It was for a cousin of mine who was a Holocaust survivor and on Schindler's list. He was at the bar mitzvah of his thirteen-year-old grandson and was telling the story of how Schindler kept them alive in the camps on potatoes, and his grandson was playing around and not paying attention, not understanding this important part of family history. After that, my cousin and I looked at each other and said, "We have to do this." It took four years. We would sit at a piano in the lobby of the New York Hilton, and I would get him talking about his experiences at one camp after the other. You can still buy his book at the Holocaust Museum in D.C.

DEAN: Did you have your company name at that time?

MICHAEL: No, we were originally the Michael Levin Writing Company back in the day. I realized it was a lot more lucrative to do ghostwriting, so it became BusinessGhost.

DEAN: What makes you different from the other ghostwriting firms?

MICHAEL: We have a process that most people don't have, getting a book done quickly and efficiently. We deliver chapters every ten days. We are a team. If you are not happy with one particular writer, we will move you over to somebody else and solve the problem. We only do books with positive messages. We don't do any *Mommy Dearest*. I also don't like working with mean people. It is a weird gift to be able to write in the voice of another person, and I am not supposed to be using it as the voice of negative people. You've got to be able to put your head on the pillow at night. I like to say I am in the greatest grad school in the world.

DEAN: Your list of clients is very impressive. I am so grateful you have taken my book as an editing project. I hope we can continue working together in the future.

MICHAEL: We will for sure.

As I was writing this variation "Bows," I spoke during the week at a meeting of the Alta Bahia Committee at Jane and Stan Grier's lovely home. This Committee was one of our first volunteer groups. Jane Grier is so important to the Philharmonic Society. She has served in every possible leadership capacity. She possesses a rich knowledge of our history and of our values. Jane has been my foundation as I have led the Philharmonic Society for the past two decades. I will love her forever. To her I owe so much. She is the Patron Saint of the Philharmonic Society. Thank you, Jane!

A bunch of folks gave a lot of money to make all of this happen. It is gratifying to receive support of foundations from people you know personally. Hearty thanks to The Segerstrom Foundation, the Shanbrom Family Foundation, and the Donna L. Kendall Foundation. We received major support from Robert and Adeline Yen Mah, Barbara Roberts, Sam Ersan, Phyllis Jacobs, Phil and Mary Lyons, Nancy Caldwell, JoAnn Leatherby, and Greg Bates, as well as George and Mary Ann Wentworth. Rick and Nancy Muth gave a gift specifically for the publication of this book. There were many others in addition. I bow to all of you in appreciation.

The star of my show, Kaly Corey, made this all happen. Without her, it wouldn't have.

As important as the Philharmonic Society contributors, volunteers, and staff are, it is you, the audience, the participants in this grand venture, who make it all worthwhile. Thank you, thank you, thank you!

Professional music teams wouldn't exist without the spectators.
—Peter Schickele

Reading List

Adorno, Theodor W. *Aesthetic Theory*. Ed. Gretel Adorno and Rolf Tiedemann. Trans. Robert Hullot-Kentor. Minneapolis: University of Minnesota Press, 1997.

Adorno, Theodor W. *Essays on Music*. Comp. Richard D. Leppert. Trans. Susan H. Gillespie. Berkeley: University of California Press, 2002.

Asprey, Robert B. *The Reign of Napoleon Bonaparte*. New York: Basic Books, 2001.

Barenboim, Daniel. *Music Quickens Time*. Ed. Elena Cheah. London: Verso, 2008.

Barzun, Jacques. *From Dawn to Decadence: 500 Years of Western Cultural Life: 1500 to the Present*. New York: HarperCollins, 2000.

Beethoven, Ludwig van. *Beethoven's Letters*. Ed. A. Eaglefield-Hull. Trans. J. S. Shedlock. New York: Dover Publications, 1972.

Beethoven, Ludwig van. *Complete String Quartets*. New York: Dover Publications, 1970.

Beethoven, Ludwig van. *Late String Quartets with Grosse Fuge*. Indianapolis: Performer's Edition, 2009.

Berlioz, Hector, and Elizabeth Csicsery-Rónay. *The Art of Music and Other Essays: (A Travers Chants)*. Bloomington: Indiana University Press, 1994.

Biss, Jonathan. *Beethoven's Shadow*. Kindle Edition, 2011.

Blom, Philipp. *Wicked Company: Freethinkers and Friendship in Pre-revolutionary Paris*. London: Phoenix, 2012.

Brendel, Alfred. *Alfred Brendel On Music: Collected Essays*. Chicago: A Cappella Books, 2001.

Buch, Esteban. *Beethoven's Ninth: A Political History*. Trans. Richard Miller. Chicago: The University of Chicago Press, 2003.

Burke, Edmund. *Reflections on the Revolution in France*. [United States]: [s.n.], 2012.

Burnham, Scott, and Michael P. Steinberg, eds. *Beethoven and His World*. Princeton: Princeton University Press, 2000.

Cairns, David. *Berlioz: The Making of an Artist*. Vol. 1. London: Allen Lane. The Penguin Press, 1999.

Cairns, David, trans. *The Memoirs of Hector Berlioz*. Ed. David Cairns. New York: Alfred A. Knopf, 2002.

Cairns, David. *Berlioz: Servitude and Greatness*. Vol. 2. Berkeley: University of California, 2000.

Erickson, Raymond. *Schubert's Vienna*. New Haven: Yale University Press, 1997.

Fiske, Roger. *Beethoven's Missa Solemnis*. New York: Charles Scribner's Sons, 1979.

Green, Hannah. *Little Saint*. New York: Random House, 2001.

Horne, Alistair. *Seven Ages of Paris*. London: Pan MacMillan, 1998.

Kerman, Joseph. *The Beethoven Quartets*. New York: W.W. Norton, 1979.

Kinderman, William. *Beethoven*. 2nd ed. New York: Oxford University Press, 2009.

Kinderman, William. *Beethoven's Diabelli Variations*. Ed. Lewis Lockwood. Oxford: Oxford University Press, 1989.

Landon, H.C. Robbins, and David Wyn Jones. *Haydn: His Life and Music*. Bloomington: Indiana University Press, 1988.

Levy, David B. *Beethoven: The Ninth Symphony*. New York: Schirmer Books, 1995.

Loesser, Arthur. *Men, Women and Pianos: A Social History*. Reprint ed. New York: Dover Publications, 1990.

Martin, Russell. *Beethoven's Hair*. New York: Broadway Books, 2001.

Mathews, Shailer A.M. *The French Revolution: A Sketch*. New York: Chautauqua, 1900.

McCullough, David G. *The Greater Journey: Americans in Paris.* New York: Simon & Schuster, 2011.

Mellers, Wilfrid. *Beethoven and the Voice of God.* London: Travis & Emery, 1983.

Moore, Lucy. *Liberty: The Lives and Times of Six Women in Revolutionary France.* New York: Harper Perennial, 2008.

Noli, Bishop Fan S. *Beethoven and the French Revolution.* New York: International Universities, 1947.

Rosen, Charles. *The Classical Style: Haydn, Mozart, Beethoven.* New York: W.W. Norton, 1997.

Rosen, Charles. *Music and Sentiment.* New Haven: Yale University Press, 2010.

Rosen, Charles. *Piano Notes: The World of the Pianist.* New York: Free Press, 2002.

Ross, Alex. *Listen to This.* New York: Farrar, Straus and Giroux, 2010.

Said, Edward W. *On Late Style: Music and Literature Against the Grain.* New York: Division of Random House, 2006.

Schnabel, Artur. *My Life and Music.* New York: Dover Publications, 1988.

Schom, Alan. *Napoleon Bonaparte.* New York: HarperCollins, 1998.

Schusser, Adelbert. *Ludwig van Beethoven.* Trans. Peter I. Waugh. Vienna: Historical Museum of the City of Vienna, n.d.

Seashore, Carl E. *Psychology of Music.* New York: Dover Publications, 1967.

Seward, Desmond. *Metternich: The First European.* New York: Viking, 1991.

Sheingorn, Pamela, Robert L. Clark, and Bernardus. *The Book of Sainte Foy.* Philadelphia: University of Pennsylvania Press, 1995.

Solomon, Maynard. *Beethoven.* New York: Schirmer Books, 1979.

Solomon, Maynard. *Late Beethoven: Music, Thought, Imagination.* Berkeley: University of California Press, 2003.

Suchet, John. *The Treasures of Beethoven.* London: Andre Deutsch, 2012.

Sullivan, J.W.N. *Beethoven: His Spiritual Development*. New York: Vintage, 1960.

Szulc, Tad. *Chopin in Paris: The Life and Times of the Romantic Composer*. First ed. N.p.: Da Capo Press, 2000.

Thayer, Alexander Wheelock. *Thayer's Life of Beethoven*. Ed. Elliot Forbes and Henry E. Krehbiel. Vol. 1. Princeton: Princeton University Press, 1967.

Tovey, Donald F. *Beethoven*. New York: Oxford University Press, 1945.

Wagner, Richard, and William A. Ellis. *Pilgrimage to Beethoven and Other Essays*. Lincoln: University of Nebraska Press, 1994.

Walker, Alan. *The Chopin Companion: Profiles of the Man and the Musician*. New York: W.W. Norton, 1973.

Walker, Alan. *Franz Liszt: The Virtuoso Years, 1811-1847*. Cornell: Cornell University Press, 1988.

About the Author

Dean Corey is President and Artistic Director of the Philharmonic Society of Orange County, California. Prior to his appointment in 1993, he held leadership positions at numerous orchestras throughout the United States, including President of the Rochester Philharmonic and Executive Director of the Jacksonville Symphony.

Mr. Corey completed his undergraduate studies at University of North Texas and earned his master's degree at Yale School of Music. He began his career as a horn player with orchestras and chamber music groups, and has taught at the Choate School, the University of Texas at Arlington, and UC Irvine.

Beethoven: The Late Great—Thirty-Three Personal Variations is Dean's first book and draws from his lifetime fascination with the history, legends and music of Ludwig van Beethoven. These essays record the impact Beethoven has had on Mr. Corey's life in music arts and on the lives of others around the world.

Dean has two grown children, Adam and Courtney; son-in-law Matt; and grandson Jack; and lives with his wife Kaly and dog Luc in Laguna Hills, California. Dean and Kaly increasingly spend their free time at their second home in Guizerix, France, where they plan to retire in 2014.

9 781939 758552